Lecture Notes in Computer Science 1756

Edited by G. Goos, J. Hartmanis and J. van Leeuwen

Springer

Berlin
Heidelberg
New York
Barcelona
Hong Kong
London
Milan
Paris
Singapore
Tokyo

Günther Ruhe   Frank Bomarius (Eds.)

Learning
Software Organizations

Methodology and Applications

11th International Conference on Software Engineering
and Knowledge Engineering, SEKE'99
Kaiserslautern, Germany, June 16-19, 1999
Proceedings

 Springer

Series Editors

Gerhard Goos, Karlsruhe University, Germany
Juris Hartmanis, Cornell University, NY, USA
Jan van Leeuwen, Utrecht University, The Netherlands

Volume Editors

Günther Ruhe
Frank Bomarius
Fraunhofer Institut, Experimental Software Engineering
Sauerwiesen 6, 67661 Kaiserslautern, Germany
E-mail: {ruhe/bomarius}@iese.fhg.de

Cataloging-in-Publication Data applied for

Die Deutsche Bibliothek - CIP-Einheitsaufnahme

Learning software organizations : methodology and applications ;
proceedings / 11th International Conference on Software Engineering
and Knowledge Engineering, SEKE '99, Kaiserslautern, Germany, June
16 - 19, 1999. Günther Ruhe ; Frank Bomarius (ed.). - Berlin ; Heidelberg ;
New York ; Barcelona ; Hong Kong ; London ; Milan ; Paris ;
Singapore ; Tokyo : Springer, 2000
  (Lecture notes in computer science ; Vol. 1756)
  ISBN 3-540-41430-4

CR Subject Classification (1998): D.2, K.6, H.5.2-3, I.2.4

ISSN 0302-9743
ISBN 3-540-41430-4 Springer-Verlag Berlin Heidelberg New York

Springer-Verlag Berlin Heidelberg New York
a member of BertelsmannSpringer Science+Business Media GmbH
© Springer-Verlag Berlin Heidelberg 2000
Printed in Germany

Typesetting: Camera-ready by author
Printed on acid-free paper   SPIN: 10719601   06/3142   5 4 3 2 1 0

Preface

Today we see many industrial companies that extend their Software Process Improvement activities to explicitly capture the knowledge gained and make it available to the entire enterprise. Organizational Learning, Organizational Memories, Knowledge Management, Data Warehouse, and Experience Factory have become important topics in industrial practice.

The 11th International Conference on Software Engineering and Knowledge Engineering (SEKE'99) was held from 16 to 19 June, 1999 in Kaiserslautern, Germany. As in the previous ten years, the conference provided a unique, centralized forum for academic and industrial researchers and practitioners to discuss the application of either software engineering methods in knowledge engineering or knowledge-based techniques in software engineering. Due to the valuable contribution of the international program committee a very attractive scientific program was presented. After a rigorous review process, 19 full-paper presentations, 19 short-paper presentations, and 16 poster presentations were held during the conference.

The workshop on Learning Software Organizations (LSO'99) brought together practitioners and researchers to discuss ongoing activities regarding the set-up of learning organizations in software industries. In order to foster interdisciplinary approaches, contributions that extend into and integrate the fields of social sciences, psychology, management science, AI, and computer science were presented.

This book provides an overview of current activities, approaches and trends in building LSOs. The first part of the book gives an overview of the topic of Learning Software Organizations. This includes the foundations of organizational learning in the Software Engineering domain, enabling techniques for organizational learning, and techniques to support learning. The most interesting papers regarding LSO issues from SEKE'99 and the adjunct workshop LSO'99 were selected and compiled into the second and third part of this book. The papers are improved and extended versions of the conference or workshop contributions. They deal with the question of how to build and run LSOs for software development organizations. Some investigate the question more from a practitioner's point of view, i.e. reporting from practical experience in industry. Others take a more academic perspective, i.e. reporting applied research results in this area.

We wish to thank DaimlerChrysler, Deutsche Telekom, Ericsson Finland, IBM Germany, Insiders, Q-Labs, sd&m, Softlab and tecinno for sponsoring the conference. We are also grateful to the authors for providing high-quality papers, and to the program committee, including all the reviewers, for their effort in ensuring the quality of the contributions.

Last, but not least, many thanks to Kornelia Streb, Fraunhofer Institute for Experimental Software Engineering (Germany) for copyediting this volume.

September 2000

Günther Ruhe
Frank Bomarius

Table of Contents

Chapter 1: Overview

Chapter 2: Methodology

Chapter 3: Applications

Introduction and Motivation

Knowledge is recognized as the crucial resource in all complex, human-based (creative) and fast changing business areas. It is the mandatory requisite for gaining and maintaining a competitive advantage and therefore requires continuous, pro-active and goal-oriented management. With continuous technological change, globalization, business reorganizations, e-migration, etc. there is a continuous shortage of the right knowledge at the right place at the right time. To overcome this shortage is the challenge for the Learning Organization.

The area of software development is characterized by a particularly rapid technological change. Virtually in all high-tech products and services software implements the majority of the latest and, from a marketing point of view, most important features. Meanwhile, the contribution of software development cost to total development costs of products and services has increased to more than 70% in several of the most important European industries. While software is of paramount importance for market success in all high-tech and service domains, software engineering practice does not yet live up to this challenge and requires tremendous improvement efforts. The need for further development of software engineering practices within companies adds to the demand for systematic knowledge management.

Software development has several characteristics that distinguish it from 'classical' production disciplines [BKRR98]:

- Software is developed, not produced or manufactured. Most development techniques cannot be automated. They are human-based and thus, rely on the individual's expert knowledge and skill.
- Each software product and process is different in terms of goals and contexts. Therefore, the software discipline is inherently experimental. This means that we constantly gain experience from development projects, and strive to provide it for reuse in future, yet different projects. Currently, there is a lack of explicit models of processes, products, and other relevant aspects of software projects that can be effectively and efficiently reused.
- Packaging knowledge and experience so as to enhance its reuse potential requires additional resources outside the normal project budget and environments.

From these characteristics we can deduce that in order to become and remain competitive in software development, there is no alternative to becoming a Learning Software Organization (LSO). A LSO is a continuous endeavor of actively identifying (discovering), evaluating, securing (documenting), disseminating, and systematically deploying knowledge throughout the software development organization.

Building and running corporate-wide knowledge management systems in the domain of Software Engineering is an idea that was initiated about 20 years ago with a more limited scope and strong emphasis on explicit knowledge. The socalled Experience Factory [Bas97] approach has gained widespread attention in recent years and software companies are more and more striving to implement Learning Software Organizations according to this approach. In the context of businesses changing ever faster, the challenges are

- to accelerate the learning processes supported by the LSO,

- to extend the scope of knowledge management to all directly or non-directly relevant processes, products, methods, techniques, tools, and behaviour in the context of software development, and
- to extend the knowledge management approach of the EF to also handle the tacit knowledge available within an organization.

This book features a collection of papers presented at the 11th International Conference on Software Engineering and Knowledge Engineering (SEKE'99) and the adjunct workshop on Learning Software Organizations (LSO'99). The contributions deal with the question of how to build and run LSOs for software development organizations. Some investigate the question more from a practitioner's point of view, i.e., reporting from practical experiences in industry, while others take a more academic perspective, i.e., reporting applied research results in this area.

All in all, this book wants to provide an overview of current activities, approaches and trends in building LSOs.

Learning Organizations in the Software Engineering Domain

Knowledge Management Terminology

The Field of LSO/Knowledge Management is developing very fast. Thus, the terminology is far from being settled and any attempt to come up with the definitive glossary is doomed to fail. Therefore, we want to provide a glossary that only covers the terminology used throughout this book.

Data is a set of discrete, objective facts about events. It says nothing about its own importance or irrelevance. It is essential raw material for the creation of information.

Information can be described as a message, usually in the form of a document or an audible or visible communication. It has a sender and a receiver. Information is meant to change the way the receiver perceives something, to have an impact on his judgement and behavior. Information moves around organizations through hard and soft networks. Data becomes information when its creator or receiver adds meaning.

Knowledge is information combined with experience, context, interpretation and reflection. It is a high-value form of information. It is ready to be applied in decision-making and action taking. Knowledge can be classified along a spectrum from tacit to explicit, ranging from knowledge the holder might not even be aware of to knowledge s/he is very well aware of (i.e., has a structured view of) or has even made available through writing, graphs, models, etc.

Tacit knowledge is personal knowledge embedded in personal experience and is shared and exchanged through direct, face-to-face contact. Subjective insights, intuitions, and hunches fall into this category of knowledge. It is hard to formalize and is generally in the heads of individuals and teams. On the other hand, it is often assumed to be the most valuable and untapped form of knowledge.

Explicit knowledge is formal or semi-formal knowledge that can be packaged as information. It can be found in the documents of an organization: reports, articles, manuals, models, lessons learned. It can also be found in the representations that an organization has of itself: organizational charts, process models, mission statements, domains of expertise.

Models are formalized representations of knowledge, often in the form of mathematical formulae, graphs, causal relationship networks, etc.

Baselines are data sets or models that provide 'typical' values, trends, mathematical dependencies, etc. from past projects in the environment under investigation against which a current project in the same environment can compare itself. Baselines are a result of systematic capturing of experiences (often through measurement programs).

Knowledge management (KM) is the formal management of knowledge for facilitating creation, access, reuse of knowledge, and learning from its application, typically using advanced technology. The goal of KM is to improve the organizational skills of all levels of the organization (individual, group, division, organization) by better usage of the resource knowledge. It is a management activity and as such goal oriented, planned and monitored. KM deals with tacit as well as explicit knowledge. A very broad definition of KM also includes human resources management activities, such as hiring new staff or to train staff in order to increase the company's capacities. If not stated otherwise, we will use the term KM for handling both knowledge and experience.

Seven **KM core processes** can be identified at the individual and organizational levels [PR98]:

- Knowledge identification
- Knowledge acquisition
- Knowledge development
- Knowledge dissemination
- Knowledge usage
- Knowledge preservation
- Knowledge evaluation.

The **body of knowledge** available within an LSO is the set of explicit as well tacit knowledge that the members are aware of and thus can 'activate' in order to solve a problem. Often, this set is called the **organizational memory**. While the definition of the OM entails also all tacit knowledge, a technical **knowledge base** can only contain the explicit knowledge and pointers to the holders of tacit knowledge (experts) who can be called when their knowledge is required.

Learning extends knowledge and enables decision making for individuals as well as for groups and entire organizations. In the context of LSO, knowledge management and learning approaches are complementary views on knowledge. Knowledge management literature usually deals with the mechanisms of knowledge handling, while learning approaches take a look at the inside of the individual, group, or organization. It is a challenge of the LSO to integrate these two approaches.

A **learning organization** is defined as a group of people who systematically extend their capacities so as to accomplish organizational goals.

Organizational Learning (OL) refers to the process of learning by individuals and groups in an organization. OL aims at a general increase of the organization's problem solving capability. From an organizational perspective, 'organizational learning' means the learning process resulting from the creation, maintenance, dissemination and exploitation of knowledge within an organization.

The **Experience Factory** (EF) supports organizational learning in the domain of software development, evolution, and application. Objects of learning are all kinds of models, knowledge and lessons learned related to the different processes, products, tools, techniques, and methods applied during the different stages of the software development process. The early application of the Experience Factory concept at the NASA Software Engineering Laboratory is described in [McGarry94] and [Bas97].

Learning Software Organization (LSO) extends the EF approach so as to accelerate the learning processes supported by the LSO, to extend the scope of knowledge management to all directly or non-directly relevant processes, products, methods, techniques, tools, and behavior in the context of software development, and to extend the knowledge management approach to handle the tacit knowledge available within an organization. The chapters 'Methodology' and 'Applications' of this book describe more recent developments in this context.

The Quality Improvement Paradigm

The Quality Improvement Paradigm (QIP) is a methodological framework for goal-oriented systematic improvement originally developed for (but by no means restricted to) software engineering organizations [BCR94a]. Since learning, on the individual as well as on the organizational level, strives for 'improvement', the QIP can very well guide the activities and goals of the LSO – this is proven by the success of the EF approach, which is based on the QIP. Also, many of the contributions in this book refer to the QIP. Thus, we provide a very brief description of the QIP in the context of knowledge management. Note that we use the terms 'learning' and 'improvement' interchangeably:

QIP was, from its very beginning, designed to explicitly identify improvement goals, capture relevant knowledge, evaluate and systematically reuse that knowledge. Therefore, a strong goal-orientation of the entire process as well as quality control of the captured knowledge are important built-in features of the QIP. The QIP is comprised of the following six steps:

- Starting point for any improvement is an appropriate **characterization** of the current status of the 'environment' which is to be improved. Only when this status is known, realistic improvement goals relative to the known status can be defined and their achievement can be controlled later on.
- Based on a given characterisation the paradigm then provides a context for **goal definition**. The Goal/Question/Metric Approach (GQM) [BCR94b] is a widely used industry-strength means to systematically capture and model goals.
- Given the status quo and the goals to be achieved, the improvement activity can be planned. This includes the **selection of methods, techniques or tools** to be applied or modified and a plan of how to monitor goal achievement.

- Actual **execution of the plan**, including the monitoring activities required to collect experiences, to control goal achievement and, if necessary, to trigger corrective actions.
- **Analysis and interpretation of experiences** made is a crucial step. It can result in abandoning irrelevant or false information, or in classifying information as questionable or hypothetical. Even contradictory observations need to be handled. In any event, the origin as well as the evaluation status is kept with the experiences that are being documented.
- Systematic reuse of experiences is what learning is all about. In the final step QIP is therefore concerned with **packaging the experiences** (documenting, structuring, abstracting, indexing, annotating, linking with other information items, etc.) to facilitate reuse.

The QIP is defined as an iterative process that repeatedly performs the six basic steps. It is very generic and thus, can be applied in many different ways and on different levels simultaneously. For instance, QIP can be applied on the project level as a means towards intra-project improvement and learning. On a higher level, QIP can be employed to implement inter-project improvement and learning, i.e., learning across a set of projects that all perform their own project-level QIP. This higher-level QIP is a step towards long-term learning and improvement in an organization (strategic level).

For the project level and strategic level, specialized versions of the QIP have been defined. They are described in Table 1. The project level improvement process is integrated with the strategic level improvement process, because achieving a long-term (strategic level) improvement goal is typically done by means of improvement in several projects or pilot studies.

QIP was further refined and operationalized by the PERFECT improvement approach [BKRR98]. More recently, the PROFES improvement methodology was developed as the first methodology to explicitly drive process improvement from product perspective. The open and modular structure of the methodology enables wide applicability and integration with existing methods, techniques and tools [JKR00].

QIP Step	Project Level Activities	Strategic Level Activities
Characterize	Characterize project and identify relevant models to be reused.	Characterize organization and identify future trends.
Set Goals	Define project goals in measurable terms and derive related metrics.	Define improvement goals and add hypotheses in measurable terms.
Choose Models	Choose appropriate processes and develop project plan.	Identify projects or pilots for investigating the hypotheses.
Execute	Perform project according to plan, collect data, and provide on-line feedback for project guidance.	Perform projects or pilots and collect data.
Analyze	Analyze project & collected data and suggest improvements.	Analyze projects and pilots and evaluation hypotheses.
Package	Package analysis results into improved reusable models.	Package experiences for use in future projects.

Table 1. Project Level and Strategic Level Activities of the QIP.

The Experience Factory Organization

Projects and organizations as a whole have different aims: Projects develop software products fulfilling predefined requirements. This has to be done within predefined time, cost and with fixed quality criteria. Organizations are encouraged to improve over time. Projects can not be expected to manage corporate experiences. An organizational infrastructure has to be established to perform the role of knowledge management from an organizational and also from a more long-term perspective. This infrastructure is constituted by the experience factory [BCR94a] as described in Fig. 1.

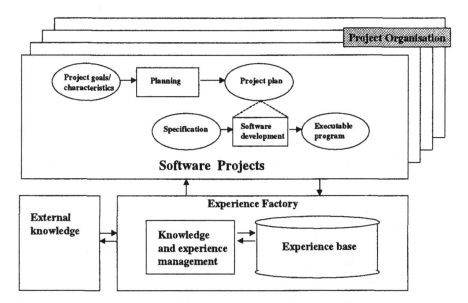

Fig. 1. Experience factory and its interaction with project organization.

The experience factory is an organizational learning infrastructure for software development. Its main part is the experience base, a corporate repository for storing relevant software engineering experience. It distinguishes the project organization in which the software development activities are performed, from the organizational improvement infrastructure, where analysis and packaging activities are carried out for project support and for maintenance and continuous evolution of the experience base.

The body of knowledge within an experience base typically includes different kinds of knowledge: know-how, know-why, know-what, and uses different representation schemes, such as explicit models, documented experiences or lessons learned, but also more or less structured tacit knowledge in the head of experts and skills. Examples are:

- Change and defect models
- Resource models and baselines
- Process definitions and models
- Lessons learned for usage of methods and techniques
- Experience from application of methods, techniques, or tools

Depending on the maturity of the organization or the project, and also depending on the underlying objectives of the corresponding analysis and interpretation of data, the content of the knowledge and experience base can be used for the following purposes:

- Characterize and understand
  Which project characteristics affect the choice of optimal selection of processes, methods, and techniques?
- Characterize and understand
  How does the inspection process lead to a reduction of rework effort?
- Predict and control

Given a set of project characteristics (size, reuse), what is the expected cost and reliability, based upon our history?

- Motivate and improve
  Which reading technique for performing software inspections is most effective and which techniques is most efficient for the different types of defects and for the different degrees of experience of the reader?

The QIP and EF are sometimes criticized for neglecting the cognitive and social aspects and organizational impact of organizational learning. This is due to a rather technical orientation of the early publications about QIP and EF. More recent publications put stronger focus on these issues [WHS00], [Gia00]. In the following section, we want to elaborate on these social and organizational questions.

Organizational Knowledge Creation

Establishing learning software organizations is not just a technical issue – it is a major cultural change within an organization. Organizations are composed of multiple interacting communities. Each of them has highly specialized knowledge, skills, and technologies. To become a LO requires for these diverse communities to bridge their differences and to integrate their knowledge and skills to create a new, shared perspective. Therefore, all the different roles and perspectives of the software development process are concerned and need to be involved appropriately.

Social sharing is not a passive process but is active perspective taking. It is often complicated by the fact that a community's shared vocabulary or domain model is tacit, making it non-inspectable and difficult for another community to understand. The social processes necessary to continuously create and share tacit as well as explicit knowledge between communities - and often also within communities - are not sufficiently developed in most organizations.

Nonaka and Takeuchi [NT95] have pointed out with their **knowledge spiral** (socialization, externalization, combination, and internalization) that knowledge creation lives from a balance in processing (creation and sharing) of tacit as well as explicit knowledge. In this process, both types of knowledge are of equal importance and are transformed into each other. Socialization, externalization, combination, and internalization are the core activities of any knowledge management system and must therefore be accommodated for. Their mutual relationship is described in Fig. 2.

During **socialization**, individuals (i) share experiences through collaboration, observation or imitation. Examples are project-touch down meetings, inspection meetings or quality circles). This is also called learning by sharing. One of the keys to sharing individual knowledge is having the appropriate incentive system for sharing knowledge.

Externalization (or learning by reflection) is the transformation of the individuals (i) tacit knowledge into explicit knowledge that can be documented and thereby understood by groups (g). Dialogue, listening, and collective reflection as performed in project post mortems are examples for how to support externalization.

Combination (or learning by integration) is the integration of different kinds of explicit knowledge from inside or outside the company (o) for the purpose of delivering appropriate knowledge at the right time to the right groups (g) of people.

Experience or knowledge bases, technical reports, quality handbooks or mathematical models are example results of combination.

Finally, **internalization** (or learning by doing) addresses the exploitation of knowledge in order to perform concrete actions. Individuals (i) identify and access the relevant knowledge and learn by adapting the knowledge to the relevant context of groups (g) or organizations (o). The participation and integration of novices in inspections is an example.

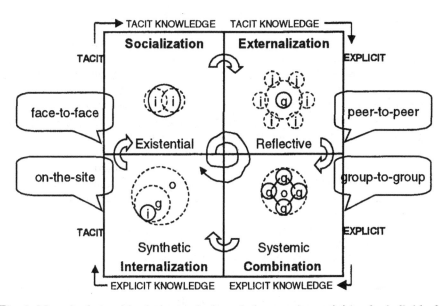

Fig. 2. Mutual relationships between the knowledge creation activities for individuals (i), groups (g), and organizations (o) as adapted from [NT95].

Nonaka and Takeuchi approach knowledge creation from the organizational and team level point of view. The individual's point of view is represented by Kolb's experimental learning theory [Kolb84], which deals with the different **learning style dispositions** of individuals. These learning dispositions of people have to be taken into account when assigning knowledge creation tasks to people.

Enabling Techniques for Learning Organizations

The evolution of scientific knowledge involves learning by observing, formulating theories, and performing experiments. Many fields like physics, medicine and manufacturing use experimentation as a means to encapsulate as well as to verify and validate knowledge. Learning is essentially based on modeling. We need appropriate abstractions from the reality of software development to learn how to improve skills and competencies. For that purpose, process, product and quality models are developed. If learning comes through experience, it follows that the more one plans guided experiments, the more one can learn. How to make the effects of experimentation transparent? Application of goal-oriented measurement facilitates to can gain new insights into the phenomena under investigation. Finally, use of information and communications technology as a tool within collaborative methods of learning will facilitate and improve the knowledge and experience exchange between the different groups and individuals of an LSO.

Experimentation

Experimentation in software engineering focuses on the building empirical software engineering models (e.g., efficiency models for inspections), and validating software engineering hypotheses (e.g., impact of object-oriented designs on maintainability) [RBS93]. The experimental process of iterative definition, testing, and enhancing model-based hypotheses provides a powerful scientific tool for the necessary advancement in knowledge and understanding. Three categories with related subcategories of experimental approaches can be identified [Zel98]:

- Historical
    - Examine previously published studies (Literature search)
    - Examine qualitative data from completed projects (Lessons learned)
    - Examine the structure of the developed product (Static analysis)
- Controlled
    - Develop multiple versions of the product (Replicated)
    - Replicate one factor in a laboratory setting (Synthetic)
    - Execute the developed product for performance (Dynamic analysis)
    - Execute the product with artificial data (Simulation)
- Observational
    - Collect development data (Project monitoring)
    - Monitor the project in depth (Case study)
    - Use ad hoc validation techniques (Assertion)
    - Monitor multiple projects (Field study)

The challenge is to find the most appropriate technique for a given situation. Typically, a sequence and/or combination of techniques will be applied.

Measurement

The motivation for performing measurement in the context of an LSO initially stems from the objective to accompany the process of knowledge asset creation. Measurement can also be used for:

- Evaluation of knowledge assets with respect to the intellectual capital of an organization for survival, renewal and growth.
- Evaluation of the performance of an organization, to get the right things to the attention of managers (for short-term and long-term decision making).
- Controlling performance of the knowledge-related activities by continuously measuring performance indicators of these activities and quality indicators of the knowledge handled as well as of the results created with the help of the knowledge.

The Goal-Question-Metrics (GQM) approach [BCR94b] is a flexible and effectively applicable approach to perform measurement of software processes, products and projects. By applying GQM, information is identified that is relevant to solve specific problems (goals), and that can be represented in a practical, applicable and interpretable way. Main features of the GQM approach are:

- Goal-orientation through top-down definition of metrics via questions;
- Careful characterization of essential environmental which influence underlying knowledge processes;
- Guiding the bottom-up analysis and interpretation of measured data; and
- Active participation of staff in definition, collection, analysis and interpretation of measured data.

Fig. 3 illustrates the essential features of GQM. The goal is formulates as a 5-tuple. The refinement of the goal into questions is supported by eliciting the implicit models of related experts (viewpoint). The questions are the guideline to find appropriate metrics to answer them.

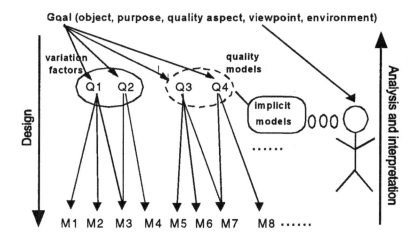

Fig. 3. Structure of the GQM approach.

Modeling

Models are abstract and simplified descriptions of reality. In the context of software development, a model is an idealized representation of a process, product, or an abstract description of quality. The different kinds of models to support individual and organizational learning are contained in an experience base of a LSO. Modeling forms the basis for understanding and improving software processes. This is especially true because of the fact that software development is a human and team-based activity.

Without a process model it is difficult to see what happens (or should happen) in a process and how to communicate this to others. Without a product model of requirements, specification, design, test plan, etc.) it is difficult to characterize what is (or should be) developed or produced at the different stages of the life cycle. Without a quality model (of effort, effectiveness, efficiency, cost, etc.) it is difficult to see how good something is developed or produced. The different kinds of models as result of an abstraction of reality are described in Fig. 4.

There are two types of modelling activities: descriptive and prescriptive. The purpose of descriptive models is to describe the actual status or behaviour of a system. The purpose of a prescriptive model is to describe the intended or optimal status or behaviour of a system.

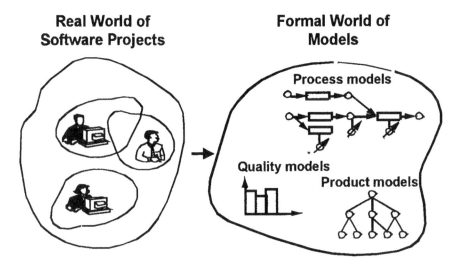

Fig. 4. Abstraction from real world to model world.

The content of a descriptive process model is mainly based on collecting knowledge from process experts and software development practitioners, i.e. the actual processes are represented, not the official ones. Entities and relationships between entities, e.g. input/output relations, activity sequences, reporting channels between roles, and role assignments to activities represent relevant real-world aspects. Entities are formalised in an operational way through attributes, which characterize the entities. Examples of attributes are size, complexity, status, time, and effort.

The task of prescriptive process modelling is to design a new process or to define an intended process improvement for the purpose of assistance. The conformance of process implementation to the prescriptive process model may be enforced through the support of a tool-based software engineering environment. The task of descriptive process modelling is to capture the current software development practices and organizational issues of a software-producing unit as a descriptive process model.

Reuse

There is a general need for reuse of know-how in all companies; however, there are strong differences about what to reuse and how to reuse [R94]. Typically, software reuse needs some kind of modification or adaptation to the new environment. The degree of modification depends on how many, and to what degree, existing object characteristics differ from those required [BR91].

There are a variety of artifacts that are candidates for reuse during both project planning and software development: requirement models and specifications, components, architectures and designs, checklists, scenarios, source code, user and technical documentation, human interfaces, data, test cases, project plans or cost and effort estimates. In Fig. 5, principal operations for reuse oriented software development are described. For more details see [ABH00].

Reuse-based software development is supported by the technical and organizational infrastructure of an Experience Factory. To accelerate the learning process supported by an LSO, support for interactions within this process is strongly needed. The experience base of the EF is an important source of knowledge for reuse within this learning process.

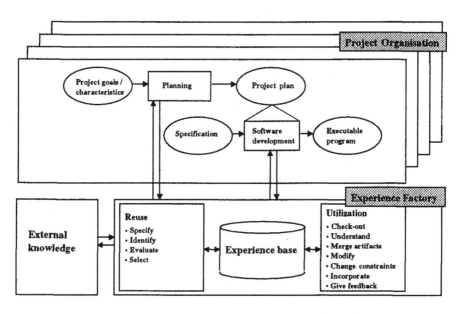

Fig. 5. Reuse-based software development.

Computer Supported Collaborative Learning (CSCL)

Since the learning needs of the participating software developers change rapidly and significantly it is important that the learning/teaching environment is flexible enough that new topics can be easily added and discussed. It would be desirable to connect the individual software developers in a way that they get aware of other people within the company who work on similar problems, technologies, projects, etc. The potential benefits for the individuals are

- to add new insights and experiences with certain methods and technologies to the information space;
- to access general training material to specific topics and technologies;
- to communicate about the knowledge and experience with their peers;
- to access „examples" of how their peers used the new method/technology within their projects;
- to develop a „best practice" description of the use for their specific part of the company they are in.

CSCL is an emerging learning paradigm that focuses on the use of information and communications technology as a tool within collaborative methods (e.g., peer learning and tutoring, reciprocal teaching, project or problem-based learning, simulations) of learning. Collaborative learning provides an environment to enliven and enrich the learning process. Introducing interactive partners into an educational system creates more realistic social contexts, thereby increasing the effectiveness of learning.

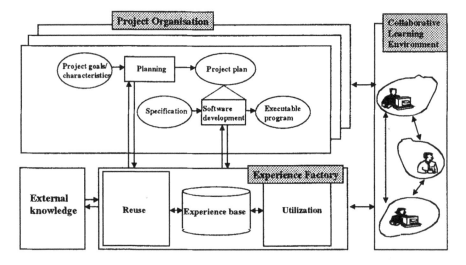

Fig. 6. The collaborative learning environment and its interaction with project organization and experience factory.

A collaborative learning environment as described in Fig. 6 concentrates on refining and integrating the learning process and the subject knowledge of the learner with the help of the collaborative partners. The promise of collaborative learning is to allow learning in relatively realistic, cognitively motivating and socially enriched learning contexts, compared to other tutoring paradigms like socratic learning, discovery learning, integrated learning, etc. With CSCL the learner can discuss these strategies with a group of fellow students who advise, motivate, criticize, compete, and direct the student towards better understanding of the subject matter [K96].

Outlook

The previous sections of this book tried to give an overview of some of the available models, methods and techniques for implementing LSOs in the software domain. As of today, we are equipped with some proven practices but are far from having a comprehensive methodology for building and running LSOs. Some of the most important future research issues in the context of LSOs are:

- Scoping of the LSO:
  What are the topic areas to be covered by the LSO? How many topics can be tackled at which effort and cost? How and how fast can the LSO scale up?
- Organizational integration:
  In which organizational unit do we seed the LSO? To which other units do we extend next? Who 'owns' the LSO? Who pays for it? Who is entitled to reap the benefits?
- Work process integration:
  Learning has to bee directed to specific needs of the different roles in software projects. The process-centered approach to learning, which is based on job-oriented skill and knowledge profiles, will provide answers to the question who (role) should learn what (content), when (process) and how (methods, techniques, tools) in software organizations.
- Integration with other 'programs':
  How do we create synergy with other 'improvement programs'? How do we avoid competition? How do we integrate different (even contradictory) approaches?
- Motivation (initial and sustained):
  How do we create buy-in on the different levels? How do we sustain motivation? Which feedback mechanisms can be employed to turn the LSO into a self-supporting endeavor?
- Cultural barriers, cultural clashes:
  How to analyze the culture of the organization? How to detect barriers early on? How to deal with a generally learning-averse cultural out-set?
- What is the required qualification of personnel involved (knowledge management, experience engineering, learning, coaching, teaching, etc.) and how can the qualification be obtained?
- To what extend do we need to deploy technology and which technology is appropriate when and for what (Intranet, Data bases, Data Mining, etc.)?

The papers featured in the 'Methodology' and 'Applications' sections provide a state-of-the art and state-of-the practice overview in building and running LSO in industrial environment.

The Contributions from SEKE '99 and LSO '99 to this Book

Methodology

In the paper [AB00], Althoff et al. introduce a tool architecture supporting continuous learning and reuse of all kinds of experience from the software engineering domain. They present the underlying methodology. As part of their approach, intelligent retrieval is realised using context-sensitive queries and similarity functions based on case-based reasoning technology.

Feldmann [Feld00] studied reuse of software development artifacts. This paper is concerned with the storage of reusable artifacts in a repository. The structure of the repository and the related reuse process are investigated. Experiences from building and maintaining an internet-based reuse repository are presented.

Althoff et al. [AN00] presents the goal-oriented method OMI for improving an organisational memory incrementally from the user's point of view. OMI consists of a general usage model, a set of indicators for improvement potential represented as protocol cases, and a cause-effect model. At each step of the general usage model, protocol cases are recorded to pinpoint improvement potential for increasing the perceived usefulness. If improvement potential is identified based on the interpretation of the protocol cases (by humans and/or by the software system), the user is asked for specific improvement suggestions.

Broomé and Runeson [BrRu00] investigate technical requirements for implementation of an experience base. The paper defines important concepts in a reuse context, elaborates a reuse scenario from which the requirements for the implementation of an experience base are derived. A list of 21 technical requirements is presented. They cover the functional aspects related to the use of an experience base. The evaluation of three alternative implementation approaches are presented, two database alternatives and one based on case-based reasoning.

Abecker et al. [ABS00] illustrates proactive knowledge delivery and context-sensitive information retrieval by presenting the KnowMore system. This prototype realises active support by providing relevant information to current tasks in enterprises' work-flows. They identify the key concepts needed in order to deal with the existing heterogeneity and sketch the architecture ontologies of the system.

The contribution of Gresse et al. [GvW00] presents a case-based approach for the retrieval of software engineering experience ware taking into account specific characteristics of the software engineering domain. domain models in practice, diversity of environments and software processes to be supported, incompleteness of data, and the consideration of "similarity" of experiences.

Birk and Kröschel [BK00] study a knowledge management lifecycle for experience packages on software engineering technologies. Their paper proposes a knowledge management lifecycle for experience on software engineering technologies and how it is packaged for reuse during the planning of software projects and improvement programs. The lifecycle model is substantiated by a tool implementation and lessons learned from an industrial trial application.

Applications

Peter Brössler [Brö00] describes the introduction of a Web-based knowledge management system at software design & management, Germany that is designed according to the 'cafeteria principle'. This principle was applied when the company was small and people did socialize a lot. The presented system stimulates such behavior by organizational and technical means. The history of the system as well as experiences from one year of operational use are presented.

When problems occur that cannot be solved experts are sought after – Conny Johannson, Patrik Hall and Michael Coquard [JHC00], from Ericsson, Sweden describe how the role of an 'Experience Broker' was defined and implemented in order to facilitate human networking. It is described how the required culture was created and experiences and results from the pilot project performed in 1998 are presented.

Eva Wieser, Frank Houdek, and Kurt Schneider [WHS00] from DaimlerChrysler, Germany focus on the cognitive models underlying learning in groups and organizations. They report experiences from three case studies, pointing out the typical cognitive tasks to be performed and the different ways of carrying them out and the situational context that can dominate the importance of the experience to be learned. Their model of organizational learning in the workplace builds upon results from the field of Computer Supported Cooperative Work (CSCW).

Hendrik M. Giaver [Gia00] from DNV, Norway discusses non-technological barriers to the success of improvement and learning programs. He suggests concrete lessons learned from a 9 month lasting improvement effort. In spite of the many improvements achieved the author questions whether success of the project matches the expenses.

Frank Houdek [HB00] from DaimlerChrysler, Germany and Christian Bunse from Fraunhofer IESE, Germany describe a process for systematic experience transfer covering the activities of acquisition, documentation and evolution, and reuse. The practical use of the proposed process is demonstrated using results from two real projects at DaimlerChrysler, Germany dealing with experience transfer in software inspections. It is also described how experience can be packaged (documented) in order to both transfer and to improve the technique packaged.

References

[ABS00]   A. Abecker, A. Bernardi, M. Sintek: Proactive Knowledge Delivery for Enterprise Knowledge Management. Lecture Notes in Computer Science Nr. 1756, Springer-Verlag 2000 (in this volume).

[AB00]   K.-D. Althoff, A. Birk, S. Hartkopf, W. Müller, M. Nick, D. Surmann, C. Tautz: Systematic Population, Utilization, and Maintenance of a Repository for Comprehensive Reuse. Lecture Notes in Computer Science Nr. 1756, Springer-Verlag, 2000 (in this volume).

[AN00]   K.-D. Althoff, M. Nick, C. Tautz: Systematically Diagnosing and Improving the Perceived Usefulness of Organizational Memories. Lecture Notes in Computer Science Nr. 1756, Springer-Verlag 2000 (in this volume).

[ANP00]   J. Arent, J. Norbjerg, M.D. Petersen: Creating Organizational Knowledge in Software Process Improvement. Proceedings 2nd International Workshop on Learning Software Organizations, June 2000, Oulu Finland, pp 81-92.

[BCR94a] V.R. Basili, G. Caldiera, H.D. Rombach: Experience Factory. In: J. Marciniak: Encyclopedia of Software Engineering, Volume 1, 1994, pp 469-476.

[BCR94b] V.R. Basili, G. Caldiera, H.D. Rombach: Goal-Question-Metric Paradigm. In: J. Marciniak: Encyclopedia of Software Engineering, Volume 1, 1994, pp 528-532.

[BR91]   V.R. Basili, H.D. Rombach: Support for comprehensive reuse. Software Engineering Journal, September 1991, pp 301-318

[Bas97]   V.R. Basili, M. V. Zelkowitz, F. McGarry, J. Page, S. Waligora, R. Pajerski: SEL's Software Process Improvement Program, IEEE Software, vol. 12, November, pp 83-87, 1995.

[BKRR98] A. Birk, R. Kempkens, D. Rombach, G. Ruhe: Systematic Improvement of Software Engineering Processes. Proceedings Frühjahrstagung Wirtschaftsinformatik 1998 (WI'98), February 26/27, 1998, Hamburg, Germany

[BK00]   A. Birk, F. Kröschel: A Knowledge Management Lifecycle for Experience Packages on Software Engineering Technologies. Lecture Notes in Computer Science Nr. 1756, Springer-Verlag 2000 (in this volume).

[Brö00]   P: Brössler: Knowledge Management at a Software Engineering Company - An Experience Report. Lecture Notes in Computer Science Nr. 1756, Springer-Verlag 2000 (in this volume).

[BrRu00]   M. Broomé, P. Runeson: Technical Requirements for the Impelentation of an Experience Base. Lecture Notes in Computer Science Nr. 1756, Springer-Verlag 2000 (in this volume).

[CORONET]   Corporate Software Engineering Knowledge Networks for Improved Training of the Work Force. 5th Framework Project of the European Commission, IST-1999-11634.

[Feld00]   R. Feldmann: On Delveloping a Repository Structure Tailored for Reuse with Improvement. Lecture Notes in Computer Science Nr. 1756, Springer-Verlag 2000 (in this volume).

[Gia00]   H. M. Giaver: Collecting, Storing and Utilizing Information about Improvement Opportunities. Lecture Notes in Computer Science Nr. 1756, Springer-Verlag 2000 (in this volume).

[GvW00]   C. Gresse von Wangenheim, K.-D. Althoff, R. M. Barcia: Goal-Oriented and Similarity-based Retrieval of Software Engineering Experienceware. Lecture Notes in Computer Science Nr. 1756, Springer-Verlag 2000 (in this volume).

[HB00]   F. Houdek, C. Bunse: Transferring Experience – A Practical Approach and ist Application on Software Inspections. Lecture Notes in Computer Science Nr. 1756, Springer-Verlag 2000 (in this volume).

[JKK00]   J. Järvinnen, S. Komi-Sirviö, G. Ruhe: The Making of the PROFES Improvement Methodology – History and Design Rationale. Proceedings PROFES 2000, Oulu, Finland, June 20-22, 2000, pp 257 - 270.

[JHC00]   C. Johansson, P. Hall, M. Coquard: Talk to Paula and Peter – They are Experienced. Lecture Notes in Computer Science Nr. 1756, Springer-Verlag 2000 (in this volume).

[Kolb84]   D.A. Kolb: Experimental Learning - Experience as the Source of Learning and Development, Prentice Hall, 1984.

[K96]   V.S. Kumar: Computer-Supported Collaborative Learning - Issues for Research. Eighth Annual Graduate Symposium on Computer Science, University of Saskatchewan, 1996.

[McGarry94]   F. McGarry, R. Pajerski, G. Page, S. Waligora, V.R. Basili, M. V. Zelkowitz. Software Process Improvement in the NASA Software Engineering Laboratory, CMU/ SEI-94-TR-22, 1994. SEI Technical Reports. Software Engineering Institute, Pittsburgh, PA.

[NT95]   I. Nonaka, I. H. Takeuchi: The Knowledge-Creating Company: How Japanese Companies Create the Dynamics of Innovation, Oxford University Press, 1995.

[PR98]   G. Probst, S. Raub, K. Romhardt: Wissen managen, Wie Unternehmen ihre wertvollste Ressource optimal nutzen, Wiesbaden: Gabler/FAZ, 1998

[RBS93]   H.D. Rombach, V.R. Basili, R.W. Selby (editors): Experimental Software Engineering Issues: A critical assessment and future directions. Lecture Notes in Computer Science Nr. 706, Springer-Verlag, 1993.

[R94]   G. Ruhe: How to organize a repository of best practices in Software Engineering: A study for the European Software Institute. Internal Report. STTI-94-01-E, Software Technology Transfer Initiative Kaiserslautern 1994.

[TK98]   I. Tervonen, P. Kerola: Towards deeper co-understanding of software quality. Information and Software Technology 39 pp. 995-1003, 1998.

[WHS00]   E. Wieser, F. Houdek, K. Schneider: Push or Pull: Two Cognitive Modes of Systematic Experience Transfer at Daimler Chrysler. Lecture Notes in Computer Science Nr. 1756, Springer-Verlag 2000 (in this volume).

[Wijg97]   K.M. Wijg: Knowledge Management: Where did it come from and where will it go? Expert systems with applications 13(1997), pp. 1-14.

[Zel98]   M.V. Zelkowitz, D.R. Wallace: Experimental Models for Validating Technology. IEEE Computer, May 1998, pp 23-31.

Systematic Population, Utilization, and Maintenance of a Repository for Comprehensive Reuse

Klaus-Dieter Althoff, Andreas Birk, Susanne Hartkopf, Wolfgang Müller,
Markus Nick, Dagmar Surmann, Carsten Tautz

Fraunhofer Institute for Experimental Software Engineering, Sauerwiesen 6
67661 Kaiserslautern, Germany
{althoff, birk, hartkopf, mueller, nick, surmann, tautz}@iese.fhg.de

Abstract. Today's software developments are faced with steadily increasing expectations: software has to be developed faster, better, and cheaper. At the same time, application complexity increases. Meeting these demands requires fast, continuous learning and the reuse of experience on the part of the project teams. Thus, learning and reuse should be supported by well-defined processes applicable to all kinds of experience which are stored in an organizational memory. In this paper, we introduce a tool architecture supporting continuous learning and reuse of all kinds of experience from the software engineering domain and present the underlying methodology.

1 Introduction

The demands on the development of software are steadily increasing: shorter time-to-market, better quality, and better productivity are critical for the competitiveness of today's software development organizations. To compound matters, the software to be developed increases in its application complexity. To meet these demands, many organizations frequently introduce new software engineering technologies. However, often there is not enough time to train project teams extensively. Experts become a scarce resource.

There are three ways to handle scarce resources [11]: automation, better planning, and reuse. The first way is the hardest: Only formalized tasks can be automated, which requires a deep understanding of the task. Unfortunately, in software development, no project is like another. Thus, formalizing tasks is hard. Moreover, many tasks are so complex that they can never be automated completely. This leaves better planning and reuse. Both are similar in the sense that they can be supported by installing an organizational memory that is capable of managing all kinds of software engineering experience.

It is widely known that an organizational memory must be maintained by an organizational unit separate from the project organizations [27, 58]. We base our approach on the experience factory concept [13, 14]. The experience factory (EF) is an organizational unit that supports reuse of experience and collective learning by developing, updating, and providing, on request, clusters of competencies to be used by the project organizations. The core of the experience factory is the experience base (EB) which acts as the organizational memory.

The experience factory not only selects what experience should be captured in the experience base, but also defines strategies on how to gain such experience (goal-oriented knowledge acquisition). Thus, the concept of the experience factory complements existing reuse approaches with a learning component for updating the EB. This is operationalized by employing a case-based reasoning [1] strategy [2] for implementing the EB[1].

The paper is organized as follows. The next section gives an overview of existing reuse approaches in software engineering. Based on existing approaches and industrial needs, we derive an open tool architecture that supports reuse and continuous learning of all kinds of experience in Sect. 3. In Sect. 4 and Sect. 5, we present our methodology for reusing and learning, respectively, and show how the architecture implements it. Sect. 6 points out important organizational aspects in the context of the installation of the tool architecture in an organization, whereas Sect. 7 lists some of the experience we gained while implementing the concept in projects. The paper ends with a summary and a conclusion in Sect. 8.

2 State of the Art

Reuse practice exhibits considerable potential for developing software faster, better, and cheaper [47, 61]. However, the full potential can only be exploited if reuse is not limited to code [17, 28]. Examples for software engineering experience besides code include requirements, design, and other software documentation as well as design method tools [39], software best practices [31], technologies [23], lessons learned [19, 46], various models (e.g., resource, product, process, quality [13], and cost models [15]), measurement plans [26, 60], and data [59].

All this experience has to be stored and retrieved. On the retrieval side, many techniques have been employed. These include classification techniques from library science such as enumerated classification, faceted classification, and information retrieval [25]. One of the problems to be dealt with is the fact that artifacts matching the reuse needs exactly are rarely found. Therefore, it must be possible to find similar artifacts. Prieto-Díaz extended the faceted classification as known in library science by the concept of similarity [44]. Case-based reasoning systems extend faceted classification further by allowing the facets to have arbitrary types [3, 16, 34]. Maarek et al. tackle the similarity problem by automatically clustering artifacts and allowing the user to browse the clusters [35]. For small sets of artifacts, browsing (e.g., using hypertext) will suffice [28]. Other techniques are specialized toward specific kinds of experience, for instance, component specifications [36, 41, 42].

There are two basic ways to characterize reusable artifacts: (1) Characteristics of the artifact itself (e.g., format, size, origin) and (2) characteristics of its application and

---

[1] By "learning" we do *not* mean "individual learning" but "collective learning" through improving the EB.

usage context (e.g., size of project, business domain, experience of project team). Ideally, an artifact is characterized using both kinds of characteristics. Characteristics of an artifact's application context can be expected to be most effective for finding relevant reuse candidates. However, finding an appropriate set of characteristics is not trivial. It requires special techniques known as *domain analysis* [10, 37, 43]. Most domain analysis work has focused on the reuse of software components only. Domain analysis for other kinds of software engineering artifacts has been addressed by quite a few authors yet (such as [18, 30]).

If more than one kind of experience is to be reused, either several retrieval systems may be used (one for each kind of experience) [44] or one generic retrieval system. The latter can take advantage of the semantic relationships among the experience items for retrieval, but requires that all kinds of experience are characterized using the same formalism. Examples include specialized knowledge-based systems [22, 39]. In addition to semantic relationships, Ostertag et al. consider similarity-based retrieval [40]. A framework for representation and retrieval techniques can be found in [24].

When choosing a representation, one cannot only consider the benefits on the retrieval side, but must also consider the cost involved in creating and maintaining the EB or "computer-supported learning" in general [24]. However, in contrast to reuse processes, learning processes have not received that much attention in the software engineering community. Research on detailed learning processes focuses primarily on identifying reusable components (e.g., [20, 21, 52]) and on building software component repositories for a given application domain (e.g., [33, 50]). But these approaches are not able to transfer experience (e.g., as lessons learned) *across* domains [29].

A community that focuses on such learning processes is the case-based reasoning community. It has its roots in Schank's work on scripts [48] and dynamic memory [49]. An evaluation of current case-based reasoning technology is given in [3]. In software engineering it has been mainly used for similarity-based retrieval and estimation tasks (an overview is given in [4]). [30] and [9] recognized that case-based reasoning can be used for implementing continuous learning in an EF-like organization. [53, 54] showed that case-based reasoning and EF are complementary, combinable concepts. A first architecture for the integration of these concepts has been presented in [4, 6].

3 Architecture of a Software Engineering Experience Environment (SEEE)

Our tool architecture is a generic, scalable environment for learning and reuse of all kinds of software engineering experience. It uses the semantic relationships among experience items to ensure the consistency of the EB, to allow context-sensitive retrieval, and to facilitate the understanding of artifacts retrieved. The environment is not restricted to retrieval and storage, but supports the complete reuse (adaptation) and learning processes as defined by our methodology in Sect. 4 and Sect. 5.

3.1 Knowledge Representation

Storage and retrieval are based on REFSENO, our *representation formalism for soft-ware engineering ontologies* [56, 55]. Pragmatic constraints impose requirements on the formalism [2]. They concern the responsibility for maintaining different types of knowledge. For example, software engineering artifacts are developed and maintained by projects. Thus, project teams should supply information about artifacts (e.g., in the form of characterizations). The EF determines what kinds of artifacts should be collected, how they are related, and how they should be characterized as to allow effective and efficient retrieval. This conceptual knowledge is captured in the EB schema. It is used to guide the storage and retrieval of artifacts. Finally, our institute "maintains" REFSENO (i.e., the way the conceptual knowledge is specified). This division is important since fast learning can only be realized if experience can be adapted quickly. Fast learning is supported by the guidance through the conceptual knowledge. The EB schema, on the other hand, evolves slowly in comparison. An evolution of schema takes place after careful analysis of reuse behaviors. More radical changes will occur only if an organization changes its strategic goals. However, REFSENO is expected to change very seldom since it is based on many projects applying the EF concept [2, 32, 45].

REFSENO basically provides constructs to describe concepts (each concept represents a class of experience items), terminal attributes (typed properties of experience items), nonterminal attributes (typed links to related experience items), similarity functions (for similarity-based retrieval) as well as integrity rules (cardinalities and value ranges for attributes, value inferences for automatically computable attributes, assertions, and preconditions). The EB schema is specified using REFSENO's constructs (Fig. 1 shows an example).

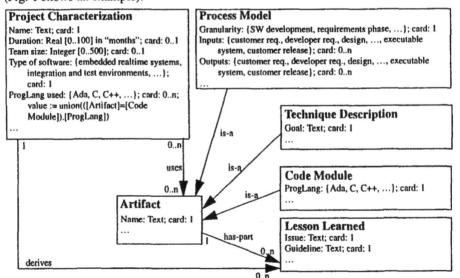

Fig. 1. Exemplary schema (not shown: similarity functions, assertions, and preconditions).

Thus, REFSENO extends the formalism of Ostertag et al. [40] by additional integrity rules and by clearly separating the schema definition and characterizations. This is in line with data modeling languages, which distinguish between data models and data, and enforce the integrity of the database by rules. However, in contrast, REFSENO allows for similarity-based retrieval.

In projects with our industrial customers we have learned that knowledge-based systems basing on completely formalized general knowledge (e.g., rule-based systems) are not necessary for our objectives. Our queries are restricted to characterizations of a particular concept selected by the user. Inferences are limited to value computations (e.g., in Fig. 1 the programming languages used in a project are automatically computed by taking the union of the programming languages of all code modules used in the project) that can be performed at the time characterizations are inserted. These simplifications result in an improvement of retrieval efficiency. The storage of experience in the form of documents (in contrast to codified knowledge) results in a significant reduction of the learning effort typically associated with knowledge-based systems [24].

The different attribute types allow to deal with various degrees of formality. In the beginning of the reuse program, it is often not clear how artifacts should be characterized. Unless a comprehensive pre-study and domain analysis work are preferred [10, 37, 43], an initial reuse infrastructure can be built gradually. Text attributes can be used to allow the storage of arbitrary information. However, in general, no meaningful queries are possible (though information retrieval techniques are conceivable). Thus, mainly browsing is possible. However, this may suffice for small collections. The browsing functionality can be enhanced by specifying nonterminal attributes enabling navigation along these semantic relationships. As the information needs become clearer or collections grow in size, text attributes can be supplemented/replaced by a set of typed attributes that allow meaningful queries (e.g., integer, real, enumeration types). This clearly extends hypertext approaches and allows to distinguish between the stored experience items.

Moreover, semantic relationships enable context-specific retrieval and facilitate the understanding of artifacts. Context-specific retrieval allows people to find useful experience they previously were not aware of (e.g., "find all process models applied in small projects of my organization" might return projects the user has not heard of before). Using semantic relationships, queries can be stated more precisely. Therefore, each concept needs to contain only a few terminal attributes to differentiate between artifacts, because artifacts also differ in their *context*. This feature reduces the effort for setting up the schema initially because a few characteristic attributes can be found easily by interviewing experts in an organization. After a specific artifact has been retrieved based on its characterization, it has to be evaluated for its applicability. To do so requires understanding of the artifact. Here, context information (provided through navigation along semantic relationships) helps to quickly identify prerequisites and rationales behind the development of the artifact.

3.2 Scalable SEEE Architecture

The installation of an EB focuses on practical problems and, therefore, has to meet different requirements. Often, the EB installation starts small, but it must be able to grow in size. Frequently, organizations already use specialized tools that must be integrated into the EB. The representation of artifact types might change in the course of an improvement program from informal to a more formal representation (e.g., process models that were represented as simple text documents in the beginning are later developed with an advanced process modeling tool). Also additional tool functionality might be supplied as the scope of the reuse program expands.

Our solution to these issues is an open architecture – an advancement of the three-layer client-server EB architectures presented in [4, 6, 2]. Fig. 2 shows this architecture with examples of artifact-specific tools that might already exist in an organization and must be integrated: a process modeling tool, a measurement tool, and another software engineering (SE) tool as well as their respective artifact-specific storage systems. The important aspects of the architecture are described in detail in the following.

The EB data (i.e., artifacts and characterizations) is distributed over an artifact-specific storage system and an EB-specific storage system. In the artifact-specific storage system, the actual artifact data (e.g., process models, measurement plans) is stored in its native format in databases or files. This artifact data consists of all collected artifacts, but not those artifacts (still) under control of a project (*project-specific artifacts*). The EB-specific storage system consists of a case base where the artifact characterizations are stored. Each characterization has a reference to the actual artifact data in the artifact-specific storage system. This distribution of the EB data over case base and artifact-specific database systems or files has the advantage that existing tools can be invoked using the reference that is stored in the characterization. Because a different server program (i.e., database management system or file system) can be used for each type of artifact according to its needs regarding the representation formalism, these different representation formalisms do not interfere with each other. In the example shown in Fig. 2, the process modeling tool and the measurement tool use the same object-relational database management system (ORDBMS), whereas the other SE tool uses a relational database system (RDBMS) for storing its data. The process modeling tool also accesses the file system for creating HTML pages for process guidance.

Fig. 2 shows our tool architecture. An EB installation has, as its core parts, a case-based reasoning tool (CBR tool) [57], a general purpose browser, and an EB server. Artifact-specific tools and storage systems can be added as needed. The CBR tool stores the artifact characterizations in the case base and allows similarity-based searching via the artifact characterizations. The general purpose browser provides searching, viewing, and manipulation of characterizations. The operations are handled by the EB server and the CBR tool. Other EB tools (e.g., for special maintenance tasks) can be added in parallel to the general purpose browser. The EB server synchronizes access to the case base, the databases, and the files. It also maintains the references from the characterizations to the artifacts. All this is only required for objects that are under the control of the EB. The project-specific artifacts are not in the scope of the EB and, thus, need not be known by the EB server. To integrate a new artifact-specific tool into our architecture, only a small synchronization module for the EB server is required. Such a module manages access to the EB-specific and artifact-specific storage. For our standard tools, synchronization modules are provided.

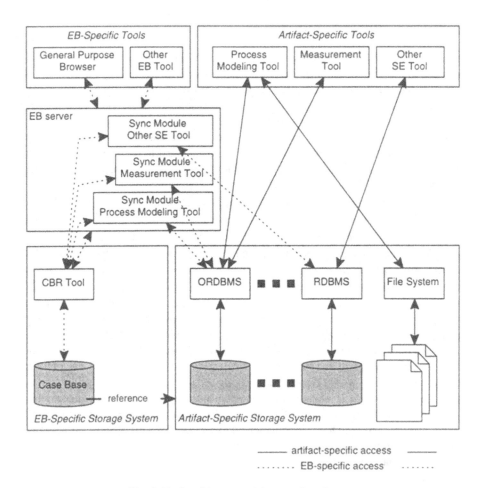

Fig. 2. Tool architecture with examples of tools

The openness of the architecture and the loose coupling of the artifact-specific tools to the EB lead to good scalability of an EB installation with reasonable effort. Because tools can be added or left out as necessary, an EB installation can start small and can be extended later where and when required.

However, the tool architecture alone will not make reuse work. In addition, defined processes for learning and reuse must exist. These processes are the focus of the next two sections.

4 Reusing Existing Experience

This section shows the decomposition of the task "reuse" and its implementation for our architecture with a simplified fictive scenario.

4.1 Decomposition of the Task "Reuse"

The task "reuse" is decomposed as shown in Fig. 3 (a refinement of the decomposition presented in [15, 2]). In the following, the objectives of the subtasks are described.

The objective of *reusing* experience is to save effort while delivering better quality in less time. This is done in several ways: First, instead of developing new artifacts from scratch, appropriate reuse candidates are *retrieved* and *utilized*. Second, tacit knowledge in a certain context is acquired from experts that are identified using the EB. Third, relevant existing information in a certain context is *retrieved* for supporting management in, for example, detecting problems and risks and making experience-based decisions.

The *retrieving* (objective: to find the most appropriate experience for the problem at hand) is decomposed into *specifying* the needed experience, *identifying* candidate experience in the EB, *evaluating* this experience, and *selecting* the best-suited experience. The objective of *specifying* the needed experience is to determine the important characteristics. These characteristics are used during the *identification* (objective: to find a set of objects with the potential to satisfy project-specific reuse requirements) in one of two ways: Either they are used to *browse* the EB or they are entered formally as a query (according to the characterization schema) to *search* the characteristizations of the artifacts stored in the EB. Once potentially useful experience has been found, the experience is evaluated in depth regarding its utility. The objective of *evaluating* experience is to characterize the degree of discrepancies between a given set of reuse requirements, and to predict the cost of bridging the gap between reuse candidates and reuse requirements. It is decomposed into the automatable task *recommend* which computes the similarity (based on the query and the characterizations of the artifacts) and the manual task *examine* during which an expert analyzes the system's recommendation based on the characterizations of the artifacts. Finally, the evaluation results are used to *select* the best-suited reuse candidate(s).

The best-suited reuse candidate(s) are then utilized. The objective of *utilizing* is to take advantage of the existing experience. It is decomposed into the following tasks: *Check-out* (optional task; objective: to copy the selected reuse candidate(s) into the project base[2]), *understand* (objective: to find out how to take advantage of the selected reuse candidate(s)), *merge artifacts* (optional task; objective: to combine several reuse

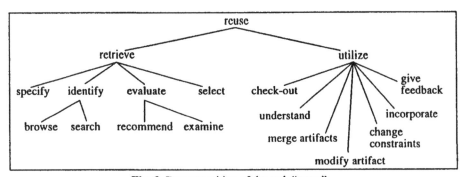

Fig. 3. Decomposition of the task "reuse".

candidate(s) to a single artifact), *modify artifact* (optional task; objective: to bridge the gap between the artifact to be utilized and the needed experience), *change constraints* (optional task; objective: to adapt a system (set of documents or development environment) so the modified artifact can be incorporated easily), *incorporate* (objective: to incorporate the (modified) artifact into a given system), and *give feedback* (objective: to improve decision making process for future utilizations of the selected reuse candidate(s)).

4.2 Scenario

The following scenario demonstrates the reuse of existing knowledge stored in the EB and the use of tacit knowledge in the organization. Thus, it exemplifies the reuse tasks of the previous section. The scenario is based on the EB schema shown in Fig. 1.

The Project "Maui". The group "fuel injection" has just signed a contract with a car manufacturer to develop the software for a new fuel injection system (an embedded real-time system). The contract demands a design review, but the group has never done a design review before.

The Planning of the Project "Maui". The planning of the project starts with a preliminary characterization of the project according to the properties known so far: a duration of 12 months, a team size of six, the software type "embedded real-time systems", and the technique "design review".

The "Maui" project manager needs information on similar projects where a design review has already been performed because he has never managed a project with design reviews before. The preliminary characterization of the project is used as a query (task *specify*) for *identifying* similar projects in the EB to reuse knowledge from these projects (task *search*). The two most similar projects "Lipari" and "Purace" both employed design reviews. The *evaluation* shows that these projects did not deal with embedded real-time systems, but experience about design reviews exists. Quite strikingly, in both projects the design reviews were combined with design inspections. The "Maui" project manager *selects* the first similar project, "Purace", for getting more in-depth, tacit knowledge by interviewing the "owner" of the project experience: the "Purace" project manager (task *understand*). It turns out that the inspections were performed for preparing the design review. The goal was to eliminate as many design defects as possible before the customer takes a look at the design, thus, increasing the confidence and/or satisfaction of the customer. Based on this discussion, the "Maui" project manager decides to employ design inspections as well and prescribes them in the project plan (task *incorporate*). The project plan itself is developed using old project plans from "Lipari" and "Purace" that are *merged* and adapted to project-specific needs (task *modify artifact*). While doing so, the "Maui" project manager recognizes that the project cannot be completed in time under the given ressource

---

[2] The project base holds all project-specific information and experience.

constraints. Therefore, he asks for an additional person working for the project (task *change constraints*).

Furthermore, he decides to check if there are process models that have been applied for developing embedded real-time systems, because the development process models that were used in the projects "Lipari" and "Purace" have not yet been applied to the development of such systems. Hence, he *specifies* the preliminary project characterization as the context for *identifying* process models that cover the whole development process (granularity "SW development", inputs "customer requirements and problem description", and output "customer release") and have been applied in a similar context (i.e., for the development of embedded real-time systems, with a team of six persons, and a duration of 12 months). This context-sensitive query is depicted in Fig. 4. Further *evaluation* shows that only one process model is suitable for the development of embedded real-time systems. This is the process model "Standard 4711", which the project manager has already used in several projects. Thus, he *selects* "Standard 4711" as best-suited reuse candidate and decides to *utilize* it. To do so, he *checks out* "Standard 4711", invokes the appropriate process modeling tool to *understand* and *modify* the process model to meet the project-specific needs. It is then extended by design inspections and reviews using parts from the process models used in the projects "Lipari" and "Purace" (task *incorporate*). The experience gained so far during the utilization (e.g., changes made to "Standard 4711" and effort needed for it) are recorded in the EB (task *give feedback*).

The Performance of Project "Maui". After the performance of the first design inspection, the project manager compares the design error rate of "Maui" (task *specify*) with the lessons learned from the *identified* similar projects "Lipari" and "Purace", which are also stored in the EB. He finds out the rate is worse than expected. The *evaluated* and *selected* lessons learned for "Lipari" and "Purace" state two potential reasons for this (task *understand*): (1) the design inspection team is less experienced; (2) the design engineers are less experienced. Obviously, the first reason matches. To check the second, the project managers of "Lipari" and "Purace" are interviewed regarding the experience of the design engineers involved (task *understand*). It turns out that they have almost the same experience as the design engineers in the project "Maui". Thus, the second reason is rejected and further training for design inspections is arranged (task *incorporate*). In the next inspections after the training, the design error rate reaches the expected level. This experience is recorded in the EB (task *give feedback*).

4.3 Benefits of Our Approach

In contrast to [15], our approach also provides knowledge maps for identifying sources of tacit knowledge (e.g., the identification of the project managers of the projects "Lipari" and "Purace" who have experience with design reviews), supports the planning and performance of projects by providing relevant information (e.g., lessons learned), and also assists in discovering unexpected knowledge (e.g., the fact that a

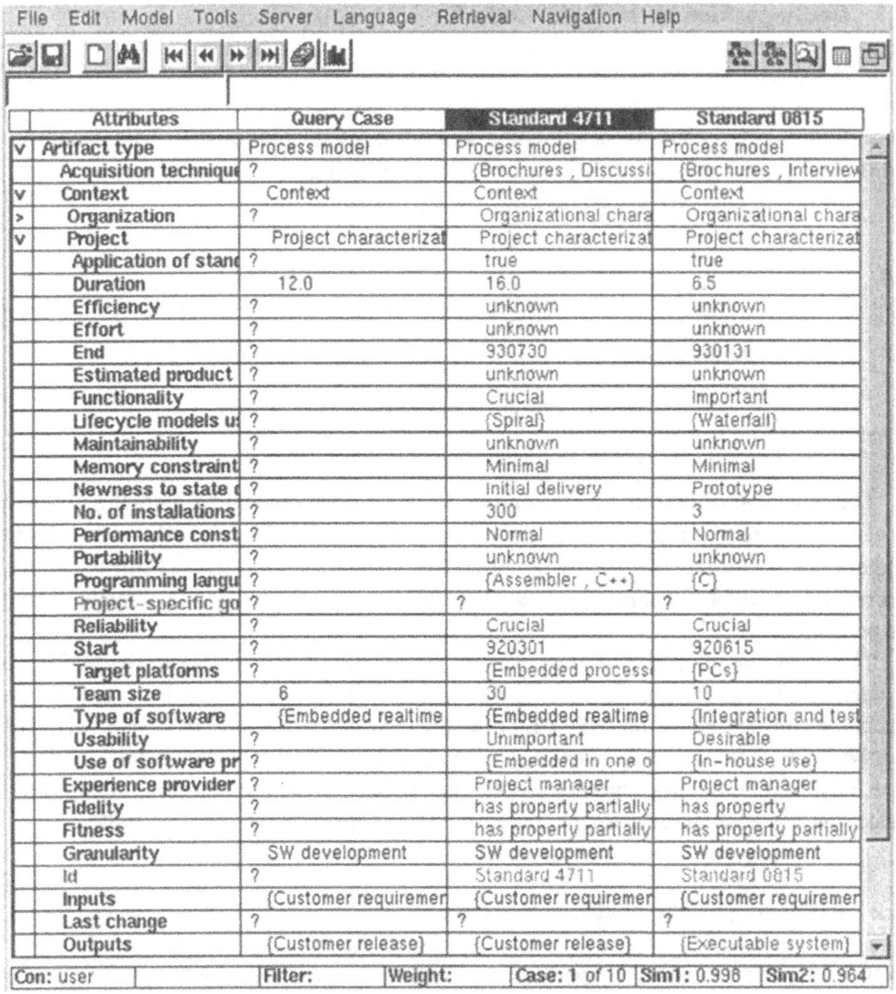

File Edit Model Tools Server Language Retrieval Navigation Help

Attributes	Query Case	Standard 4711	Standard 0815
Artifact type	Process model	Process model	Process model
Acquisition technique	?	{Brochures , Discussi	{Brochures , Interview
Context	Context	Context	Context
Organization	?	Organizational chara	Organizational chara
Project	Project characterizat	Project characterizat	Project characterizat
Application of stand	?	true	true
Duration	12.0	16.0	6.5
Efficiency	?	unknown	unknown
Effort	?	unknown	unknown
End	?	930730	930131
Estimated product	?	unknown	unknown
Functionality	?	Crucial	Important
Lifecycle models u	?	{Spiral}	{Waterfall}
Maintainability	?	unknown	unknown
Memory constraint	?	Minimal	Minimal
Newness to state	?	Initial delivery	Prototype
No. of installations	?	300	3
Performance const	?	Normal	Normal
Portability	?	unknown	unknown
Programming langu	?	{Assembler , C++}	{C}
Project-specific go	?	?	?
Reliability	?	Crucial	Crucial
Start	?	920301	920615
Target platforms	?	{Embedded process	{PCs}
Team size	6	30	10
Type of software	{Embedded realtime	{Embedded realtime	{Integration and test
Usability	?	Unimportant	Desirable
Use of software pr	?	{Embedded in one o	{In-house use}
Experience provider	?	Project manager	Project manager
Fidelity	?	has property partially	has property
Fitness	?	has property partially	has property partially
Granularity	SW development	SW development	SW development
Id	?	Standard 4711	Standard 0815
Inputs	{Customer requiremen	{Customer requiremen	{Customer requiremen
Last change	?	?	?
Outputs	{Customer release}	{Customer release}	{Executable system}

Con: user   Filter: Weight: Case: 1 of 10   Sim1: 0.998   Sim2: 0.964

Fig. 4. Identification of the process model with the general purpose browser.

design review requires a design inspection).

Unlike many other approaches, reuse is also comprehensive, that is, reuse is not restricted to artifacts of one or a few types (e.g., component specifications [36, 41, 42]).

5 Learning for Future Projects

This section shows the decomposition of the task "learn" and its implementation for our architecture with a simplified scenario that continues the scenario from the previous section.

5.1 Decomposition of the Task "Learn"

In [15] learning was decomposed into recording and packaging. Because it was (1) too abstract to be applied systematically in practice and (2) lacking a task for removing superfluous experience, we developed a more detailed decomposition. This decomposition is depicted in Fig. 5 and described in the following.

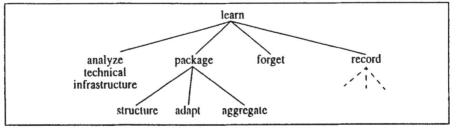

Fig. 5. Decomposition of the task "learn".

The objective of *learning* is to improve software development by allowing efficient and effective reuse. Therefore, we create a repository of well-specified and organized experience. Learning is done by continuously analyzing the technical infrastructure, recording available experience as well as packaging and forgetting already stored experience.

The objective of *analyzing the technical infrastructure* (consisting of the SEEE, its contents, and the schema underlying the contents) is to find potential to improve the technical infrastructure regarding its effectiveness and efficiency (see also [8]). The analysis can result in various actions: reorganizing existing experience (task *package*; see Sect. 5.3), removing superfluous experience (task *forget*), or *recording* new experience that has been made available through ongoing projects (see next section).

5.2 Recording Newly Available Experience

New experience is added by performing the task *record*. The objective of *recording* experience is to fill the EB with well-specified and organized experience according to the needs of the EB's users. It is decomposed into *collecting* the experience, *storing* it in the EB, ensuring its reusability by *qualifying* it, making it available for users' queries (i.e., *publishing* it), and *informing* interested users about its existence (see Fig. 6).

The objective of *collecting* experience is to capture new or improved experience. The EF can do this actively by searching for artifacts and information that might be worth recording for future reuse (in projects and in the world at large). "Worth" means, for example, that the item is the kind of knowledge that is expected to be used in future projects, or that the item is regarded useful by the project team. The project teams can also make suggestions for new artifacts or updates of already stored artifacts and/or their characterizations.

In general, there is a wide range of ways for collecting experience. The following four ways are typical:

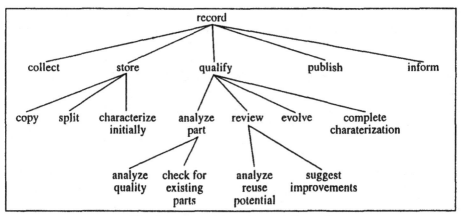

Fig. 6. Decomposition of the task "record"

- *Spontaneous collection,* where only the scope is defined (e.g., spontaneous record-ing of lessons learned during project performance, suggestions by project teams for reusable software components)
- *Event-driven collection* at milestones of a project (e.g., shipping of a release, com-pletion of an inspection or review) and at the end of a project (e.g., the analysis of a project in a post-mortem meeting with the project team)
- *Periodical collection* (e.g., periodic checking of projects for new code modules)
- *Exactly-planned collection,* where exactly specified experience is developed and/or collected (e.g., an EF-initiated project that develops code modules for reuse, a con-trolled experiment by the EF for testing a new design inspection method)

Each of these ways has certain advantages and prerequisites. For example: For short projects it is practicable to collect experience only at the end of the project to keep the effort for learning low. For long-term projects, event-driven collection at milestones makes new experience available earlier. The periodical collection also allows to make artifacts available relatively early when the period of time between milestones is long; on the other hand, this could also lead to more effort for qualifying the artifacts because they might not have passed all tests in the project.

All experience collected needs to be stored. The objective of *storing* experience is to make a new artifact and its characterization available in the EB so that it can be quali-fied and published if it is accepted. Experience is stored in *experience packages (EPs)* [15] that consist of an artifact and its characterization. To store an artifact, it is first *copied* from the storage system of the project into the EB to avoid further modifica-tions by the project team. For some artifacts it is appropriate to *split* them into reusable parts (e.g., a program into components). Afterwards, the artifacts or each of the parts it has been split into, is *characterized initially* as far as the characteristics are known.

The objective of *qualifying* experience is to check and modify (if necessary) a new artifact and its characterization to have it "fit" for reuse (or reject it during the qualify process). The *quality* of each EP (or parts thereof) has to be *analyzed* to ensure that it has the required minimal quality. In addition, it is *checked* whether similar EPs (or parts thereof) already *exist*. The information about the quality and similar existing experience is input to the manual *review* process. During the *review,* the *reuse potential* of the artifact (or parts thereof) is *analyzed* and *improvements* are *suggested* by the reviewers. Improvement suggestions include how to change the artifact to increase its reuse potential, which artifacts that are already stored in the EB should be replaced by the new artifact (meaning that the task *forget* needs to be performed after the *recording*), and which of the already stored artifacts should be merged with the new one. Then the artifact is *evolved* according to the improvement suggestions. Also, the *characterization* has to be *completed*. Note that evolving an artifact can require another quality analysis and/or review (depending on the changes).

The objective of *publishing* experience is to make a stored and qualified EP available for its intended users. Before the experience is published, it is only available within the context of the recording of the artifact (e.g., for testing the characterization of the artifacts with some retrievals). Draft versions can be *published preliminarily* when useful.

The objective of *informing* is to notify potential users of the new artifacts. Several strategies can be used, including broadcasting (informing all users about every new artifact), subscribing (users subscribe to the kinds of artifacts they would like to be informed about), and event-driven (e.g., if a checked-out artifact has been improved by someone else, the person who checked out the artifact is informed).

Scenario. The scenario demonstrates how the learning process is supported by tools. It continues the scenario from Sect. 4. The characterization schema of the EB is shown in Fig. 1.

Planning and Performance of the Project "Maui". During the planning phase, the preliminary characterization of the project "Maui" is *recorded*. The advantages of this are that the project "Maui" can be notified when, for example, errors are found in artifacts reused by "Maui", that the EB can be used as knowledge map on tacit knowledge in currently running projects, and that the preliminary characterization can be specified as context for all experiences from the project that are recorded during planning and performance of "Maui". For example, lessons learned cannot be added without a project characterization. This is specified in the schema (see Fig. 1) by the cardinality of the "derives" relationship between lessons learned and project characterizations.

During project performance, a lesson learned for the reused code module "db-access" about a problem with a database management system ABC-Access and its solution is spontaneously *recorded* as follows: The lesson learned including its characterization is provided by the project team as a suggestion for the EB (*collect* and *store*). The *quality analysis* regarding the EB standards for lessons learned showed no violations. Also, no parts similar to those of the lesson learned were found (task *check for existing parts*). Afterwards, the lesson learned is *reviewed* to see whether it is a wanted, potentially useful artifact. Except for some editorial changes, no *improvements* have been *suggested*. Because ABC-Access is expected to be used in many future projects, the lesson learned is regarded as useful and, thus, *evolved* and *published*. Finally, potential users (e.g., all those who checked out the module "db-access") are informed about the problem.

Post-Mortem Meeting of Project "Maui". After the project "Maui" was finished, a post-mortem meeting showed that the new process model, which has been developed in the project, is worth being stored in the EB. The post-mortem analysis also showed that instead of six people, seven had been working on the project. The project duration was also prolonged by one month.

The preliminary project *characterization* is updated and *completed* based on the results of the post-mortem analysis. Then it is validated by a *review*. Finally, the updated, validated project characterization is *published*. Note that an analysis of its reuse potential is not necessary because the project characterization is required as context information for any experience from the project that is stored in the EB. Thus, recording project characterizations is mandatory for all projects.

The process model is *copied* to the EB and *initially characterized*. The process model is stored as a whole. Thus, it does not have to be *split* into parts. Then the process model and its characterization are *analyzed for their quality*. It is noticed that standards regarding names are not fulfilled completely. Moreover, similar artifacts already stored are identified (task *check for existing parts*). In this case "Standard 4711" is retrieved to ease the analysis of the reuse potential. For the *review*, a process modeling tool is used for viewing the process model. The model is *analyzed* regarding its *reuse potential*: The process model has been used in a project with a small team. The reuse scenarios show that process models for projects should be available for projects with small and large teams. Thus, the process model is *evolved* by adding recommendations about how the process model can be used in a project with a large team. Moreover, the non-standard-compliant names are replaced with standard-compliant names using the process modeling tool. Finally, the *characterization is completed*, all project managers are *informed* about the new process model, and the EP "Standard 4711 with Design Inspections and Review" is *published* (see Fig. 7).

This publishing can even be done remotely with our WWW interface as shown in Fig. 7. The use of WWW-based technology also allows to scale the EB system from use in a single intranet (e.g., for a small company) up to global networks (e.g., for a globally operating company). For global reuse and learning appropriate artifact-specific storage systems are also required that can deal with world-wide access. Simple text or HTML documents can be viewed directly using the WWW browser.

5.3 Organizing and Maintaining Existing Experience

Over time, it may become necessary to reorganize the experience in the EB. There are several reasons that can lead to such a reorganization:

- The reuse potential was predicted wrong, i.e., an artifact is not as attractive for reuse as judged by the reviewers during the *recording*. This can be "diagnosed" using access statistics (e.g., how often the artifact was returned as the result of a user's query or how often an artifact was actually checked out) [8]. In this case, the reusability of the corresponding artifact should be increased, e.g., by modifying the artifact.
- The experience may not have been available in the form needed. For instance, it is difficult to write a handbook on a software engineering technology from scratch.

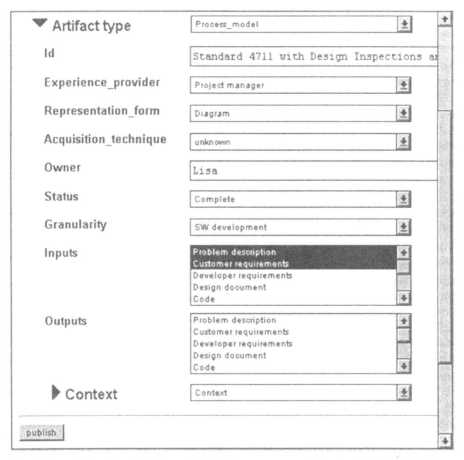

Fig. 7. Example for characterizing and publishing a process model using the WWW interface.

Before a comprehensive and (in practice) useful handbook can be written, the technology needs to be applied in pilot projects, observations and measurements need to be made, and analysis results need to be documented and merged [6, 23]. In this case, many experience items need to be merged to a single new artifact.

- The user requirements may change. As the users of an EB utilize the contents, they begin to better understand their real needs. This may result in requests to change (a) the contents and/or (b) the structure of the EB.
- The environment may change. External market pressures (e.g., the need to be ISO 9000 conform) may have an impact on both the contents and the structure of the EB.

The reorganization is subject of *packaging*. The objective of *packaging* experience is to increase its reuse potential. This can be done by, for example, merging artifacts (task *aggregate*), improving the EB characterization schema (task *structure*), finding out what kinds of packages are required in future projects (new reuse requirements, processes, and scenarios) and acquiring these packages (new criteria for *collecting* and *quality analysis*) or modifying existing EPs to meet these new requirements (task *adapt*).

Scenario. After the completion of "Maui", it became evident that many projects took longer to complete than originally planned (in case of "Maui" one month, see Sect. 5.2). It is decided to analyze this further and to find out by how much (expressed as a percentage) a project took longer than planned. Unfortunately, this kind of analysis was not taken into account at the time the EB schema was developed. Therefore, the planned duration has not been recorded as part of the project characterization.

To enable the analysis, the schema needs to be extended (task *structure*): An attribute "Planned duration" and a concept "Duration Model" (holding the average overtime of a manually defined set of projects) are added (see Fig. 8). The attribute "Overtime factor" of the concept "Duration Model" uses the value inference mechanism of REFSENO. Since all relationships are bidirectional, the formula is able to access all "Project Characterizations" that are linked to the particular "Duration Model". These "Project Characterizations" are referred to as "projects" in the formula (see name on arrow connecting "Project Characterization" with "Duration Model"). The formula calculates the average overtime factor of all projects linked to the particular duration model. If either the attribute "Duration" or "Planned duration" of any of the linked projects is changed, the duration model will be updated automatically.

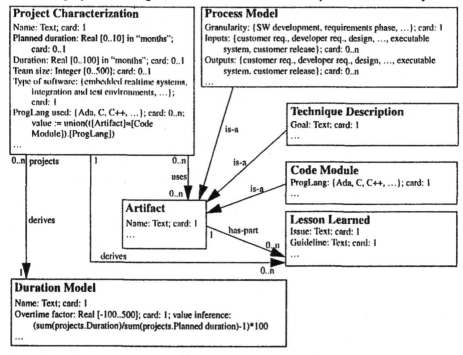

Fig. 8. Extended schema.

The next step is to fill the new attribute "Planned duration" with data, i.e., *adapt* the corresponding characterizations of the projects. This is done by retrieving the corresponding project plans (invoking a specialized project planning tool) and entering the planned duration manually. Once all characterizations have been adapted, the projects must be *aggregated* for their duration models (for each group a separate duration model will be constructed). This allows to distinguish between, for example, embedded and software development systems which are very different in nature.

5.4 Benefits of Our Approach

So far, learning has often been neglected in reuse approaches. We have presented a detailed description of recording, a subtask of learning. For developing and collecting experience, a viable approach has been described. The qualifying actively ensures that the stored artifacts are of high quality and relevant for future (re)use. The detailed description of the recording process allows to support the tasks with tools, which also makes learning faster, better, and cheaper through, for example, guidance for characterizing new artifacts by the use of schemas, automatically controlled integrity rules ensuring consistency of the EB, and usage of existing artifact-specific tools. The use of WWW-technology for the general purpose browser makes our approach scalable from local to global use to support world-wide learning in a company that is distributed around the globe.

The scenario presented also shows a very simple *packaging* scenario to give the reader an idea what *packaging* (another subtask of learning) means. The tasks, however, can be much more complex than outlined in the scenario. For example, the simple value inference can be replaced by a formula of trend analysis that considers more recent projects with a higher weight than older projects. This would make improvements visible in the value of the "Overtime factor" sooner by slowly "forgetting" the older projects. Also, the *structure* task can involve many stakeholders each having their own interests in the contents (and therefore schema) of the EB. These interests need to be prioritized and converted to a schema [51]. Finally, processes that guarantee the availability of the needed information must be defined. The latter amounts to a detailing of the *recording* task for each kind of artifact stored in the EB.

With the tasks of *analyzing the technical infrastructure, forgetting, packaging,* and *recording* (as well as its subtasks), the *learning* is not limited to recording and deleting simple "data sets" as known from traditional database systems. Instead, it is possible (and supported by the flexible SEEE) to also improve the EB itself in a *goal-oriented* fashion. Value inferences help in keeping maintenance effort low and ensuring the consistency of the EB's contents.

6 Running an Experience Base

The scenario in the previous sections has shown how the tasks of continuous learning and reuse can be supported by an EB. An actual deployment of an EB also requires that the EB is embedded into an organizational infrastructure that provides funding and strategies to consolidate reuse and learning [44].

The organizational infrastructure is divided into project organization and EF [13] according to the responsibilities of each organizational unit. The *project organization* consists of several project teams and focuses on software development while reusing experience and gaining it. The *EF* provides the technical infrastructure of the EB and records and packages experience for future projects. We identified the roles manager, supporter, engineer, and librarian within the EF. The *manager* defines strategic goals, initiates improvement programs, acquires and manages resources. He also determines the structure and contents of the EB (e.g., the schemas) and controls its quality. The *supporter* is mainly responsible for collecting new experience from projects and supporting the project teams. He collects, stores, and qualifes artifacts (e.g., he analyzes and reviews a process model and its characterization, evolves a process model) according to reuse requirements and goals given by the engineer. He assists the project team on request in retrieving and utilizing experience. The *engineer* is responsible for analyzing the technical infrastructure as well as for adapting, aggregating, and forgetting stored experience. He analyzes the technical infrastructure to find improvement potential. Together with the manager, he identifies new reuse requirements und defines new goals for the EB to record EPs according to them. The *librarian* is responsible for technical tasks like the creation and maintenance of the EB. He stores and publishes EPs and informs potential users of the new EPs.

Fig. 9 shows the elements of the organizational infrastructure and the information and control flow among them. Here, the supporter is the interface between the project organization and the EF. For the project organization, he works as a team member. For the EF, he collects, characterizes, and qualifies artifacts of the project. For this work, the supporter is paid from the EF (which, in turn, is partly funded by the project). However, the border line between the project organization and the EF (i.e., whether the tasks of the supporter are mainly performed by the project organization or the EF) is

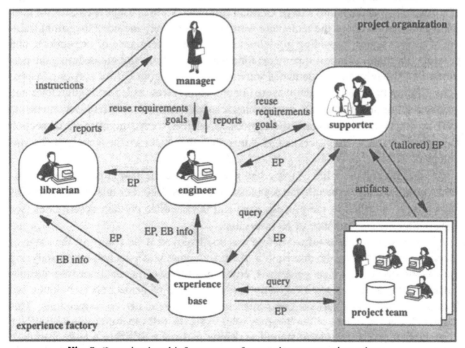

Fig. 9. Organizational infrastructure for running an experience base

based on the needs and characteristics of a company, and can vary from company to company [13].

The implementation of the infrastructure can grow incrementally. First, one person can perform all roles of the EF beginning with a single, small project. As more projects participate, more people undertake the different roles. However, right from the start, management commitment is necessary. Elements in convincing management might be the incremental introduction of the infrastructure or reports about the benefits and costs of reuse [28]. A key to create commitment from project teams is training in reuse [28]. This is done by the supporter who assists the project teams in reusing experience. He also pays attention to the quality of the EPs to strengthen the project teams' confidence in the reliability of the EPs. Another important point is that the EF gives incentives for recording and reusing experience.

Through the organizational infrastructure the tasks of continuous learning and reuse are assigned to the above mentioned roles. A role is responsible for its assigned tasks. So, it is ensured that no task is forgotten. Finally, the instantiation of the roles with real persons depends on the specific company.

7 Projects

The approach described in this paper has been applied in several projects. In this section, we present some of them.

In an industrial project, one of the authors was involved in transferring the technique of software inspections into a large German company. Various usage scenarios for querying information about the technique were identified. They included the initial training of project teams, providing guidelines during the performance of inspections, and providing problem-solution statements for mastering difficult situations during the performance. The information demands were met by building an EB for software inspections. Classes of experience items were (among others) lessons learned (guidelines and problem-solution statements), project characterizations, and auxiliary documents as well as descriptions of intermediate products (defect forms, minutes of inspection meeting etc.), roles, and process steps. Altogether, they make up the technique description [23].

Because no complete list of important guidelines and difficult situations was available a priori, we had to enable the organization to *learn itself*. For this purpose, lessons learned were attached to the process steps and intermediate product descriptions (see above) after the performance of an inspection.

Although our technical infrastructure was not deployed at the company, the usage of schemas for structuring the description of the technique was very helpful in analyzing the lessons learned to create guidelines, problem-solution pairs, and improvement suggestions. Currently, we are integrating several variants of inspection techniques and lessons learned from various companies into one single EB on inspections. This requires the enforcement of the integrity rules using the full capabilities of REFSENO.

In another project, we have started to deploy parts of a SEEE in a large insurance company. In that project, we initially developed a schema for the process model, lessons learned, and project characterizations. It is planned to gradually extend the schema to also include measurement plans, measurement results, milestone plans, and project schedules. Other kinds of experience may follow. Through this project we have learned that schemas with many text attributes are difficult to fill out because it is not always clear under which attribute a given piece of information must be placed. Guidelines for filling out schemas can be devised to alleviate this problem.

Within a publicly funded project we had the opportunity to prove that our approach can be applied to experience handling in other domains, too [5]. In this project we implemented a prototype of a system that supports continuous improvement programs in the health care domain. The EB stores knowledge about improvement ideas that comprises not only a context description, but also a diary of the implementation and data that helps to control the improvement program. The schema developed with REF-SENO has a well-balanced number of formalized and not formalized (free text) attributes. A thorough elicitation of the vocabulary used in hospitals guided the implementation of taxonomies that are used to create the context description of an improvement idea. A trial phase with hospitals in the summer 1999 confirmed the envisioned expressiveness of the schema. Free text attributes are used to record diary entries and attach lessons learned to improvement ideas, which are handled as characterizations in the system. The prototype version of the IPQM system (Intelligent Process and Quality Management) is publicly available[3]. The web interface of this system was built as an instance of our general purpose browser. In this project we have learned that the initial structuring of the experience base can be accelerated by rapid prototyping using the general purpose browser. This improves the communication among (EB) manager and (experience) engineers during structuring because the prototype can be used for trials with existing artifacts.

Apart from the above mentioned projects we have created two other prototype applications that are showcases for our tool architecture (the general purpose browser in particular) and serve as publicly available product experience bases.

The first prototype, called CBR-PEB[4] (Case-Based Reasoning Product Experience Base), enables users to search for CBR systems [7]. There are characterizations about two kinds of CBR systems in the EB: CBR applications (running software systems that can be reused, but must be adapted to new requirements) and CBR tools (software systems that can be used to generate CBR applications). CBR-PEB is also an example where context-sensitive search was rated important by the users that were interviewed for the initial definition of the schema (technical criteria and general information) [12].

Using this prototype we learned through goal-oriented measurement and usage trials that the quality of the artifacts and the accuracy of their characterizations are essential with respect to the perceived usefulness of the experience provided by the retrieval system [38]. This means that any artifact stored must exhibit a minimal quality (to be defined by the user) and be associated with a complete, correct, and up-to-date characterization [4].

The second prototype, called KM-PEB[5] (Knowledge Management Product Experi-

---

[3] URL: http://demolab.iese.fhg.de:8080/Project-KVP-EB/
[4] URL: http://demolab.iese.fhg.de:8080

ence Base), has been set-up recently and shall help users retrieve information about knowledge management tools. The comprehensive description of tools allows the users to perform a context-sensitive search with a high probability to receive useful results even in a rather loosely defined domain.

Both prototypes demonstrate that the architecture presented in this paper can support organizational learning in a globally distributed environment.

8 Conclusion

In this paper we presented our tool architecture and its underlying methodology for reuse and continuous learning of all kinds of software engineering experience. Our architecture extends existing ones by supporting the whole process of reuse and learning for arbitrary experience items.

The retrieval mechanism includes a context-sensitive search and is based on a schema that guides the characterizations of experience items. This means that users need not be knowledge engineers. It also enables them to find useful experience they previously were not aware of. The consistency of the experience base is ensured through integrity rules. This reduces the effort for maintaining the experience base. The schema allows a gradual upscaling from informal to formal characterizations as collections grow in size. In addition, the schema ensures helpfulness and good quality of service for a diverse set of users (e.g., developers, project managers, experience factory personnel). This has been demonstrated through scenarios.

By allowing arbitrary representations for storing artifacts (in contrast to their characterizations), new artifacts (and tools to view and edit them) can be incorporated at any time. Tools existing in the organization can be integrated easily. It is even possible to store earlier versions of an artifact as text files and later versions in a tool-specific format without the need to switch to a new environment. This makes our approach flexible with regard to the formality of the artifacts stored. The World Wide Web interface allows to scale up our infrastructure for global use as demonstrated by our prototypes CBR-PEB and KM-PEB.

Currently, we are extending our learning process through an engineering approach for developing organization-specific schemas. The basic idea is to derive an initial version from a core set of schemas (the counterparts to our artifact-specific tools) and then to iterate this version by monitoring the usefulness (and its influencing factors) perceived by the users.

Acknowledgments

We thank Frank Bomarius for fruitful discussions on the presented tools architecture and Sonnhild Namingha for reviewing an earlier version of this paper.

---

[5] URL: http://demolab.iese.fhg.de:8080/KM-PEB/

References

1. Agnar Aamodt and Enric Plaza. Case-based reasoning: Foundational issues, methodological variations, and system approaches. *AICom - Artificial Intelligence Communications*, 7(1):39–59, March 1994.
2. K.-D. Althoff, F. Bomarius, and C. Tautz. Case-based reasoning strategy to build learning software organizations. *Journal on Intelligent Systems, special issues on "Knowledge Management and Knowledge Distribution over the Internet"*, 1999.
3. Klaus-Dieter Althoff. Evaluating case-based reasoning systems: The Inreca case study. Postdoctoral thesis (Habilitationsschrift), University of Kaiserslautern, 1997.
4. Klaus-Dieter Althoff, Andreas Birk, Christiane Gresse von Wangenheim, and Carsten Tautz. Case-based reasoning for experimental software engineering. In Mario Lenz, Brigitte Bartsch-Spörl, Hans-Dieter Burkhard, and Stefan Wess, editors, *Case-Based Reasoning Technology - From Foundations to Applications*, number 1400, chapter 9, pages 235–254. Springer-Verlag, Berlin, Germany, 1998.
5. Klaus-Dieter Althoff, Frank Bomarius, Wolfgang Müller, and Markus Nick. Using case-based reasoning for supporting continuous improvement processes. In Petra Perner, editor, *Proceedings of the Workshop on Machine Learning*, pages 54–61, Leipzig, Germany, September 1999. Institute for Image Processing and Applied Informatics.
6. Klaus-Dieter Althoff, Frank Bomarius, and Carsten Tautz. Using case-based reasoning technology to build learning organizations. In *Proceedings of the the Workshop on Organizational Memories at the European Conference on Artificial Intelligence '98*, Brighton, England, August 1998.
7. Klaus-Dieter Althoff, Markus Nick, and Carsten Tautz. Cbr-peb: An application implementing reuse concepts of the experience factory for the transfer of cbr system know-how. In *Proceedings of the Seventh Workshop on Case-Based Reasoning during Expert Systems '99 (XPS-99)*, Würzburg, Germany, March 1999.
8. Klaus-Dieter Althoff, Markus Nick, and Carsten Tautz. Systematically diagnosing and improving the perceived usefulness of organizational memories. elsewhere in this book, 1999.
9. Klaus-Dieter Althoff and Wolfgang Wilke. Potential uses of case-based reasoning in experienced based construction of software systems and business process support. In R. Bergmann and W. Wilke, editors, *Proceedings of the Fifth German Workshop on Case-Based Reasoning*, LSA-97-01E, pages 31–38. Centre for Learning Systems and Applications, University of Kaiserslautern, March 1997.
10. G. Arango. *Domain Engineering for Software Reuse*. PhD thesis, University of California at Irvine, 1988.
11. Bruce H. Barnes and Terry B. Bollinger. Making reuse cost effective. *IEEE Software*, 8(1):13–24, January 1991.
12. Brigitte Bartsch-Spörl, Klaus-Dieter Althoff, and Alexandre Meissonnier. Learning from and reasoning about case-based reasoning systems. In *Proceedings of the Fourth German Conference on Knowledge-Based Systems (XPS97)*, March 1997.
13. Victor R. Basili, Gianluigi Caldiera, and H. Dieter Rombach. Experience Factory. In John J. Marciniak, editor, *Encyclopedia of Software Engineering*, volume 1, pages 469–476. John Wiley & Sons, 1994.
14. Victor R. Basili and H. Dieter Rombach. The TAME Project: Towards improvement–oriented software environments. *IEEE Transactions on Software Engineering*, SE-14(6):758–773, June 1988.

15. Victor R. Basili and H. Dieter Rombach. Support for comprehensive reuse. *IEEE Software Engineering Journal*, 6(5):303–316, September 1991.

16. R. Bergmann and U. Eisenecker. Case-based reasoning for supporting reuse of object-oriented software: A case study (in German). In M. M. Richter and F. Maurer, editors, *Expertensysteme 95*, pages 152–169. infix Verlag, 1995.

17. Ted J. Biggerstaff and Charles Richter. Reusability framework, assessment, and directions. *IEEE Software*, 4(2), March 1987.

18. Andreas Birk. Modelling the application domains of software engineering technologies. In *Proceedings of the Twelfth IEEE International Automated Software Engineering Conference.* IEEE Computer Society Press, 1997.

19. Andreas Birk, Peter Derks, Dirk Hamann, Jorma Hirvensalo, Markku Oivo, Erik Rodenbach, Rini van Solingen, and Jorma Taramaa. Applications of measurement in product-focused process improvement: A comparative industrial case study. In *Proceedings of the Fifth International Software Metrics Symposium*, pages 105–108. IEEE Computer Society Press, 1998.

20. Gianluigi Caldiera and Victor R. Basili. Identifying and qualifying reusable components. *IEEE Software*, 8:61–70, February 1991.

21. A. Cimitile and G. Visaggio. Software salvaging and the call dominance tree. *Journal of Systems and Software*, 28(2):117–127, February 1995.

22. Premkumar Devanbu, Ronald J. Brachman, Peter G. Selfridge, and Bruce W. Ballard. LaSSIE: a knowledge-based software information system. *Communications of the ACM*, 34(5):34–49, May 1991.

23. Raimund L. Feldmann and Carsten Tautz. Improving Best Practices Through Explicit Documentation of Experience About Software Technologies. In C. Hawkins, M. Ross, G. Staples, and J. B. Thompson, editors, *INSPIRE III Process Improvement Through Training and Education*, pages 43–57. The British Computer Society, September 1998. Proceedings of the Third International Conference on Software Process Improvement Research, Education and Training (INSPIRE'98).

24. W. B. Frakes and P. B. Gandel. Representing reusable software. *Information and Software Technology*, 32(10):653–664, December 1990.

25. Wilhelm Gaus. *Documentation and Classification Science (in German)*. Springer-Verlag, Berlin, 1995.

26. C. Gresse von Wangenheim, A. von Wangenheim, and R. M. Barcia. Case-based reuse of software engineering measurement plans. In *Proceedings of the Tenth Conference on Software Engineering and Knowledge Engineering*, San Francisco, 1998.

27. Martin L. Griss. Software reuse experience at Hewlett-Packard. In *Proceedings of the Sixteenth International Conference on Software Engineering*, page 270. IEEE Computer Society Press, May 1994.

28. Martin L. Griss, John Favaro, and Paul Walton. Managerial and organizational issues - starting and running a software reuse program. In W. Schäfer, R. Prieto-Diaz, and M. Matsumoto, editors, *Software Reusability*, chapter 3, pages 51–78. Ellis Horwood Ltd., 1994.

29. S. Henninger. Developing domain knowledge through the reuse of project experiences. In Mansur Samadzadeh, editor, *Proceedings of the Symposium on Software Reusability SSR'95*, pages 186–195, April 1995.

30. S. Henninger, K. Lappala, and A. Raghavendran. An organizational learning approach to domain analysis. In *Proceedings of the Seventeenth International Conference on Software Engineering*, pages 95–103. ACM Press, 1995.

31. Scott Henninger. Capturing and formalizing best practices in a software development organization. In *Proceedings of the Ninth Conference on Software Engineering and Knowledge Engineering*, pages 24–31, Madrid, Spain, June 1997.

32. Frank Houdek, Kurt Schneider, and Eva Wieser. Establishing experience factories at Daim-

32. Frank Houdek, Kurt Schneider, and Eva Wieser. Establishing experience factories at Daimler-Benz: An experience report. In *Proceedings of the Twentieth International Conference on Software Engineering*, pages 443–447, Kyoto, Japan, April 1998. IEEE Computer Society Press.

33. Kyo C. Kang, Sajoong Kim, Jaejoon Lee, Kijoo Kim, Euiseob Shin, and Moonhang Huh. FORM: A feature-oriented reuse method with domain-specific reference architectures. *Annals of Software Engineering*, 5:143–168, 1998.

34. P. Katalagarianos and Y. Vassiliou. On the reuse of software: A case-based approach employing a repository. *Automated Software Engineering*, 2:55–86, 1995.

35. Y. S. Maarek, D. M. Berry, and G. E. Kaiser. An information retrieval approach for automatically constructing software libraries. *IEEE Transactions on Software Engineering*, 17(8):800–813, August 1991.

36. Rym Mili, Ali Mili, and Roland T. Mittermeir. Storing and retrieving software components: A refinement based system. *IEEE Transactions on Software Engineering*, 23(7):445–460, July 1997.

37. James M. Neighbors. The draco approach to constructing software from reusable components. *IEEE Transactions on Software Engineering*, SE-10(5):564–574, September 1984.

38. Markus Nick, Klaus-Dieter Althoff, and Carsten Tautz. Facilitating the practical evaluation of organizational memories using the goal-question-metric technique. In *Proceedings of the Twelfth Workshop on Knowledge Acquisition, Modeling and Management*, Banff, Alberta, Canada, October 1999.

39. Markku Oivo and Victor R. Basili. Representing software engineering models: The TAME goal oriented approach. *IEEE Transactions on Software Engineering*, 18(10):886–898, October 1992.

40. Eduardo Ostertag, James Hendler, Rubén Prieto-Díaz, and Christine Braun. Computing similarity in a reuse library system: An AI-based approach. *ACM Transactions on Software Engineering and Methodology*, 1(3):205–228, July 1992.

41. John Penix and Perry Alexander. Toward automated component adaptation. In *Proceedings of the Ninth Conference on Software Engineering and Knowledge Engineering*, pages 535–542, Madrid, Spain, June 1997.

42. Aarthi Prasad and E. K. Park. Reuse systems: An artificial intelligence-based approach. *Journal of Systems and Software*, 27(3):207–221, December 1994.

43. R. Prieto-Diaz. Domain analysis for reusability. In *Proceedings of the Eleventh Annual International Computer Software and Application Conference (COMPSAC)*, pages 23–29, 1987.

44. Rubén Prieto-Díaz. Implementing faceted classification for software reuse. *Communications of the ACM*, 34(5):89–97, May 1991.

45. H. Dieter Rombach. New institute for applied software engineering research. *Software Process Newsletter*, pages 12–14, Fall 1996. No. 7.

46. Charisse Sary. Recall prototype lessons learned writing guide. Technical Report 504-SET-95/003, NASA Goddard Space Flight Center, Greenbelt, Maryland, USA, December 1995.

47. Wilhelm Schäfer, Rubén Prieto-Díaz, and Masao Matsumoto. *Software Reusability*. Ellis Horwood, 1994.

48. R. Schank and R. Abelson. *Scripts, Plans, Goals, and Understanding*. Erlbaum, Northvale, NJ, USA, 1977.

49. Roger C. Schank. *Dynamic Memory: A Theory of Learning in Computers and People*. Cambridge University Press, 1982.

50. M. Simos. Organization domain modeling (odm): Formalizing the core domain modeling life cycle. In Mansur Samadzadeh, editor, *Proceedings of the Symposium on Software Reusability SSR'95*, pages 196–205, April 1995.

51. Mark Simos, Dick Creps, Carol Klingler, Larry Levine, and Dean Allemang. Organization Domain Modeling (ODM) guidebook, version 2.0. Informal Technical Report STARS-VC-A025/001/00, Lockheed Martin Tactical Defense Systems, Manassas, VA, USA, June 1996.

52. Guttorm Sindre, Reidar Conradi, and Even-André Karlsson. The REBOOT approach to software reuse. *Journal of Systems and Software*, 30(201–212), 1995.

53. Carsten Tautz and Klaus-Dieter Althoff. Using case-based reasoning for reusing software knowledge. In D. Leake and E. Plaza, editors, *Proceedings of the Second International Conference on Case-Based Reasoning*. Springer Verlag, 1997.

54. Carsten Tautz and Klaus-Dieter Althoff. Operationalizing comprehensive software knowledge reuse based on CBR methods. In Lothar Gierl and Mario Lenz, editors, *Proceedings of the Sixth German Workshop on Case-Based Reasoning*, volume 7 of *IMIB Series*, pages 89–98, Berlin, Germany, March 1998. Institut für Medizinische Informatik und Biometrik, Universität Rostock.

55. Carsten Tautz and Christiane Gresse von Wangenheim. REFSENO: A representation formalism for software engineering ontologies. Technical Report IESE-Report No. 015.98/E, Fraunhofer Institute for Experimental Software Engineering, Kaiserslautern (Germany), 1998.

56. Carsten Tautz and Christiane Gresse von Wangenheim. A representation formalism for supporting reuse of software engineering knowledge. In *Proceedings of the Workshop on Knowledge Management, Organizational Memory and Knowledge Reuse during Expert Systems '99 (XPS-99)*, Würzburg, Germany, March 1999. http://www.aifb.uni-karlsruhe.de/WBS/dfe/xps99.proc.htm.

57. CBR-Works. URL http://www.tecinno.de/english/products/cbrw_main.htm, 1999. tec:inno GmbH, Germany.

58. Will Tracz. International conference on software reuse summary. *ACM SIGSOFT Software Engineering Notes*, 20(2):21–25, April 1995.

59. Giuseppe Visaggio. Process improvement through data reuse. *IEEE Software*, 11(4):76–85, July 1994.

60. Christiane Gresse von Wangenheim, Klaus-Dieter Althoff, and Ricardo M. Barcia. Goal-oriented and similarity-based retrieval of software engineering experienceware. elsewhere in this book, 1999.

61. Mansour Zand and Mansur Samadzadeh. Software reuse: Current status and trends. *Journal of Systems and Software*, 30(3):167–170, September 1995.

On Developing a Repository Structure Tailored for Reuse with Improvement

Raimund L. Feldmann

University of Kaiserslautern, Department of Computer Science,
Software Engineering Group, Postfach 3049,
D-67653 Kaiserslautern, Germany
r.feldmann@computer.org

Abstract. Learning from experience gained in past projects is seen as a promising way to improve software quality in upcoming projects. Thus, reusing components to support software development is widely accepted in research and industry. Some approaches even require not only the reuse of (directly) reusable components, but, for instance, the reuse of techniques, methods, tools, processes, or even metrics. This calls for a repository that organizes all kinds of reusable elements and offers them, on demand, to the (re-)user in accordance with the applied reuse processes. Furthermore, such a repository should also support processes to learn about, and improve, the quality of its stored artifacts. This paper describes how a comprehensive reuse repository is developed and tailored for an organization. The discussion is detailed by an example, namely the development of the SFB 501 repository at the University of Kaiserslautern. Resulting structures and aspects of the implementation are discussed.

1 Introduction

Learning from experience gained in past projects is seen as a promising way to improve software quality in upcoming projects. Thus, reusing (code) components to support software development is widely accepted in research and industry. But learning is not only limited to successful projects. Failures, especially, that occurred in past projects have to be carefully analyzed and documented in order to be avoided in the future. As a result, (anti-) patterns and frameworks [17], for instance, are being developed to capture the gained experience of already developed software. Nevertheless, experience is not only represented in the form of (directly) reusable software artifacts. To allow comprehensive reuse, as, for example, proposed in [7], some approaches require the reuses of other forms of knowledge that go far beyond mere software artifacts, in order to determine success factors and reasons for failure. This includes, for instance, the reuse of techniques, methods, tools, or even metrics that have already been successfully used in projects. Process descriptions are used to precisely describe how to develop software in a certain domain. In addition, lessons learned [8] are often used to document qualitative experience for future use. Hence, reusable elements can be found in heterogeneous representations and different types of quality. Because the main focus of this paper lies on the development of repositories and not on the reusable elements themselves, every kind of (software engineering) experience, independent of its type of documentation, is regarded as *experience element* [14], and not analyzed in depth, in the remainder of this paper.

However, to be easily accessible for later (re-)use, the experience elements have to be systematically collected and stored, for example, in a repository. Unfortunately, there exists no universal (reuse) repository that is suitable for all kinds of organizations. The reason for this is that a repository has to be individually adapted and tailored to the applied improvement (i. e., learning) and reuse processes of an organization. It can not be expected that a solution that holds for one organization works for another.

At the University of Kaiserslautern the Sonderforschungsbereich 501 (SFB 501) 'Development of large Systems with Generic Methods', a long-term strategic research activity funded by the Deutsche Forschungsgemeinschaft (DFG) was established in 1995 [2]. Since then, several reuse approaches have been developed and tested in different *experiments*.[1] To store the gained knowledge, the SE Laboratory of the SFB 501 develops and maintains a repository that can be adapted and tailored to specific needs of all participating research groups, and that supports learning about and improvement of its stored experience elements. The process used to define and implement the structures of the SFB 501 repository is discussed in this paper. Details of resulting structures and aspects of the implementation are given. They can be seen as a starting point for defining and tailoring such a repository for other organizations.

The remainder of this paper is organized as follows: Section 2 shortly describes the basic learning cycle in which the SFB 501 repository is integrated. A short usage scenario motivates the intended functionality of the repository. In Section 3 the process used to define and tailor the SFB 501 repository structure is presented. How the structure evolved in time, before it was suitable for use as a database-supported implementation of the repository, is discussed in detail. Some implementation aspects, of the HTML-based prototype installation and the current ORDBMS-based implementation, are discussed in Section 4. Finally, related work is described in Section 5 and the results are summarized in Section 6.

2 An Example for Integrating a Repository in a Basic Reuse Cycle

We shortly describe a repository integration into a learning cycle, as it is used for the SFB 501, and presents a usage scenario to motivate the development of the repository structure.

All SFB 501 experiments use a basic learning cycle in which the SFB 501 repository is integrated as illustrated in Fig. 1. The learning cycle is an adaptation of the Quality Improvement Paradigm (QIP) as described by Basili et. al. [6], where each experiment is conducted in four steps: plan, execute, analyze, and package. At the

---

[1] All SFB 501 software development projects are regarded as *experiments* because their main focus is to learn about, and improve, the new approaches (i. e., the developed techniques, methods, or tools), and their minor focus is on the (software) product development itself.

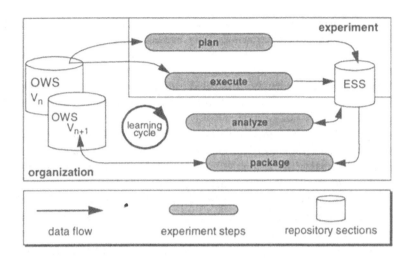

Fig. 1: Integration of a repository in a basic learning cycle

beginning, a new experiment is carefully planned, and its (learning) goals are defined before it is executed. During these first two steps, already existing experience can be reused. In the next step, the result of the experiment is analyzed, before the newly-gained experience is fixed in the last step. The experience can then serve as input for the planning of new experiments, and the learning cycle starts again.

A distinction is made between two (logically, not physically) different sections of the repository: the *experiment-specific section (ESS)* and the *organization-wide section (OWS)*. The ESS stores all information concerning single experiments, and therefore, is filled while an experiment is planned, executed, and analyzed. It can be compared to a project database. The ESS serves as a basis for the last step of the learning cycle, which packages the gained experience into the OWS that stores experience relevant to several experiments of the organization. The OWS then, on demand, offers the experience as input for new projects in the planning and executing steps. Note that both sections together form the repository and need not be physically disjunct. The following scenario motivates the chosen distinction between the ESS and the OWS for the repository.

Let us assume that a new experiment (remember, in the SFB 501 each software development project is seen as an experiment) is planned according to the four steps of the described learning cycle (see Fig. 1). As in common project environments, the new experiment first has to be characterized, for example, by means of *"What are the deliverables?"*, *"In which environment is it to be conducted?"*, and *"Are there any time restrictions?"*. This characterization serves as a basis for searching the OWS for reusable artifacts. Hence, each experience element should be stored with additional information, to allow easy formulation of such search queries. Most of the time, there will be no exact match between the formulated search request and experience elements in the repository. Therefore, similarity-based search and retrieval should be offered, to retrieve experience elements that are relatively close to the requested ones. To gain more information about the retrieved reuse candidates, it would be useful to see experiments in which they have been successfully used, or from which they have been derived in the package step. A closer look at the old experiments, which are stored completely in the ESS of the repository, could even result in further reusable experience elements. As an example, one could find information about tools that have been successfully used together with a process model that is going to be reused in the new experiment.

According to the underlying reuse process, more reusable experience elements (e. g., patterns or code fragments) are retrieved and used during the execution of the new experiment. Again, the complete experiment documentation is recorded and stored together with the results of the analyzing step in the ESS. The analyzed data is then used to systematically improve and/or adapt experience elements that were (re-) used in the actual experiment (e. g., technologies, process descriptions, or patterns). Even if no problems occurred and everything worked out fine, the results are useful for future experiments: this is because the reused experience elements can be trusted more, since they have been successfully tested in practice, and therefore, can guarantee a minimum of quality assurance in an experiment, if they are selected for reuse. As a result of the package step, patterns, for example, that have been successfully used in several experiments might be raised to a higher maturity level [12] that provides higher quality and improves reusability.

3 Development of the Repository Structure

In Sec. 3.1 a process for defining and implementing a suitable repository structure, tailored to specific needs of an organization, is introduced. Subsequently, examples of a resulting logical repository structure (Sec. 3.2) and relations and attributes for the characterization of experience elements (Sec. 3.3) are given, using the SFB 501 repository example.

3.1 A Process for Tailoring a Repository Structure

To define a repository for reuse with improvement, it is important to receive fast feedback on how parts of the repository are accepted (i. e., used). Hence, the suggested process for defining and implementing such a repository aims to quickly run a prototype. Based on the gained experience with the running prototype, the repository structure is then iteratively tailored to the specific needs of the organization. Fig. 2 illustrates the intended process. First, the initial repository structure is defined by the process steps of part A. Then, an iterative implementation and evaluation of the repository structure is proclaimed by the process step cycle of part B.

Note that the described process does not take into account any actions needed to integrate a repository into the specific learning and/or reuse processes of an organization. This integration must be achieved before the process can start and depends strongly on the culture of the organization. In the upcoming discussions of the process

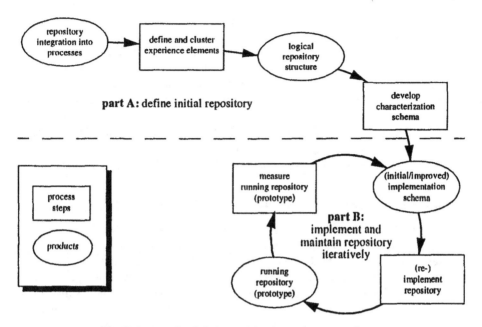

Fig. 2: Process for defining and implementing a repository

steps and the description of the SFB 501 repository example, we assume the repository integration into the basic learning and reuse process as introduced in Sec. 2. Taking this into account, we now describe the single process steps.

Process steps of part A: define initial repository.

- *define and cluster experience elements:* The intended integration of the repository into the reuse and improvement processes of the organization provides first information about the types of experience element that should be stored in the repository. The list of experience elements mentioned in the process descriptions should be completed by interviews with developers and all other groups of possible repository users. Based on this information, it is now possible to define an initial logical repository structure by clustering the experience elements. They can be clustered, for example, according to the process steps they are used in, or the representation type used for the experience element documentation. At this point in time, one should avoid to take into account (technical) implementation aspects of the repository. Do not think in database tables! This will be done in a later process step.

- *develop characterization schema:* Just storing the different experience elements according to the defined logical repository structure would not allow the installation of an advanced search and retrieval system. This is especially true when the experience elements are represented in heterogeneous formats (e. g., PostScript files, GIFs, or word processor binary files) that can not easily be searched for keywords. But not only information about the contents of an experience element must be thought of when developing the characterization schema for a repository. Common information about the experience element, for instance, standard describing attributes like size or creation date that can normally be found in a file system, have to be integrated into the schema. In addition, information describing the environment in which an experience element can be (re-)used must be provided. Program code, for example, has to be accompanied by information about the programming language used. The characterization schema together with the logical repository structure is the basis for an initial implementation schema. This can be represented using object oriented techniques, like UML [24], or special representation formalisms like REFSENO as suggested in *'Systematic Population, Utilization, and Maintenance of a Repository for Comprehensive Reuse'* by Althoff et. al. in this book.

Process steps of part B: implement and maintain repository iteratively.

- *(re-)implement repository:* Using the initial implementation schema, a technology for the repository implementation is selected. It is defined which functionality is offered or has to be added to meet specific needs of the repository. Based on the selected technology, suitable (graphical) user interfaces are developed, and, if needed, database tables are defined. Here, one should consider using a simple technology to allow rapid prototype implementation of the repository, and not offer the complete functionality yet. This will support the idea of gaining fast feedback from the repository users. The gained feedback will then help to tailor the repository to specific needs. An advanced technology can be introduced in a later reimplementation of the repository based on an improved implementation schema, when the logical repository schema and the characterization schema have become quite stable. Nevertheless, the technology chosen for the running repository has to be steadily evaluated and compared to available technologies that might have improved in time.

- *measure running repository (prototype):* As indicated before, it is important to gain feedback on how the running repository (especially its prototype) is accepted by the users. Tailoring the repository is facilitated best by such feedback based on practical experience. Hence, the repository (i. e., its structure and implementation), as well as the experience elements stored in the repository, have to be under permanent evaluation. Therefore, qualitative and quantitative measurement data has to be collected when the repository is running. Requests for extended functionality of the repository, for example, should be collected frequently from the users and may result in an improved implementation schema.

The more theoretical process steps of part A can only guarantee a minimum up front tailored repository structure based on the processes the repository is integrated in. Some repository structure examples can support faster implementation of a repository prototype. Therefore, we will exemplify some results of the process steps *define and cluster experience elements* and *develop characterization schema* using the SFB 501 repository in the next sections. The process steps *implement repository* and *measure running repository (prototype)* strongly depend on the chosen technologies. Here, no general advise can be given on which one will be most suitable for an organization. Nevertheless, some implementation aspects used for running and maintaining the first

HTML-based repository prototype, as well as the current ORDBMS-based implementation of the SFB 501 repository, will be given later in Section 4. They might help in selecting suitable technologies for one's own repository implementation.

3.2 Defining a Modular Repository Structure

In this section we use the SFB 501 repository's initial logical repository structure as an example to illustrate possible results of the process step *define and cluster experience elements*. It is reported in detail how the structure evolved over time, when we were running the first prototype implementation of the SFB 501 repository to tailor the structure according to our specific needs.

We decided to further subdivide and structure the two repository sections OWS and ESS by clustering similar types of experience elements together into different logical *areas* [14] that are utterly disjunct. This kind of modularization was chosen mainly for three reasons: First, to allow an iterative implementation and growth of the repository, by simply adding one area after the other. Second, to give users of the repository a first orientation on which types of experience element can already be found in the repository, and where they can be found, since it was not planned to develop and offer an advanced search and retrieval mechanism for this first prototype implementation. And third, to support the definition and development of the repository structure. The last point needs some more explanation: Before an experience element is added to the repository, it can be classified with the help of the areas (since all areas are disjunct and store only experience elements of a similar type). When an experience element does not fit exactly into one of the already defined/implemented areas, there are two solutions:

- If the experience element does not fit into one area because it contains characteristics of more than one area, it must be split into smaller pieces that belong to the different areas.

- If the experience element does not fit into any of the areas at all, a new area is detected that must be added to the repository.

Both solutions help by either finding the right granularity of an experience element, or by extending and completing the structure of the repository.

At the end of the process step *define and cluster experience elements*, the ESS was subdivided into two areas called *case studies* and *controlled experiments*, which store the experiments of the respective types.[2] For each area a template was defined in accordance with the first three steps of the learning cycle, providing a structure for documenting complete experiments. These predefined templates are filled out while an experiment is conducted (i. e., planned, executed, and analyzed). The current structure of the ESS remains more or less the same. The only changes over time occurred in the template structure. Here, as a result of the process step *measure running repository*

---

[2] SFB 501 experiments are either *case studies*, as defined in [22], or *controlled experiments* (sometimes also denoted as 'formal experiments').

Table 1. Changes in the SFB 501 repository's module structure of the OWS

models	technologies	qualitative experience	SE glossary	literature	domain-specific knowledge		
models -process -product -resource	technologies -techniques -methods -tools			literature -research group 1 : -research group n			
			glossaries -SE -SDL -GQM	literature -references -on-line documents -contact addresses		component repositories -code -SDL patterns	
process modeling -domain-specific -domain-independent	technologies -techniques -methods -tools	qualitative experience		background knowledge -glossaries -literature -domain-specific knowledge		component repositories -code -SDL patterns	measurement

prototype, three more specific templates replaced the initial one for the case studies area [11]. This fact allowed improved structuring of the area, tailored to our specific needs, by further subdividing it into three (sub-)parts, one for each kind of experiment documentation according to the new templates. Such *area refinements* were introduced not only in the case studies area, but also in several areas of the OWS of the repository.

The structure of the OWS was initially subdivided into six different areas, each without area refinements. How the SFB 501 repository's module structure looked like at end of the process step *define and cluster experience elements* is illustrated in the first row in Table 1. Columns represent the different areas. A row indicates another major version of the logical repository structure based on results of the process steps *measure running repository prototype*. Note that each definition of an area is valid for the rows below, unless it is replaced by an other definition. The last row represents the logical repository structure that serves for the current database supported implementation.

At the beginning, the *models area* was defined to store all kinds of models that are developed or used in the SFB 501. Soon it turned out that this definition could be redefined more precisely, since only experience elements related to process modeling topics were stored in this area. First, renaming the complete area was avoided, because other types of models were still expected to occur over time. Therefore, the area was subdivided into three area refinements called *process models*, *product models*, and *resource models*. This would still allow to store other models by simply adding another area refinement to the structure. But finally, after two major structure changes, and the request to store the (process / product / resource) models according to domain-specific and domain-independent models, the area was renamed into *process modeling area* subdivided into two area refinements.

Different descriptions of techniques, methods, and tools are stored in the *technologies area*. Therefore, the area is subdivided into three area refinements. Experience elements stored in this area contain basic information about the technologies and help select the appropriate techniques when setting up a new experiment. The RCS package, for instance, helps newcomers get into the RCS system [29] and is therefore stored in the area refinement called *tools*.

All experiences that were not planned to be made in an experiment, but turned out to be useful, are represented in the *qualitative experience area*. This is the only area in the SFB 501's logical repository structure of the OWS that remained stable right from the beginning of the process step *define and cluster experience elements*. Several attempts were made to further refine the area, but no satisfactory solution has been developed until now.

The three areas *SE glossary, literature,* and *domain-specific knowledge* were defined and implemented separately in the first version of the repository's prototype. They where meant to provide all kinds of knowledge about our domain: real-time house automation and the technologies used in the SFB 501. Knowledge concerning, for instance, methods or techniques used, consistent definitions of (software engineering) terms, or expert knowledge, such as a collection of thermodynamic formulas for heating systems, are stored here. When it turned out that changes in the structure of these areas occurred in almost every new version of the running repository prototype because the definition of these areas and their refinements were too specific, it was decided to pack them together into one big area called *background knowledge*.

One area that was not part of the initial logical repository structure is the *component repositories area*. It contains directly reusable components and was added soon after the first prototype was running. Currently, it is subdivided into two area refinements for *code* and *SDL patterns* [12].

The newest area in the OWS is called *measurement area*. It stores predefined measurement goals and product measures that can be easily adapted to new experiments. Currently, this area is not further refined.

As described, areas are the main building blocks of the SFB 501's logical repository structure. It turned out that this kind of modularization was a good choice, not only in combination with the chosen HTML-based prototype implementation (see Sec. 4.1). Furthermore, the module structure can be used to build specialized repositories inside the global one, simply by using only some areas or area refinements [15], [18]. Hence, the described current logical repository structure can serve as a generic logical repository structure for the process step *define and cluster reuse artifacts* when tailoring a repository for another organization.

3.3 A Characterization Schema for Experience Elements

Based on the logical repository structure of the SFB 501 repository example, we now illustrate some outcomes of the process step *develop characterization schema*.

In the initially developed characterization schema, copies of the experience elements were only accompanied by a short description and a so called *context vector* [14]. The context vector characterizes the environment / type of experiment in which the experience element is valid (i. e., can be reused). It simply consists of a collection of attribute-value-pairs, for example, ⟨(project effort, 50.000 h), (programming language, JAVA), ...⟩. Soon it became obvious that additional information must be associated and stored with each experience element, to provide the basis for an advanced search and retrieval system. Relations, for instance, indicating how experience elements in different areas interrelate, must be added (e. g., when an experience element was split into smaller pieces), or attributes that not only describe the context of the experience element, but the experience element itself (e. g., its creation date , represen tation type, or author).

As a result, the concept of the *characterization vector (CV)* was developed. CVs are used to store all information concerning experience elements. Therefore, they are a major concept in the characterization and implementation schema of the SFB 501 repository. The information contained in a CV can be divided into three segments. One for references to the different representations of the experience element, one with attributes that describe the experience element and its validity, and one holding information about relations from the experience element to other experience elements.

References. CV references are a *set of links* to different possible representations of one experience element. For instance, if the experience element is a requirements document, one link could reference the original word processor binary-file in which the document was written. Another one could be a reference to an HTML version or a graphical representation, to allow direct viewing of the experience element. A third one might be a PostScript version to allow easy printouts of the document.

Attributes. CV attributes serve as the basis for all search functions offered by the repository. They integrate the attributes of the former context vectors as well as all other describing attributes, including the ones offered by standard file systems (e. g., size, creation / modification date, file name). Additionally, attributes that describe which section, area, or area refinement an experience element belongs to have to be included, too. This is because of the intended final implementation of the repository with the help of an database system. Here all attributes have to be integrated into the database schema. Hence, they have to be defined in the CV as well, since per definition they store *all* information concerning an experience element! A detailed list with all CV attributes can be found in [13].

Relations. CV relations are attributes that are used to express relationships from a single experience element to other experience elements. Since the CV relations connect the different areas of the logical repository structure, they are discussed in detail. Currently, the SFB 501 repository defines six different types of CV relations:

1. `measures/measured_by`: This type of relation is defined between experience elements of the measurement area and experience elements stored in the process modeling, technologies, qualitative experience, or component repositories areas. It is used to identify the experience elements that are measured (e. g., by a standardized questionnaire stored in the measurement area). In the other direction, it helps the planner of an experiment to find an experience element that measures a certain element s/he is reusing.

2. `is_about/has_part`: This type of relation is defined between lessons learned stored in the qualitative experience area and experience elements of the process modeling, technologies, component repositories, or measurement areas. It is used to identify the experience element(s) that the lesson learned is concerned with. In the

other direction it helps to find lessons learned that deal with a certain experience element. The number and/or the content of the lessons learned can be used to trigger further improvement processes to raise the quality of the experience element that they are concerned with.

3. `used_in/uses`: This type of relation is defined between experience elements of the OWS and the experiment documentations in the ESS (i. e., the case studies area and the controlled experiments area) of the SFB 501 repository. It allows to identify the experiments in which an experience element has been used, or which experience elements have been used in a certain experiment. Note that since it can be assumed that an experience element that has been (successfully) reused often is quite valid, the number of `used_in` relations for an experience element gives a first impression about its validity.

4. `gained_in/gains`: This type of relation is defined between a lesson learned in the qualitative experience area and the experiment documentations in the ESS. It identifies in which experiment a lesson learned was gained, or which lessons learned have been gained in a certain experiment.

5. `uses/used_with`: This type of relation is defined between experience elements of the process modeling area and the component repositories area. It documents that a certain experience element is used in the description of a process model. The opposite direction gives hints as to which process descriptions a certain experience element is used or suggests its usage. This type of relation is further defined between experience elements of the process modeling area and the technologies area, and between experience elements of the technologies area and the component repositories area.

6. `explains/explained_in`: This type of relation is defined between an experience element of the background knowledge area and experience elements of all other areas. It describes where background knowledge about a certain experience element can be found, or helps to find examples where the background knowledge is used (this gives first hints, if the offered background knowledge is useful at all).

Fig. 3 summarizes the framework defined by the different areas and CV relations in the SFB 501 repository example. With these defined relations it is now possible to offer another search and retrieval functionality. Let us assume that a first search, based on the CV attributes, retrieved several experience elements that all meet the search requirements to exactly the same extent. Now one can follow the CV relations to get further information that helps to decide which experience element should be reused. Furthermore, the described CV relations document the improvements gained by the applied learning processes. By following the `used_in/uses` relations, for instance, one will find the experiments in which a certain experience element has been reuses. From the experiments one can follow the `gained_in/gains` relations to see the lessons learned of the experiment. If one of the lessons learned is about the reused experience element this is documented by the `is_about/has_part` relation. Hence, each successful applied learning process is represented within the repository by a cycle formed by of the CV relations.

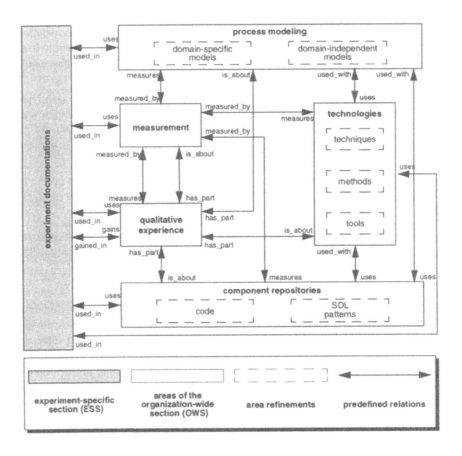

Fig. 3: CV relations between the different sections/areas of the logical repository structure
(background knowledge area not included)

The described characterization schema in combination with the generic logical repository structure of the SFB 501 repository (see Sec. 3.2), can be used as a starting point when developing a similar repository for another organization. This would allow faster implementation of a repository prototype, by shortening the initial effort needed for the process steps *define and cluster reuse artifacts* and *develop characterization schema*, since they define a basis for an initial implementation schema. It might even result in less changes in the repository structure when running the first repository prototype. Nevertheless, we strongly recommend to implement a repository prototype to tailor the repository to the specific needs of the organization.

4   Implementation Aspects of the Repository

This section discusses elements of the HTML-based prototype implementation

(Sec. 4.1), and the current ORDBMS-based implementation (Sec. 4.2) of the SFB 501 repository.

4.1 Elements of the HTML-Based Prototype Implementation

As described in [16], the prototype implementation of the SFB 501 repository uses a Unix file system to store the experience elements. Copies of the experience elements are only accompanied by HTML pages representing the CVs. Basic descriptive attributes, like creation date, last modification date, or the owner/author of an experience element, were used directly from the file system. All CV references were realized by HTML links to the experience elements in the file system, the same hold for the CV relations. In addition, some HTML pages, denoted as *overview pages* [16], are used to implement the logical repository structure. An overview page acts as a table of contents for each section, area, or area refinement. The basic search and retrieval system of the SFB 501 repository prototype is based on these pages.

The chosen HTML-based prototype implementation turned out to be extremely useful. First, because all changes to the logical repository structure are accessible to all repository users as soon as they are implemented (i. e., integrated into the overview pages), without any further actions. This is due to the fact that the changes must only be made centrally in the file system on which the web server is operating. They will be automatically distributed to all users who are using the repository (i. e., requesting information from the web server). Second, because all requests for experience elements stored in the repository can be logged by the web server that provides the repository. With the help of this information it is possible to create usage statistics of the repository, as needed for the process step *measure running repository prototype*. The access to newly-structured or added areas of the repository, especially, can be visualized. Consequently, a tool was developed that automatically generates the usage and access statistics to the SFB 501 repository prototype [19]. From this statistics we learned that no problem was caused by the fact that a prototype of the repository, offering only a simple usage functionality, was provided. The interest of the users in the SFB 501 repository remains stable over time and does not get less because some requested functionality was not implemented. For example, only a simple full text search is supported, as provided for many home pages in the WWW. Although, a similarity-based search and retrieval of experience elements was requested by some users.

Overall, the HTML-based prototype implementation of the repository positively influenced the development of the characterization vector concept. This is especially true for the CV references and CV relations. On the other hand, the HTML-based implementation showed some shortcomings in defining the complete list of attributes that have to be included into the CVs for a database implementation. But this shortcoming might also be influenced by the fact that it was never intended to provide an advanced search and retrieval system functionality with the prototype implementation.

4.2 An ORDBMS-Based Implementation of the Repository

When the logical repository structure and the characterization schema (i. e., areas, area refinements, and CVs) became quite stable, it was time to think about a suitable database management system (DBMS) to store the experience elements. In cooperation with the Database and Information Systems research group that is part of the SFB 501, it was evaluated which kind of DBMS would best serve our purpose [13], [23]. Both, relational database systems (RDBMS) and object-oriented database systems (OODBMS) offer features that are useful for the implementation of such a repository. Transactions, queries, and views, for instance, as offered by RDBMS are needed to support the search and retrieval of experience elements. Complex objects and user-defined data types, on the other hand, as offered by OODBMS are helpful to implement the logical repository structure. Therefore, it was decided to use an object-relational database system (ORDBMS) [26]. ORDBMS integrate features of both, OODBMS and RDBMS, and are currently considered to be the most successful trend in DBMS technology. To avoid the cost of new construction from scratch, it was further decided to use one of the commercially available ORDBMS and extend its functionality to meet our needs. Next is a description of how some of the features of ORDBMS can be directly exploited for a repository implementation.

Different types of experience elements (e. g., PostScript-files, GIFs, or word processor binary-files) can be considered as large objects, which are stored in the database by using the management features for CLOBs (character large objects) or BLOBs (binary large objects). To be more precise, each experience element is regarded as a set of CLOBs or BLOBs. This is because of the fact that there can be many CV references for one experience element to allow easy access to its different available representations stored in the repository.

During the execution of an experiment, different tools are used to create, extend or change experience elements that are all to be stored in the corresponding experiment documentation of the experiment-specific section. Most of these tools store data in proprietary formats by using the file system and can not directly access the DBMS. While this was no problem for the HTML-based prototype implementation where the experience elements are stored in a Unix file system, problems might occur in a DBMS-based implementation. The problem of the proprietary formats is already met by storing the experience elements as BLOBs or CLOBs. Luckily, ORDBMS offer several mechanisms to extend database processing to data that is not directly stored in the database, but, for example, is held in the file system. These mechanisms are bridging the gap between the database storage system and the (external) file system. Hence, the tools can store experience elements in files, but, simultaneously, they can be accessed and controlled via the database interface of the repository. This concept offers referential integrity, access control, and coordinated backup and recovery for database related file system data. A file system filter intercepts file system requests to the linked experience elements and, thereby, controls access (w. r. t. the database access rights). This means that the different tools can further access experience elements in the file system, but they are closer integrated with the experience elements in the database. In cases where the experience elements written by tools are not in a binary format, it is even possible to extend the full-text search offered by the database to these 'external' experience elements. Nevertheless, a 'simple' full-text search is not always possible.

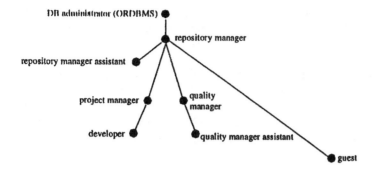

Fig. 4: Role hierachy in the current ORDBMS-based SFB 501 repository implementation

Therefore, a similarity-based search system is implemented that operates on the CV attributes associated with each experience element. Here, again, ORDBMS render a substantial contribution. Similarity functions can be realized as so-called *user-defined functions*.

Another advantage of ORDBMS, which is extensively used for the SFB 501 repository, is the predefined infrastructure for connecting a database to the WWW. Thus, appropriate interfaces for a distributed, heterogeneous system environment can be offered. For the user of the SFB 501 repository there is not much of a change in the user interface of the new ORDBMS-based implementation and the former HTML-based implementation of the repository. The query used to access the database behind the link is transparent for the user.

Together with the ORDBMS-based implementation, we integrated an access control system into the SFB 501 repository. An authorization mechanism based on user names and a role concept is used. Whether or not a certain experience element or functionality is available to a user, is determined by the role s/he uses to access the repository. Currently, the following roles are defined:

- *DB administrator* (running and maintaining the ORDBMS)
- *repository manager* (managing experience elements in the OWS)
- *repository manager assistant* (supporting the repository manager)
- *project manager* (managing data of a concrete experiment in the ESS)
- *developer* (attending an experiment, for instance, as tester)
- *quality manager* (assuring quality of the development process and corresponding products of a concrete experiment in the ESS)
- *quality manager assistant* (supporting the quality manager)
- *guest* (viewing selected parts of the ESS and/or OWS)

To each role, a set of rights concerning the access to stored experience elements in the repository (e. g., read, create, update) is assigned. A user can grant a (sub)set of his/her access rights to other users with assigned roles that are lower in the hierarchy tree.

Fig. 4 illustrates the hierarchy tree. Currently, we do not consider more roles than the listed ones, since we believe that all roles can be integrated into our hierarchy. Traditional software development roles (e. g, requirements engineer, coder, or tester) can be mapped to our roles 'project manager' or 'developer'. The same holds for all roles that are concerned with quality management activities. They are represented by our roles 'quality manager' or 'quality manager assistant'. Repository-specific roles, as for instance described in the article *'Systematic Population, Utilization, and Maintenance of a Repository for Comprehensive Reuse'* by Althoff et.al.in this book, can be mapped to our 'repository manager' or 'repository manager assistant' roles, respectively.

5 Related Work

The description of related work is twofold: First, we take a look at structures of existing repositories (Sec. 5.1) and compare them with the resulting SFB 501 repository example. Then, we will compare the technical realization of other repositories with our current implementation, based on an ORDBMS (Sec. 5.2). Due to space restrictions, a comparison with AI systems (like Case-based reasoning systems [1]), which could be used to support the intelligent search and retrieval of experience elements, is beyond the scope of this paper. The same holds for approaches that focus on integrating repositories into a certain (learning) process, in order to build up a corporate memory.

5.1 Repository Structures

In [21] Henninger discusses a *repository for reusable software components*. The paper focuses on the indexing structure of such a repository. A method is suggested of how the index of a repository can be implemented *"with a minimal up-front structuring effort"* and be incrementally refined while the components are reused. The evolutionary construction of such repositories starts with the *"Repository Seeding"*. That is, a rudimental set of reusable components is stored in the repository with a simple, basic index structure to get the reuse activities started. Then, while the components are being reused, the index structure, which is used for finding components in the repository, is incrementally improved, according to the practical needs of the repository users. The idea of starting the reuse process in a state of incompleteness to gain practical results as the basis for incremental improvement is similar to our approach. The information stored in the SFB 501 repository example becomes more detailed, as more experience elements are being reused, caused by the growing number of relations (e. g., the used_in/uses relation) between the experience elements. However, Henninger offers no predefined relation structure between the components, which is an essential part of our suggested repository structure.

The *Experience Factory (EF)* approach by Basili et. al. [5] describes an organizational approach for building up software competencies in a company and transferring them systematically into projects. As a central part of the approach, a repository called *Experience Base* stores all relevant knowledge and offers it to new projects of the organization on demand. The idea of comprehensive reuse of all kinds of software engineering experience manifested by the Experience Base is also realized in our approach (process step *define and cluster experience elements*). In contrast to Basili, our SFB 501 repository example includes the single project databases in the form of complete experiment documentations in the ESS. Nevertheless, the logical repository structure of the SFB 501 repository can be seen as a specialized instantiation of an Experience Base tailored to the SFB 501 environment. However, the main concern of an Experience Factory is the establishment of a global organizational improvement process, thus, no fixed structure for the repository (i. e., the Experience Base) is given. Our focus, on the other hand, is on the repository itself, and the process for developing and tailoring repository structures to the specific needs of an organization.

Finally, the *ASSET Reuse library WSRD* [25] is an example of a web-based implementation of an object repository. The WSRD reuse library is a domain-oriented reuse repository that contains more than 1,000 experience elements, dealing with topics such as software reuse practice or the Y2K problem. The repository is organized according to certain domains and collections that offer a mixture of different experience elements, like lessons learned, process models, or code fragments. Therefore, a certain domain (or collection) that stores experience elements from similar, but yet different projects in one entry can be compared to an experiment documentation in the ESS of the SFB 501 repository example. However, complete project documentations are not an integral part of WSRD. Cross-references that interrelate the entries in the collections are offered, but they are much more general and unstructured than the relations defined in the SFB 501 repository.

5.2 Technical Realizations of Repositories

Here, we first compare our SFB 501 repository example with a repository of the *Arcadia project* [28], in which several *object management systems* [20], [27], [31] have been developed to support the various needs of their process-centered software engineering environment. *Triton* [20] is one of those object managers. The whole system is based on the *Exodus* [9] database system toolkit to avoid the cost of new construction from scratch, just like we are using the standard functionality of a commercially available ORDBMS and extend it, in accordance with our needs. Heimbigner describes Triton in [20] as follows: "*It is a serverized repository providing persistent storage for typed objects, plus functions for manipulating those objects*". Whereas we, on demand, link the stored experience elements from the ORDBMS to the file system, so that different (commercial) tools can use them, Triton uses Remote Procedure Calls (RPC) for communication between clients programs (tools) and the repository. Therefore, the server offers a procedural interface to its clients, acting as a kind of library of stored procedures. They are accessible from programs written in a variety of programming languages (such as Ada, C++, or Lisp). But this is a limitation that we can not accept, since most of the (commercial) tools that we are using in our environment do not offer the needed functionality to use RPC's and can not be modified because their source code is mostly not available. To overcome this problem, we could have introduced mediators as described in [30] to bridge the gap between a repository like Triton and our tools. But this would call for a wide variety of mediators, basically one mediator for each tool of our environment. For the same reason, we consider experience elements as CLOBs and BLOBs to keep the original storage formats required by the different tools. Triton, on the other hand, uses a homogeneous storage schema to provide efficient representation for the wide variety of software artifacts. Consequently, all data that is shared by two or more tools has to be converted to the Triton schema, even if a direct data exchange via a format like RTF is available between the tools. Again, this is acceptable in an environment like the Arcadia project, where most of the tools have been developed from scratch, but it is not suitable for an environment like ours where commercially available tools are heavily in use.

In [3] a hybrid system for delivering marketing information in heterogeneous formats via the Internet is described. An *object-oriented client/server document management system* based on a RDBMS is used for storing the documents of the repository. Standard attributes, like creation date, author, or a version number are automatically assigned to the repository entries by the document management system. Additional attributes, which further characterize a document, have to be included as HTML metatags. Web servers are running search engines to index the repository with the help of these tags. Since we are not using HTML metatags in the ORDBMS-based repository implementation, or the HTML-based prototype implementation, all describing attributes are summarized in the characterization vectors assigned to each experience element. Based on these characterization vectors, we offer tailored search mechanisms, including similarity-based search functions, for the different tasks, whereas the system described in [3] offers the standard web functionality for search and retrieval.

6 Conclusion

In this paper, an approach for developing a comprehensive repository tailored for reuse with improvement was presented. First, a learning cycle that integrates the repository as one of its central parts was introduced. Based on this learning cycle, a process for defining and implementing the structures of such a repository was given. The described process suggests to quickly implement and run a first prototype of the repository to gain feedback of its users, and thus, to tailor the repository structures to the specific needs of the given organizational context. Next, some of the process steps were detailed by an example, namely the development of the SFB 501 repository at the University of Kaiserslautern. Beside some (technical) aspects of the used HTML-based prototype implementation and the current ORDBMS-based implementation, the resulting logical repository structure of the SFB 501 repository example was discussed. Using the repository development process presented in combination with the logical repository structure described and the characterization vector concept of the SFB 501 repository, will promote fast development of a repository for reuse with improvement in other organizations. Finally, related work concerning existing repository structures and technical realizations of repositories were reflected.

As future work, we intend to integrate additional services, for instance, versioning of experience elements and complete experiments, into the ORDBMS-based repository. Furthermore, it is intended to use the repository as a basis for different tools that support the software development process. For example, a process modeling tool, as described in [4], or a specialized SDL pattern editor [10], could use the repository to directly (re-)use existing experience elements from the OWS in new experiments, and store the newly-created experience elements in the corresponding areas of the ESS.

Acknowledgment

Part of this work has been conducted in the context of the Sonderforschungsbereich 501 'Development of Large Systems with Generic Methods' (SFB 501) funded by the Deutsche Forschungsgemeinschaft (DFG). Thanks go to my colleagues from the SFB 501, who have been involved in realizing this project and to my students, who implemented large parts of the HTML-based prototype. Especially Norbert Ritter and Wolfgang Mahnke from the 'Database and Information Systems Group (DBIS)' at the University of Kaiserslautern gave valuable insights into the different database systems. My gratitude is extended to our project leader Prof. Dr. H. D. Rombach. Last but not least, I would like to thank Sonnhild Namingha and Frank Bomarius from the Fraunhofer Institute for Experimental Software Engineering (IESE) for reviewing the first version of this paper.

References

1. A. Aamodt, E. Plaza: Case-based reasoning: Foundational issues, methodological variations, and system approaches. *AICom - Artificial Intelligence Communications*, 7(1):39–59, March 1994.

2. J. Avenhaus, R. Gotzhein, T. Härder, L. Litz, K. Madlener, J. Nehmer, M. Richter, N. Ritter, H. D. Rombach, B. Schürmann, G. Zimmermann: Entwicklung großer Systeme mit generichen Methoden - Eine Übersicht über den Sonderforchungsbereich 501 (in German). *Informatik, Forschung und Entwicklung*, 13(4):227–234, December 1998.

3. V. Balasubramanian, A. Bashian: Document Management and Web Technologies: Alice Marries the Mad Hatter. *Communications of the ACM*, 41(7):107–115, July 1998.

4. J. Münch, B. Dellen, F. Maurer, M. Verlage: Enriching software process support by knowledge-based techniques. *Special issue of International Journal of Software Engineering & Knowledge Engineering*, 1997.

5. V. R. Basili, G. Caldiera, H. D. Rombach: Experience Factory. In: J. J. Marciniak (ed.), *Encyclopedia of Software Engineering*, Vol. 1, pages 469–476. John Wiley & Sons, 1994.

6. V. R. Basili, H. D. Rombach: The TAME Project: Towards improvement–oriented software environments. *IEEE Transactions on Software Engineering*, SE-14(6):758–773, June 1988.

7. V. R. Basili, H. D. Rombach: Support for comprehensive reuse. *IEE Software Engineering Journal*, 6(5):303–316, September 1991.

8. A. Birk, C. Tautz: Knowledge Management of Software Engineering Lessons Learned. In: *Proc. of the Tenth Int. Conference on Software Engineering and Knowledge Engineering (SEKE'98)*, pages 116–119, San Francisco Bay, CA, USA, June 1998. Knowledge Systems Institute, Skokie, Illinois, USA.

9. M. Carey, D. Dewitt, G. Graefe, D. Haight, J. Richardson, D. Schuh, E. Shekita, S. Vandenberg: The EXODUS Extensible DBMS Project: an Overview. In: S. Zdonik, D. Maier (eds.), *Readings in Object-Oriented Databases*. Morgan Kaufman, 1990.

10. D. Cisowski, B. Geppert, F. Rößler, M. Schwaiger: Tool Support for SDL Patterns. In: *Proc. of the 1st Workshop of the SDL Forum Society on SDL and MSC (SAM98)*, pages 107–115, Berlin, Germany, 1998. ISSN: 0863-095.

11. M. Fechtig: Fixing the case studies' structure for the access and storage system of the experiment-specific section in the SFB 501 Experience Base (in German). Projektarbeit, Dept. of Computer Science, University of Kaiserslautern, Germany, 67653 Kaiserslautern, Germany, January 1998.

12. R. L. Feldmann, B. Geppert, F. Rößler: Continuous Improvement of Reuse–Driven SDL System Development. In: *Proc. of the Eleventh Int. Conference on Software Engineering and Knowledge Engineering (SEKE'99)*, pages 320–326, Kaiserslautern, Germany, June 1999. Knowledge Systems Institute, Skokie, Illinois, USA.

13. R. L. Feldmann, W. Mahnke, N. Ritter: (OR)DBMS-Support for the SFB 501 Experience Base. Technical Report 12/98, Sonderforschungsbereich 501, Dept. of Computer Science, University of Kaiserslautern, 67653 Kaiserslautern, Germany, 1998.

14. R. L. Feldmann, J. Münch, S. Vorwieger: Towards Goal-Oriented Organizational Learning: Representing and Maintaining Knowledge in an Experience Base. In: *Proc. of the Tenth Int. Conference on Software Engineering and Knowledge Engineering (SEKE'98)*, pages 236–245, San Francisco Bay, CA, USA, June 1998. Knowledge Systems Institute, Skokie, Illinois, USA.

15. R. L. Feldmann, C. Tautz: Improving Best Practices Through Explicit Documentation of Experience About Software Technologies. In: C. Hawkins, M. Ross, G. Staples, J. B. Thompson (eds.), *INSPIRE III Process Improvement Through Training and Education*, pages 43–57. The British Computer Society, September 1998. Proc. of the Third Int. Conference on Software Process Improvement Research, Education and Training (INSPIRE'98).

16. R. L. Feldmann, S. Vorwieger: Providing an Experience Base in a research Context via the Internet. In: *Proc. of the ICSE 98 Workshop on "Software Engineering over the Internet"*, http://sern.cpsc.ucalgary.ca/ maurer/ICSE98WS/ICSE98WS.html, April 1998.

17. E. Gamma, R. Helm, R. Johnson, J. Vlissides: *Design Patterns – Elements of Reusable Object-Oriented Software*. Addison-Wesley, 1995.

18. B. Geppert, F. Rößler, R. L. Feldmann, S. Vorwieger: Combining SDL Patterns with Continuous Quality Improvement: An Experience Factory Tailored to SDL Patterns. In: *Proc. of the 1st Workshop of the SDL Forum Society on SDL and MSC (SAM98)*, pages 97–106, Berlin, Germany, 1998. ISSN: 0863-095.

19. M. Habetz: Tools for supporting the Software Engineering Laboratory of the SFB 501. Technical Report 04/99, Sonderforschungsbereich 501, Dept. of Computer Science, University of Kaiserslautern, 67653 Kaiserslautern, 1999.

20. D. Heimbigner: Experiences with an object manager for a process-centered environment. In: *Proc. of the Eighteenth VLDB Conference, Vancouver, British Columbia, Canada*, August 1992.

21. S. Henninger: Supporting the Construction and Evolution of Component Repositories. In: *Proc. of the Eighteenth Int. Conference on Software Engineering*, pages 279–288. IEEE Computer Society Press, March 1996.

22. B. A. Kitchenham: Evaluating software engineering methods and tools, part 1: The evaluation context and evaluation methods. *ACM SIGSOFT Software Engineering Notes*, 21(1):11–15, January 1996.

23. N. Ritter, H.-P. Steiert, W. Mahnke, R. L. Feldmann: An Object-Relational SE-Repository with Generated Services. In: *Proc. of the 1999 Information Resources Management Association Int. Conference (IRMA99)*, pages 986–990, Hershey, Pennsylvania, USA, May 1999.

24. J. Rumbaugh, I. Jacobson, G. Booch. *The Unified Modeling Language Reference Manual.* Addison-Wesley, 1999.

25. The ASSET staff: Reuse Library, December 1997. http://www.asset.com/WSRD/indices/domains/REUSE_LIBRARY.html.

26. M. Stonebraker, P. Brown, D. Moore: *Object-Relational DBMSs.* Morgan Kaufman, 2nd edn., 1998.

27. P. Tarr, L. A. Clark: PLEIADES: An object management system for software engineering environments. In: D. Notkin (ed.), *Proc. of the First ACM SIGSOFT Symposium on the Foundations of Software Engineering*, pages 56–70. ACM Press, December 1993. Published as ACM SIGSOFT Software Engineering Notes 18(5), December 1993.

28. R. N. Taylor, F. C. Belz, L. A. Clarke, L. Osterweil, R W. Selby, J. C. Wileden, A. L. Wolf, M. Young. Foundations for the arcadia environment architecture. In: P. Henderson (ed.), *Proc. of the Third ACM SIGSOFT/SIGPLAN Symposium on Practical Software Development Environments*, pages 1–13, November 1988. Appeared as ACM SIGSOFT Software Engineering Notes 13(5), November 1988.

29. W. Tichy. RCS–a system for version control. *Software–Practice and Experience*, 15(7):637–654, July 1985.

30. G. Wiederhold: Mediators in the architecture of future information systems. *IEEE Computer*, 25(3):38–49, March 1992.

31. J. C. Wileden, A. L. Wolf, C. D. Fisher, P. L. Tarr: PGraphite: An Experiment in Persistent Typed Object Management. In: *Third Symposium on Software Development Environments (SDE3)*, 1988.

Systematically Diagnosing and Improving the Perceived Usefulness of Organizational Memories

Klaus-Dieter Althoff, Markus Nick, Carsten Tautz

Fraunhofer Institute for Experimental Software Engineering (IESE)
Sauerwiesen 6, 67661 Kaiserslautern, Germany
Email: {althoff, nick, tautz}@iese.fhg.de

Abstract. The benefits of an organizational memory are ultimately determined by the usefulness of the organizational memory as perceived by its users. Therefore, an improvement of an organizational memory should be measured in the added perceived usefulness. Unfortunately, the perceived usefulness has many impact factors. Hence, it is difficult to identify good starting points for improvement.

This paper presents the goal-oriented method OMI (Organizational Memory Improvement) for improving an organizational memory incrementally from the user's point of view. It has been developed through several case studies and consists of a general usage model, a set of indicators for improvement potential, and a cause-effect model. At each step of the general usage model of OMI, the indicators are used to pinpoint improvement potential for increasing the perceived usefulness and asking the user for specific improvement suggestions where feasible.

1 Introduction

The management of knowledge is a critical factor of an enterprise´s success. The objective of knowledge management is the optimal use of the resource »knowledge« for enabling learning from experience, continuous process improvement, and the extension of a company's creativity potential [1]. To support these objectives, a company's knowledge has to be explicitly stored in a so-called organizational memory (OM). While building up such an OM is already a challenging task and involves difficult subtasks like knowledge acquisition, modeling, evaluation, and reuse, the improvement of an OM through user feedback is of essential importance if an OM shall be a continuous source of a company's benefit.

The benefits of an OM are ultimately determined by the usefulness of the OM as perceived by its users. Therefore, an improvement of an OM should be measured in the added perceived usefulness. Unfortunately, the perceived usefulness has many impact factors (e.g., the precision of the user query, the urgency with which the user needs information, the coverage of the underlying knowledge base, the quality of the schema used to store knowledge, and the quality of the implementation). Hence, it is difficult to identify good starting points for improvement.

This paper presents the goal-oriented method OMI (Organizational Memory Improvement) for improving an OM incrementally from the user's point of view. It has been developed through several case studies [6] and consists of a general usage model, a set of indicators for improvement potential, and a cause-effect model. At each step of the general usage model of OMI, data are recorded to pinpoint improvement potential for increasing the perceived usefulness. If improvement potential is identified, the user is asked for specific improvement suggestions.

Since OMI bases on a continuous diagnosis of the usefulness of the OM, this method can help to adapt the OM to the needs of the users – even if the environment, for which the OM was designed, changes. Thereby the OMI method allows to overcome the general problem that users are often not available during the development of the OM. The basic idea underlying OMI is to start with an »intelligent guess« (not focus of this paper) and to improve the OM incrementally by systematically collecting and analyzing focused user feedback (focus of this paper).

In spirit OMI is comparable to evolutionary constructions of repositories (e.g., [22]) and approaches based on Failure Mode and Effect Analysis (FMEA) [23, 32, 31], which also try to avoid failure situations, that is in case of OMI, a decrease of the perceived usefulness.

OMI can also be compared to approaches for diagnostic problem solving, especially case-based diagnosis [2, 39, 3], because a classification problem has to be solved based on collected symptoms. By contrast, OMI is intended to be human-based. Only if the OM maintenance team size and number of protocol cases to be processed require additional support, case interpretation will be more and more automated.

The paper is structured as follows. Based on the description of our approach for implementing an OM in [5], Section 2 and Section 3 of this paper present OMI's cause-effect model for usefulness as perceived by the user and the general usage model, respectively. Section 4 describes OMI's diagnostic process for improving an OM, whereas Section 5 gives some information about its validation. Finally some conclusions are drawn.

2 Perceived Usefulness

The success of an OM can be measured in many ways. Examples for specific views on evaluation mainly from the knowledge-based system and related fields are [4, 3, 15, 18, 19, 24, 34, 36]. Also, some evaluation work has been done in the area of software reuse (programs), mainly regarding economic success [9, 25, 21]. Many of the economic models for software reuse can also be used to evaluate organizational memories, because OMs are also about reuse. Only in the case of an OM, reuse is not restricted to software development artifacts. Other evaluation criteria, most importantly *recall* and *precision*, come from library and information science [33].

However, using a goal-oriented measurement and evaluation approach where experts participate in the definition of a measurement program [14], we found out that the usefulness, as perceived by the user of the OM, is the most important measure for the success of an OM management system (OMMS) [30, 28]. This is not surprising since an OM is worthless if it fails to deliver information that is of value to its users. These findings are also supported by Harter [20] (there called »psychological relevance«) and Cooper [16] (there called »personal utility«).

Therefore, we will judge whether any change is an actual improvement based on the perceived usefulness *before* and *after* the change. If the usefulness improved, the change is regarded as an improvement.

As pointed out by Cooper, the ideal measurement of the usefulness as perceived by the user is practically and economically impossible [16]. Therefore, we have to simplify the measurement procedure. To do so, we recall the meaning of similarity. Ideally, the similarity between an experience item in an OM and the needed experience (specified by the query) is an a-priori approximation of the a-posteriori usefulness as experienced by the user [39, 7]. If the OMMS returns the instances i_1, ..., i_n in response to a query q, where i_1 is most similar to q and i_n least similar, the user should select (ideally) i_1 or – if more than one instance is perceived as useful – the set i_1, ..., i_m with $m \leq n$. Ideally, $m = n$. This implies also an assignment of the degree of usefulness to the instances on an ordinal scale, that is, i_1 is the most useful instance, i_2 the second most useful, etc.

Since it is difficult to determine a minimal similarity value (this depends among others on the background knowledge of the user[1]), an OMMS could return a fixed number of instances, e.g., $n = 10$. If i_m denotes the last *useful* instance, then the system is optimally useful if an OMMS never returns an instance $i \in \{i_1, ..., i_m\}$ that is not useful. The more often an OMMS returns such an instance, the less useful it will be. Using this definition, the user can simply mark all instances i_1, ..., i_n as either useful or not useful. Based on this data, the usefulness of an OMMS can be computed (e.g., relative to the number of queries issued by users). Another important aspect of usefulness is that an OMMS returns useful instances at all, i.e., m should be greater than 0.

Unfortunately, there is no single parameter with which the usefulness of an OMMS can be changed. Rather, there is a large number of variation factors. Fig. 1 shows the variation factors we have identified so far. However, we do not claim that the list is exhaustive. In the following, we will go into detail for the main branches of the cause-effect model.

– **User.** The intentions and abilities of the user will greatly influence the usefulness of the experience items returned by the OMMS. For instance, if a user does not specify his needs correctly, the OMMS might return experience items adequate for the needed experience as specified by the query, but not for the actual experience needed (which is in the mind of the user). But even if the query is specified correctly, it may be underspecified (user gives too little attribute values to allow a meaningful differentiation among the stored experience items) or overspecified (the user gives too many attribute values – no experience item in the OM can be found which matches the query). An overspecification is only possible in an OMMS that is only capable of retrieving exact matches or an OMMS computing a cutoff-value (i.e., threshold) for similarities. For a similarity-based OMMS that returns a fixed number of instances, an overspecification is practically impossible.

---

[1] See [37] for an example where similarity thresholds are used.

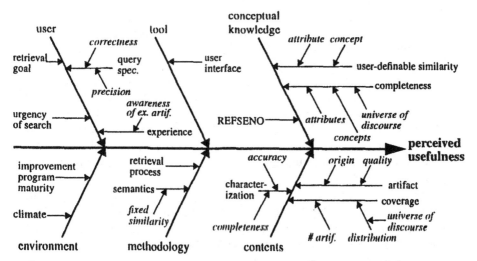

Fig. 1. OMI's cause-effect model: The usefulness as perceived by the user is influenced by many factors.

Also of importance for the usefulness of an experience item is the purpose for which the user retrieves the experience (denoted as »retrieval goal« in Fig. 1). A characterization may contain all information that is necessary to apply a lesson learned (thus the lesson learned will be perceived as useful), but may fail to provide hints how to adapt its solution to other situations (thus the lesson learned might be perceived as not useful if it needs to be changed).

Quite interestingly, the urgency of the search [20] and the experience of the user (e.g., the user might perceive only new experience, that is, experience he was not aware of, as useful) [16] will also affect the perceived usefulness.

– **Environment.** The environment in which the OMMS operates may be mature. In this case the OM tends to be filled with more experience that has been gained by the organization itself. Typically, own experience is more valuable than experience that is part of textbooks, because it can be tailored more easily to new situations since the contexts between the situation in which it was gained and the situation in which it is applied do not differ as much (or at least, the differences are better known) [12, 11]. Also, the climate in an organization influences how willingly people are to share their experience with their colleagues over an OMMS. In organizations where mistakes are not viewed as chances to learn, valuable information will remain in the minds of the people – mistakes will be repeated [17].

– **Tool.** For the user, the tool (OMMS) is mainly characterized through its behavior and its user interface. The behavior is determined through all other branches (except for the »environment« branch) and is not considered further at this point. The user interface constitutes a sort of barrier for the usage of a system. If a system is hard or cumbersome to use, people will try avoid using the system [26, 27, 30, 28]. And, if a system is not used, it is perceived as not useful and cannot yield any benefit.

– **Methodology.** It is the methodology that is supported by the OMMS. If the underlying methodology (e.g., the retrieval process supported by the OMMS or the semantics of REFSENO's primitives) is not optimal, it cannot be expected that the system is perceived as useful as it could be.

– **Conceptual Knowledge**. Clearly, the behavior of an OMMS is not solely determined by its implementation, but also by its contents and the organization of these. As the conceptual knowledge determines what and how experience is stored in the OM, it plays a major role regarding the usefulness of a system. First of all, the concepts and their attributes define a universe of discourse that the OM *can* cover. In contrast to this universe stands the universe of discourse the OM *shall* cover. The concepts and attributes may not cover all kinds of experience to be stored or all information needed to perform certain predefined tasks. In addition, the similarity functions may not approximate the perceived usefulness appropriately. And finally, certain characteristics of the universe of discourse may not be expressible using the primitives of REFSENO.

– **Contents**. Even if the conceptual knowledge is defined optimally regarding the usefulness, the contents of the OM may cause the system to fail. Just as with databases, the information stored in an OM must be accurate and complete [29]. Otherwise, users will lose their confidence in the experience provided by the system. This will lower the overall perception of the system's usefulness.

Also, the universe of discourse the OM shall cover is not covered simply by defining the universe in terms of experience types to be stored. The actual experience has still to be stored! The coverage of a universe of discourse is influenced by two characteristics: the number of artifacts in the OM and their distribution. The more artifacts are stored, the *more likely* it is that the system will return useful information. However, it is possible that many artifacts are stored, but the stored artifacts do not match the users' queries good enough (they are not similar enough). Thus, the distribution of the artifacts must match the distribution of the users' queries.

The usefulness of experience offered by the OMMS is also determined by the known quality of its artifacts. Quality can be measured in many ways, e.g., in terms of popularity or importance [16]. In addition, confidence in the origin of an artifact (e.g., the author) may influence the perceived usefulness. For instance, assume that the user issues a search request on software inspections. Let us further assume that the OMMS returns experience on software inspections whose author is known to the user to be an expert in software testing. The user may now value the usefulness of this particular experience item very high, because he may suspect a connection between software inspections and testing. In a consecutive query, the user may now also want to include experience regarding software testing.

3 Usage Model

As can be seen from the variation factors presented in the previous section, the usage of an OMMS cannot be described by a sequential process. The result of a query may lead to new insights and thus to additional queries. Queries leading to unsatisfactory results will be changed and issued again. To analyze these situations further, we first describe the »ideal« (i.e., sequential) usage scenario for an OMMS. Later, we describe under which circumstances the user might go back and repeat some of the steps.

Fig. 2 shows the sequential usage model. The process starts with the specification the user has in mind for the experience needed. The user specifies a query based on this specification guided by the schema. This query is input for the OMMS. It identifies potential experience items (e.g., if the user requests a project schedule, all project schedules are potential experience items). The identified experience items are then evaluated by computing a similarity value (as defined by the schema) from each of the experience items to the query. The resulting list is ordered by decreasing similarity and cut off at a fixed number (e.g., after the tenth experience item). The characterizations of the ten artifacts are displayed to the user who evaluates (manually) the offered expe-

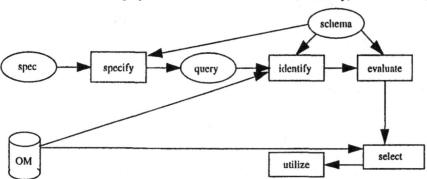

Fig. 2. The »ideal«, sequential usage model of an OMMS.

rience items. The user selects and retrieves all useful artifacts from the OM based on the provided characterizations. Finally he utilizes the artifacts.

Most of these reuse tasks have already been introduced in [5]. However, for this paper we will detail the tasks »evaluate« and »select« as illustrated in Fig. 3 (a complete version is described in [35]). The figure shows that the step »evaluate« is subdi-

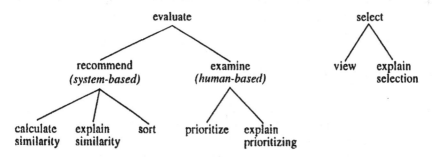

Fig. 3. The steps »evaluate« and »select« can be detailed further.

vided into one part that is performed automatically (step »recommend«, objective: suggest an ordering of the potential artifacts based on their characterizations by the system) and another part that is performed manually (step »examine«, objective: prioritize set of potential artifacts by the user). The step »recommend« is subdivided into the steps »calculate similarity« (computation of the similarity from the characterization of the stored artifact to the query), »explain similarity« (an optional breakdown by the retrieval tool how it came up with the final similarity value), and »sort« (ordering of the characterizations in descending order of their similarity), whereas the step »examine« is subdivided into »prioritize« (ordering of the artifacts based on their characterizations by the user) and »explain prioritizing« (reasons why the user ordered the artifacts the way he did).[2] The step »select« is subdivided similarly into »view« (viewing of the artifacts in the order determined by »evaluate«) and »explain selection« (reasons why the user selected the artifacts he did or why the user did not select any artifact at all).

In practice, this idealized process does not take place. It starts with the fact that users try to optimize the effort for maximum information gain [20]. This means for our usage model that the user will not specify a query with all known information (from the specification in the user's mind), but rather specify only some attribute values (in interviews, experts stated that at most ten values ought to suffice for a query) [27]. This may result in underspecified queries which in turn lead to an unsatisfactory retrieval result. If the user thinks that the system can do better, he will go back to step »specify« and supply additional information and reissue the search request.

Also, it is unlikely that a user will solely select artifacts on the basis of their characterizations. Typically, he will view the artifacts using some editor to make the decision on whether to utilize them, or not (e.g., Is the artifact well documented? Can it be easily understood?). However, aim of the characterization knowledge is to limit the number of artifacts that have to be inspected in this way as well as to reduce the effort needed to inspect the artifacts (by supplying information that can only be extracted using large amounts of effort, e.g., correctness of a technical design with respect to its specification). After the viewing of the artifact the rating of the usefulness of the artifacts may change. The deepened understanding may also lead to additional queries, starting a new usage process.

Finally, it may turn out *after* utilizing the artifact that it was not the best candidate for the purpose. If the task could not be performed by utilizing a retrieved artifact, the user may want to reissue his (possibly refined) query to find more suitable artifacts.

4 Diagnosing for Improvement

At each step of the usage model presented in the previous section, indicators may be examined to identify improvement potential. The basic idea is to diagnose situations that lead to suboptimal usefulness. These situations can be described using the variation factors of usefulness as they have been presented in Section 2. Based on the diagnosis, changes can be suggested that (hopefully) will lead to improvements of the OMMS. As we have already seen in Section 2, not all of the variation factors can be changed by purely technical means. Although some of these variation factors influence the usefulness of an OMMS substantially, the diagnosis and change of these factors is beyond the scope of this paper.

---

[2] Also a two-step CBR approach can be used to identify the most relevant attributes based on user characteristics (see, e.g., [38]).

To ease the understanding of situations that can be changed by tailoring the OMMS, Fig. 4 shows the usage model enhanced by change steps to the OMMS. In the following, each of the steps of the usage model is examined in detail.

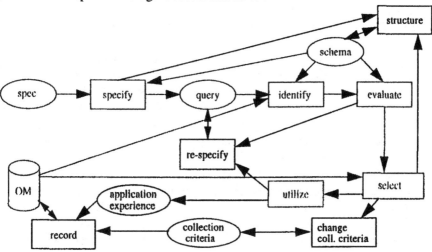

Fig. 4. The usage model (shown in grey) can be enhanced by change steps to the OMMS.

- **Specify.** At this step it may turn out that the universe of discourse to be covered by the OM, is actually not covered. For instance, if no concept for lessons learned is part of the conceptual knowledge, it is not possible to specify lessons learned for retrieval. If lessons learned are needed by the users, they should be part of the universe of discourse of the OM. Therefore, a new concept for lessons learned should be introduced. At the same time, existing lessons learned (e.g., in form of memos and minutes) should be analyzed and characterized for their retainment as artifacts in the OM.
- **Identify.** This step is performed without user interaction. Hence, no situation for improving the usefulness can be identified (by the user) during this step.
- **Evaluate.** As outlined above, this step has an automatic (step »recommend«) and a manual part (step »examine«). As with the step »identify«, »recommend« cannot be used for identifying improvement potential (by the user). Considering the extended usage model where the user employs some editor to inspect candidate artifacts to decide on their usefulness, the objective of »examine« is to decide which artifacts to view in which order (artifacts that are deemed useless based on the characterizations are neglected). This is done in step »prioritize«.

    If not enough useful artifacts have been found, the user may decide to reissue a revised query.

    During »examine«, the user may not be able to decide whether to view an artifact or declare it as »useless«. As the inspection of an artifact can require considerable effort (imagine, you have to decide whether a textbook actually contains information important to your research work), the user wants to inspect only those artifacts that have a high potential of being useful. If the user is not able to make this decision, some information about the artifact is missing. This can be supplied as part of the characterization. Therefore, for all artifacts the user cannot decide on, the user should articulate the missing information. This feedback can be used to improve the conceptual knowledge of the OM in a goal-oriented way by adding new attributes. If the missing information is supplied by the OM maintenance team (i.e., including the values for new attributes), the user will be able to decide next time he issues a similar query. The usefulness of the system will have been improved.

The output of »examine« is the order in which potentially useful artifacts are viewed. If the viewing of the artifacts is invoked under the control of the OMMS, the OMMS can record this order. Ideally, the order should be the same as the one determined during »recommend«/»sort« (as pointed out in Section 2). If it is not or if artifacts which are placed high up in the similarity-based ordering although they were deemed useless by the user, the user can be asked why he chose a different ordering (step »explain prioritizing«). The reasons may be either (a) underspecified queries (the user knows more than he has specified, and he matches the characterizations with the unspecified but known information; in this case nothing needs to be improved) or (b) improper similarity functions (either because of inadequate local or global similarity functions or because of undocumented knowledge known/assumed by the user; in the latter case additional attributes should be defined capturing the undocumented knowledge and the new knowledge should be considered by the similarity functions).

– **Select.** After prioritizing the artifacts based on their characterizations, the artifacts are viewed in the order of the priorities assigned to them. As soon as one or more artifacts have been viewed, the best suitable artifact is selected to be utilized. If the user shall not be bothered with too many questions (these will arise especially after the initial set-up of an OMMS), the questions can be restricted to the artifact actually utilized, that is, the step »explain prioritizing« is skipped – only »explain selection« is performed.[3] This alternative will not be able to identify situations in which artifacts were originally judged to be useful (based on the characterization), but later judged to be useless (based on the artifact's viewing).

At any rate, if the selection step yields no selected artifact, the user should be asked to give a reason why the most similar artifact was not chosen. In this case, a hole in the coverage of the OM has been identified. The artifact needed to fill this hole is both specified by the original query supplied by the user and the reason why the most similar artifact does not cover the requirements. Based on this feedback, the collection criteria for the type of the requested experience should be analyzed. Do they allow the collection of an artifact similar enough to the requested one? If not, the collection criteria should be changed. If the missing artifact is deemed to have a high application potential in the future by other users, either a separate project for creating such an artifact may be started or – if the artifact is created as part of the project the user belongs to – the artifact may be stored after the project has been completed.

---

[3] There are systems that implement this strategy. For instance, KONTEXT is a tool that logs justifications for made selections (see [13]).

– **Utilize.** During the utilization of an artifact, experience should be recorded about the effort for understanding and modifying the artifact as well as how the artifact could/should (not) be changed. Such experience can then be attached (in form of an extended characterization) to the artifact after its utilization. In this way, the applicability information is improved continuously with each utilization of an artifact.

During the artifact's utilization, it may turn out that the artifact is not as useful as originally estimated. If this is the case, one of four choices can be made:

1. Ignore the fact and continue utilizing.
2. Stop utilizing and do nothing more (e.g., if it turns out that a lesson learned is not applicable in the current situation).
3. Stop utilizing and create the needed artifact from scratch (e.g., a project schedule).
4. Stop utilizing and retrieve another (hopefully more useful) artifact (e.g., a project schedule).

In the latter case, the old query may serve as an entry point.

The descriptions above show how improvements in the conceptual knowledge and contents of an OM can be pinpointed by automatically collecting data and asking the user for feedback if the system behaves not as expected (based on the usage model). Tab. 1 shows a summary of the improvement actions described in this section.

Tab. 1. Indicators, causes of suboptimal usefulness, and corresponding improvement actions

Step	Indicator	Cause	Improvement action
specify	Type of needed artifact cannot be specified	Conceptual knowledge (schema) is incomplete, that is, universe of discourse does not match defined concepts	Extend schema by a new concept
evaluate/ examine	Not enough useful artifacts in the result of the query	1. Imprecise or incorrect query 2. Coverage too low	1. Re-specify query 2. Record new artifacts
evaluate/ examine	User cannot decide whether an artifact is useless or should be considered for (viewing and) utilizing	1. Conceptual knowledge (schema) is incomplete, that is, universe of discourse does not match defined attributes for the respective concepts 2. Characterizations of artifacts are incomplete, that is, not all attribute values are specified	1. Extend schema by new attributes; adapt characterizations of stored artifacts 2. Adapt/complete characterizations of affected artifacts

Tab. 1. Indicators, causes of suboptimal usefulness, and corresponding improvement actions

Step	Indicator	Cause	Improvement action
select	Order in which user views artifacts is not the order recommended by the retrieval tool	1. Imprecise query 2. Improper user-definable similarity or there are missing attributes that have not been considered for the similarity computation, but should be (error in conceptual knowledge)	1. None 2. Add attributes (if needed) and redefine similarity
select	User does not select any artifact	Coverage too low	Ask user why most similar artifact was not selected; check collection criteria (and change them if necessary); make artifacts similar to the requested one available and record them
utilize	Artifact is not as useful as originally estimated	Wrong user estimation	1. Ignore and continue utilizing 2. Stop utilizing and do nothing more 3. Stop utilizing and create artifact from scratch 4. Stop utilizing and retrieve another (hopefully more useful) artifact

Changes regarding other branches of Fig. 1 (e.g., user interface and missing experience items the user is aware of) can be suggested based on answers to questions posed to the user after each (or after each n-th) retrieval attempt at the end of step »select«. However, in contrast to the situations outlined above, these questions cannot be posed based on some (automatic) analysis and, thus, must be posed unconditionally. This might lead to an overburden on the user who has to devote his time in answering the posed questions.

Finally, the variation factors listed in the »user« branch deserve a closer look. While the precision and the correctness of the query has been taken care of by allowing the user to reissue a revised query, the variation factor »retrieval goal« may not be underestimated. Different retrieval goals have different information needs and the usefulness of the retrieval result is measured (at least partly) in terms of how well the presented experience items are suited to perform some predefined task. Consequently, both the information need (represented by a set of attributes) and the similarity functions (estimating the usefulness) may differ. Therefore, all optimizations of the OMMS must be performed with respect to the retrieval goal. Otherwise, an improvement done for one retrieval goal may result in a change to the worse for another retrieval goal (see also [37]).

As a consequence, an OMMS should ask the user for his retrieval goal at the beginning of the session. Based on the retrieval goal, the query attributes can be restricted to the relevant ones. Thus, the user is guided more effectively which in turn also helps to reduce the risk of incorrect and/or meaningless queries. In addition, optimal similarity functions can be selected. Finally, the retrieval goal can be used to tailor the OM for specific retrieval goals – the optimizations do not influence the behavior of the OMMS for other retrieval goals. However, besides the (marginal) additional effort on part of the user to specify the retrieval goal, a new error source is introduced. Now, not only the query may be incorrect but also the specification of the retrieval goal. Hence, it may not be enough for the user to change his query in case the system does not behave as wanted, but perhaps the user must correct his retrieval goal as well. An empirical investigation is needed to find out whether an average user is capable of recognizing what to change.

5 Validation of OMI

OMI was validated using CBR-PEB (Case-Based Reasoning Product Experience Base) [30], a publicly accessible OM[4] on case-based reasoning tools and applications [10]. CBR-PEB has been developed for supporting CBR system development. Emphasis is placed on providing decision support for reusing existing CBR system know-how for the development of new systems.

During its last major evaluation [27], experts (i.e., managers of CBR system developments) were interviewed to find out about their expectations about CBR-PEB, resulting in an adaptation of the schema underlying the OM. The experts articulated under what circumstances they would view CBR-PEB as useful. The interviews showed that the characterizations need to be accurate (i.e., up-to-date) and complete (validating the »characterization« branch of »contents« in Fig. 1). In addition, the experts listed some information that was essential for providing good decision support. Some of this information was not captured as part of the characterization yet, making the decision which CBR system to use as the basis for a new CBR system very difficult. This corresponds to the »attributes« branch of the »completeness« of the »conceptual knowledge« in Fig. 1. The »coverage« was seen as a major influence factor for the usefulness of CBR-PEB. For example, the number of artifacts was named explicitly.

After changing the schema and adapting the characterizations of the CBR systems stored in CBR-PEB (improvement action of second »examine« entry in Tab. 1), the experts trialed the revised OMMS. The observations concerning the way they interacted with CBR-PEB confirmed the usage model of OMI (cf. Fig. 2) [27].

The indicator/cause/improvement actions listed in Tab. 1 have been validated partly. For example, the second »examine« entry has been validated as outlined above. Other table entries are either obvious (e.g., the »specify« entry) or can be validated in a similar fashion.

---

[4] http://demolab.iese.fhg.de:8080/

In summary, through CBR-PEB we validated the cause-effect model, the general usage model as well as parts of Tab. 1. Currently, we are validating the other table entries. In addition, we are currently validating OMI with other ongoing in-house and industrial projects.

6 Conclusion

In this paper we have presented a method for improving the perceived usefulness of an organizational memory incrementally through user feedback. It is based on a general usage model, a cause-effect-model for usefulness as perceived by the user, and a set of indicators for improvement potential. The organizational memory improvement method OMI considers the practical constraints typically encountered in industrial environments, e.g., limited time of users.

To apply OMI in practice, it must be supported technically. This can be done by logging the human-computer interaction and capturing the user improvement suggestions in protocol cases [8].

Currently both our general organizational memory approach as well as the improvement method are validated within a number of industrial and in-house projects. It is expected that the method will lead to quick improvements after the introduction or extension of an organizational memory. Later on, the change rate will decrease. Thus, the additional effort requested from the users for their feedback will be limited in time.

Acknowledgements

The authors would like to thank Frank Bomarius for providing feedback on an earlier version of this paper.

References

1. Andreas Abecker, Stefan Decker, and Otto Kühn. Organizational memory (in German). *Informatik-Spektrum*, 21(4):213–214, August 1998.
2. K.-D. Althoff and S. Wess. Case-based knowledge acquisition, learning and problem solving in diagnostic real world tasks. *Proceedings of the Fifth European Knowledge Acquisition for Knowledge-Based Systems Workshop*, pages 48–67, 1991.
3. Klaus-Dieter Althoff. *Evaluating Case-Based Reasoning systems*. LNAI. Springer-Verlag, 2000. to appear.
4. Klaus-Dieter Althoff and Agnar Aamodt. Relating case-based problem solving and learning methods to task and domain characteristics: Towards an analytic framework. *AICom - Artificial Intelligence Communications*, 9(3):109–116, September 1996.
5. Klaus-Dieter Althoff, Andreas Birk, Susanne Hartkopf, Wolfgang Müller, Markus Nick, Dagmar Surmann, and Carsten Tautz. Systematic population, utilization, and maintenance of a repository for comprehensive reuse. elsewhere in this book, 1999.

6. Klaus-Dieter Althoff, Frank Bomarius, and Carsten Tautz. Using case-based reasoning technology to build learning organizations. In *Proceedings of the the Workshop on Organizational Memories at the European Conference on Artificial Intelligence '98*, Brighton, England, August 1998.

7. Klaus-Dieter Althoff, Markus Nick, and Carsten Tautz. Cbr-peb: An application implementing reuse concepts of the experience factory for the transfer of cbr system know-how. In *Proceedings of the Seventh Workshop on Case-Based Reasoning during Expert Systems '99 (XPS-99)*, Würzburg, Germany, March 1999.

8. Klaus-Dieter Althoff, Markus Nick, and Carsten Tautz. Improving organizational memories through user feedback. In *Workshop on Learning Software Organisations at SEKE'99*, Kaiserslautern, Germany, June 1999.

9. Bruce H. Barnes and Terry B. Bollinger. Making reuse cost effective. *IEEE Software*, 8(1):13–24, January 1991.

10. Brigitte Bartsch-Spörl, Klaus-Dieter Althoff, and Alexandre Meissonnier. Learning from and reasoning about case-based reasoning systems. In *Proceedings of the Fourth German Conference on Knowledge-Based Systems (XPS97)*, March 1997.

11. Victor R. Basili, Gianluigi Caldiera, and H. Dieter Rombach. Experience Factory. In John J. Marciniak, editor, *Encyclopedia of Software Engineering*, volume 1, pages 469–476. John Wiley & Sons, 1994.

12. Victor R. Basili and H. Dieter Rombach. The TAME Project: Towards improvement–oriented software environments. *IEEE Transactions on Software Engineering*, SE-14(6):758–773, June 1988.

13. Andreas Birk and Felix Kröschel. A knowledge management lifecycle for experience packages on software engineering technologies. In Frank Bomarius, editor, *Workshop on Learning Software Organisations at SEKE'99*, pages 115–126, Kaiserslautern, Germany, June 1999. Fraunhofer IESE.

14. Lionel C. Briand, Christiane M. Differding, and H. Dieter Rombach. Practical guidelines for measurement-based process improvement. *Software Process*, 2(4):253–280, December 1996.

15. P. R. Cohen. Evaluation and case-based reasoning. In K. Hammond, editor, *Proceedings of the Second DARPA Workshop on Case-Based Reasoning*, pages 168–172. Morgan Kaufman, 1989.

16. William S. Cooper. On selecting a measure of retrieval effectiveness. In K.S. Jones and P. Willet, editors, *Readings in Information Retrieval*, pages 191–204. Morgan Kaufmann Publishers, 1997.

17. Leela Damodaran. Development of a user-centered IT strategy: A case study. *Behavior and Information Technology*, 17(3):127–134, 1998.

18. J. Gaschnig, P. Klahr, H. Pople, E. Shortliffe, and A. Terry. Evaluation of expert systems: Issues and case studies. In F. Hayes-Roth, D.A. Waterman, and D.B. Lenat, editors, *Building Expert Systems*, pages 241–282. Addison-Wesley, Reading, Mass., USA, 1983.

19. Avelino Gonzales, Lingli Xu, and Uma Gupta. Validation techniques for case-based reasoning systems. *IEEE Transactions on Systems, Man, and Cybernetics*, 28(4):465–477, July 1998. Part A: Systems and Humans.

20. Stephen P. Harter. Psychological relevance and information science. *Journal of the American Society for Information Science*, 43(9):602–615, October 1992.

21. B. Henderson-Sellers. The economics of reusing library classes. *Journal of Object-Oriented Programming*, (4):43–50, 1993.

22. Scott Henninger. An evolutionary approach to constructing effective software reuse repositories. *ACM Transactions on Software Engineering and Methodology*, 6(2):111–140, April 1997.

23. Matthias Jarke and Ralf Klamma. Innovation based on computer-aided failure management: Results of the BMBF project FOQUS (in German). In *Proc. Wirtschaftsinformatik*, 1998.

24. S. Kirchhoff. *Mapping Quality of Knowledge-Bases Systems: A Methodology for Evaluation (in German)*. Josef Eul Verlag, Bergisch-Gladbach, Germany, 1994.

25. Wayne C. Lim. Reuse economics: A comparison of seventeen models and directions for future research. In Murali Sitaraman, editor, *Proceedings of the Fourth International Conference on Software Reuse*, pages 41–50, Orlando, Florida, USA, April 1996. IEEE Computer Society Press.

26. Michael G. Morris and Andrew Dillon. How user perceptions influence software use. *IEEE Software*, 14(4):58–64, July/August 1997.

27. Markus Nick. Implementation and Evaluation of an Experience Base. Diploma thesis, Fraunhofer IESE, University of Kaiserslautern, 1998.

28. Markus Nick, Klaus-Dieter Althoff, and Carsten Tautz. Facilitating the practical evaluation of organizational memories using the goal-question-metric technique. In *Proceedings of the Twelfth Workshop on Knowledge Acquisition, Modeling and Management*, Banff, Alberta, Canada, October 1999.

29. Markus Nick and Carsten Tautz. Practical evaluation of an organizational memory using the goal-question-metric technique. Technical Report IESE-Report No. 063.98/E, Fraunhofer Institute for Experimental Software Engineering, Kaiserslautern (Germany), 1998.

30. Markus Nick and Carsten Tautz. Practical evaluation of an organizational memory using the goal-question-metric technique. In *XPS'99: Knowledge-Based Systems - Survey and Future Directions*. Springer Verlag, Würzburg, Germany, March 1999. LNAI Nr. 1570.

31. T. Pfeifer, editor. *Knowledge-Based Systems in Quality Management (in German)*. Springer-Verlag, 1996.

32. T. Pfeifer and T. Zenner. Using experience during failure analysis - the application of case-based techniques (in German). In R. Grob and J. Spickermann, editors, *Workshop at the Third German Conference on Expert Systems*, pages V1–V12. Technical Report LSA-95-04, University of Kaiserslautern, 1996.

33. Gerard Salton and Michael J. McGill. *Introduction to Modern Information Retrieval*. McGraw-Hill Book Co., New York, 1983.

34. J. R. Slagle and M. R. Wick. A method for evaluating candidate expert system applications. *AI Magazine*, 9(4):44–53, 1988.

35. Carsten Tautz. *Customizing Software Engineering Experience Management Systems to Organizational Needs*. PhD thesis, University of Kaiserslautern, Kaiserslautern, Germany, 2000. to appear.

36. Bert van Wegen. *Impacts of KBS on Cost and Structure of Production*. PhD thesis, 1996.

37. Christiane Gresse von Wangenheim, Klaus-Dieter Althoff, and Ricardo M. Barcia. Goal-oriented and similarity-based retrieval of software engineering experienceware. elsewhere in this book, 1999.

38. Stephan Weibelzahl and Gerhard Weber. User modeling of customer demands through Case-Based Reasoning (in German). In Stefan Wrobel et al., editor, *Proceedings of the Workshop Days on Learning, Knowledge Discovery, and Adaptivity (LWA '99)*, pages 295–300, Otto-von-Guericke-Universität Magdeburg, Germany, September 1999.

39. S. Wess. *Case-Based Reasoning in Knowledge-Based Systems for Decision Support and Diagnostics (in German)*. PhD thesis, University of Kaiserslautern, 1995.

Technical Requirements for the Implementation of an Experience Base

Mikael Broomé[1] and Per Runeson[2]

[1] Q-Labs, IDEON Research Park, SE-223 70 Lund, Sweden,
`mikael.broome@q-labs.se`

[2] Dept. of Communications Systems, Lund University, P. O. Box 118, SE-221 00 Lund, Sweden,
`per.runeson@tts.lth.se`

Abstract. Reuse of different types of experience is a key issue in successful improvement in software engineering. The approach taken in the Quality Improvement Paradigm (QIP) and its supporting organisation, the Experience Factory (EF), is to define an Experience Base (EB), where all types of reusable objects are organised and stored. The objects may be of any type related to software development, for example, code, methods, quality models and specifications. Furthermore, not only objects identical to the target object needed can be reused, but also similar ones. This paper defines important concepts in a reuse context, elaborates a reuse scenario from which the requirements for the implementation of an Experience Base are derived. A list of 22 technical requirements is defined which cover the functional aspects related to the use of an Experience Base. The evaluation of three alternative implementation approaches are presented as an example: two database alternatives and one based on Case-Based Reasoning (CBR). Future work is to investigate the costs for extending the functionality to fulfil the requirements and to use the requirements in a real setting.

1 Introduction

Experience is a key issue for the improvement of any engineering activity. In software engineering, the reuse of experience is a crucial asset for continuous learning and improvement of the development process and consequently, the resulting products. Reuse of software artefacts, for example, code and specifications, has been promoted as a way to improve productivity in software development [4, 6]. However, a more general perspective is taken in the Quality Improvement Paradigm (QIP) [3] where all kinds of experience are reused.

There are two feedback loops in the QIP. In the *project loop*, experience gained during the project course is analysed and small changes to the execution of the project are applied. In the *corporate loop*, packaged experience is used when setting up the framework for a new project. Not only concrete objects like, for example code documents and requirement documents, but also any experience can be reused to reduce rework and improve quality, thus improving the productivity in software development. Examples of reusable experiences are processes, quality models, products and tools. Furthermore, also objects that are not identical, but similar to the target objects needed, can be reused with modifications.

To support the application of the QIP, a suitable organisation is defined, the Experience Factory (EF) [3]. The EF is a separate organisational unit with the goal of serving a long-term perspective on the software development by collecting and maintaining experience. A key component of the EF is the Experience Base (EB), where all types of reusable objects are organised and stored.

This paper focuses on technical requirements for the implementation of an Experience Base. The key question is: what requirements should be set on the implementation of an EB to support reuse of experience? The requirements are derived from usage scenarios for an experience base. Note that the requirements refer to technical requirements with respect to the usage scenarios, not on general database requirements or company-specific requirements concerning, for example, computer platform and cost.

The paper is outlined as follows. Section 2 elaborates the reuse of software experience. Section 3 presents a typical, but fictitious scenario for reuse of experience. The background in Section 2 and the scenario in Section 3 are used to derive the technical requirements on an Experience Base, which are presented in Section 4[1]. Three different implementation approaches are investigated and briefly reported in Section 5 and finally a summary and directions for future work are presented in Section 6.

2 Reusing software experience

The objects to be reused in the QIP and EF context are not limited to concrete objects like source code or design documents, but may be any piece of knowledge considered valuable for a software organisation. The evolutionary nature of software development implies that the different kinds of objects used in a current software development project are very seldom *identical*, but far more often *similar* to objects used in previous projects. A reuse approach capable only of reusing objects *as is* will likely fail in general due to the fact that every software development project is unique in some sense [2].

An efficient reuse of objects under such circumstances must involve retrieval of existing objects similar to the desired one, followed by necessary modification in order to bridge the different kind of discrepancies. Questions natural to arise in this situation are:
- What is the discrepancy between an existing object and the target object needed in the current project?
- Which existing object requires the least modification effort in order to become the target object needed in the current project?

These questions reflect common problems in reuse of objects in software organisations, namely the difficulty in describing the discrepancy between objects and especially judging the modification effort required to bridge the discrepancy [2].

---

1. In the following, references to the associated requirement in Section 4 are made by the notation [Rx.y], where x.y is a requirement ID.

2.1 Understanding the discrepancy between objects

The discrepancy between two objects is in general of three types [2]:
1. Discrepancies in the properties of the *object itself*.
2. Discrepancies in the *object interfaces*, i.e. the two objects are interacting differently with surrounding objects. Independent of the type of object, an object will in general not be used alone, but used as part of a system interacting with surrounding objects.
3. Discrepancies in the *context* of the two objects. An existing object has been developed in a context (for example, in a certain development environment aimed at producing software for a certain application domain). This original context also affects the object, although these influences may often not be visible on the object itself.

In order to model the discrepancy between two objects completely, in general all three kinds above must be used, as depicted by the three-layer model in Fig. 1 [2].

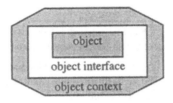

Fig. 1. Three-layer model enabling a complete understanding of discrepancies between objects in software projects

A proper characterisation of an object is to be based on the three-layer model as exemplified by the fictitious Characterisation Scheme for Reading Techniques shown in Table 1.

2.2 Understanding the modification effort for an existing object

In the situation of choosing which object to reuse, the focus is on the effort required to modify an existing object into the needed target object. Since automated support in this phase is preferable, a formal, implementable measure of modification effort is needed. The importance of a proper organisation of objects in an Experience Base to the success of reuse is discussed in [8].

A measure of modification effort naturally consists of components representing the modification effort associated with the object's individual attributes, which in general need to be assigned different weights to reflect their relevance for the total modification effort. A thorough description of a modification effort measure is given by Ostertag [13].

The modification effort can be formalised into a measure D with the following properties:

Table 1. An example of Characterisation Scheme for Reading Techniques

Layer	Name of attribute	Description of attribute
Object	Name	File path to document containing the entire description of the Reading Technique.
	Technique	Type of technique used in the reading, for example Checklist Reading.
	Document type	Type of document, which the Reading Technique is tailored for, for example, textual requirements documents.
	Representation	Form used to represent the Reading Technique, for example, as a general description or a company-specific one.
Object interface	Input/output	List of input and output documents used and produced by the Reading Technique.
	Experience level	Level of experience among the users of the Reading Technique.
Object context	Application domain	Domains in which the developed software is to be used, for example, aerospace software or banking software.
	Document size	Size of documents to which the Reading Technique can be applied; for example, small (less than 10 pages), medium-sized (10-100 pages) or large (more than 100 pages).
	Review yield	Percentage of the total number of defects found with the Reading Technique.

- $D_{AB}= k*\{$effort to modify object A into object B$\}$, where k denotes a constant of proportionality
- $D_{AB} \neq D_{BA}$ in general [R1.1]
- D contains for each attribute a_i a distance $d_{i|k,l}$ = effort$\{$modify attribute a_i from value k to $l\}$
- D defines $d_{i|k,l}$ as a creation distance or removal distance respectively if k or l is undefined (θ)
- D assigns value zero to $d_{i|k,l}$ if $k=l$
- D assigns a weight w_i for every attribute a_i denoting its relevance for D,

$$D = \sum_{\forall a_i} w_i \cdot d_{i|k,l}$$

The distance values and weights to use in a measure for modification effort, are determined by a process called domain analysis, explored in [15].

A formal modification effort measure as described above can significantly support the retrieval of objects to reuse. Starting with a description of the desired target object, for example, the Reading Technique with the desired characteristics, the modification effort measure can be used to retrieve the objects from the Experience Base most similar to the target object, i.e., those which require the least modification effort.

The concepts of a Characterisation Scheme and a modification effort measure as introduced above can significantly support reuse if appropriately implemented in the Experience Base.

2.3 Storing valuable knowledge

Appropriate retrieval of knowledge in the form of objects is an important part of reuse. The proper storage of knowledge must, however, also be taken care of in order to achieve efficient reuse of knowledge in software organisations.

An object, considered to represent knowledge valuable to future projects, must in general be adapted to the need of future projects (for example, formalised and generalised) and supplied with information facilitating its reuse [2]. This additional information to be packaged with the object into an *experience package* is basically:

- A *characterisation* of the object according to a Characterisation Scheme along with its *relations* to other objects in the Experience Base [12, R6.7].
- Description of available *Modification Approaches* for the object, for example, how it can be tailored for different purposes and environments [R4.2].
- *Lessons Learned* describing characteristics experienced during its use in projects [12, R4.2].

Objects to store in an Experience Base can be of any type, for example, cost estimation models, process models and design documents. The way a process model is characterised differs significantly from the way a design document is characterised. Consequently, different Characterisation Schemes and modification effort measures must be used for different types of object [R6.2, R6.3]. Further, new object types are likely to be derived as specializations of existing object types. An example is the object types Reading Technique and Unit Testing Technique, which both have some properties in common with the more general type Defect Detection Techniques. Such a specialisation into subtypes can be considerably supported in an Experience Base by inheritance of common properties as present in object-oriented modelling [10, R6.1, R6.4, R6.5, R6.6].

3 Reuse Scenario

3.1 Introduction

In order to make it clearer how reuse of objects can be carried out and to constitute a basis for derivation of requirements for an Experience Base, this Section provides a fictitious reuse scenario. The reuse scenario is based on the activities involved in reuse, see Fig. 2. This reuse model is further described in [7, 2].

The type of objects to be used throughout this scenario is techniques for reading of software artefacts. The scenario consists of three parts, which are partly based on experiments in the area [5, 14]. In the first part, existing experience is reused in a current project (Section 3.2) and in the second part, experience from a current project is extract-

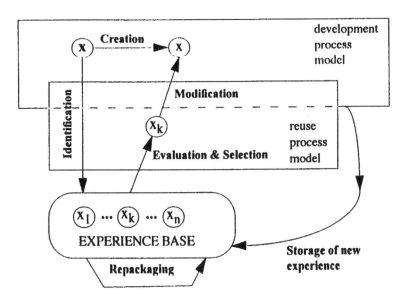

Fig. 2. An object reuse model

ed and stored into the Experience Base (Section 3.3). The third part describes the repackaging of experience in the Experience Base (Section 3.4).

3.2 Reuse of existing experience in a current project

This section describes a scenario of reuse of existing experience in a current project. The specification phase in the development process has produced informal specifications of the required objects of type Reading Techniques according to:

A Reading Technique in a company-specific representation to be used when inspecting textual requirements documents of medium size in the aerospace domain. The technique should have a yield of at least 60% when used by experienced inspectors.

The reuse of Reading Techniques is carried out in the activities Identification, Evaluation & Selection and Modification shown in Fig. 2 and presented in the sub-sections below.

Identification. The identification activity uses a formal modification effort measure to retrieve objects from the Experience Base based on similarity. The modification effort measure for Reading Techniques is shown in Fig. 3. The three attributes used are found in the shaded fields in Table 2. A transition from the θ node represents creation of an attribute value whereas a transition to the θ node represents the case where the attribute is not specified for the target object (don't care). The figures on the arcs denote the distance values $d_{i|k,l}$ [R1.1, R1.2, R1.3, R1.4].

Based on the modification effort measures shown in Fig. 3 and the informal target descriptions presented above, the target object needed is classified as:

Representation = Company-Specific, Document Type = Requirements, Yield≥ 60%.

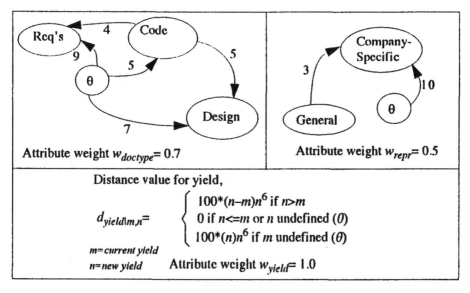

Fig. 3. Fictitious example of modification effort measures for Reading Techniques

Assume that the Experience Base contains three objects of the Reading Technique type, characterised as shown in Table 2. If any objects belonging to subtypes derived as specializations of the type Reading Techniques would be available, those objects would also have to be considered [R2.2]. Please note that the modification effort measure is only based on the attributes in the shaded fields in Table 2.

Similarity-based retrieval uses the modification effort measures in Table 2 and the target classification above to order the existing objects in decreasing similarity to the target classification [R2.1] as defined by the modification effort [13]. The order of the objects of the current sub-type is [R2.4]:

Table 2. Characterisations of Reading Technique available in the Experience Base

Attribute	Candidate Reading Techniques		
	1	2	3
Name	CBR_code	DBR_req	PBR_req
Technique	Checklist-based reading	Defect-based reading [14]	Perspective-based reading [5]
Document size	Medium	Small	Small
Document Type	Code	Requirements	Requirements
Representation	Company-Specific	General	General
Yield	50%	60%	?

*For Reading Techniques: Candidate 2 with modification effort D= 1.5, candidate 1
with modification effort D= 3.3 and candidate 3 with modification effort D= 4.3 [R1.5].*

Evaluation & Selection. The candidates obtained by Identification are further investigated in order to select the most appropriate ones to reuse. At this stage, *all attributes
in the characterisation* (Table 2) are taken into account (not only the attributes in the
shaded fields) [R2.3, R4.1] as well as *properties only seen on the objects themselves.*
The *Modification Approaches* and *Lessons Learned* introduced in section 2.3 are also
considered when evaluating an existing Reading Technique [R4.2].

*When information from Table 2 is taken into account, candidate 2 is still favoured,
although it has not been applied to* medium-sized *documents. It is expected that the
technique will scale up from small to medium-sized documents.*

All types of information described above must be considered when deciding if to reuse and which candidate to reuse, and is summarised in Table 3 for available Reading
Techniques. Let us assume that such a consideration arrives at the conclusion that: *The
candidate most suitable to reuse is Reading Technique candidate 3, since it is the only
technique that applies to textual requirements documents.*

Table 3. Properties for the available Reading Techniques not found in their characterisations

Properties	Candidate Reading Techniques		
	1	2	3
Input parameter	Code documents	Requirements docu-ments in SCR tabular notation [9]	Textual require-ments documents
Output parameter	List of defects	List of defects	List of defects
Modification Approaches	Description of how the model can be adapted to different document types		Description on how the technique can be adapted to different document sizes
Lessons Learned	Well established technique	Not suitable for other notations than the SCR [9]	Promising approach when applied by experts

Modification. The candidate selected in Evaluation & Selection is modified to fit the
requirements in the current project.

*The Reading Technique chosen, candidate 3, has an unknown yield. Since this yield
is important (and must be at least 60%) it should be estimated for candidate 3. Further,
it has a Modification Approach for different document sizes. If the chosen candidate
seems to be capable of delivering the required yield, it does not have to be modified with
respect to yield, but only with respect to representation and document size according to
its Modification Approach.*

If the modified object obtained does not fulfil the initial requirements, another candidate might be chosen for modification.

3.3 Storage of new experience

This section describes a scenario of storage of a Reading Technique, used in a current project, into the Experience Base. This storage is guided by informal descriptions of the objects needed in future projects. These descriptions are in general organised in the Experience Base according to their corresponding object subtype [R5.1]. The need of additional Reading Techniques in future projects is:

The Reading Techniques to be used in future projects are applied to code reading of large documents by medium-experienced people. They should be easy to adapt to changing project environments and display a yield of at least 70%.

The objects used in current projects are investigated and compared to the informal description of the future need above. When deciding if an object is worth storing, Lessons Learned when using the object are also taken into account:

Two different Reading Techniques are candidates for storage. Technique A is an improved checklist-based technique applied to large Java code documents by experienced staff. Lessons Learned reveals that the technique is easy to use and gives a yield of 55% by inexperienced people and 70% by experienced people. Technique B is a formal technique, reading by step-wise abstraction [11], which has shown to give a yield of 75% on small documents. Lessons Learned tells that the technique is rather hard to learn and will hardly scale-up to large documents. Both techniques are represented in general format. Technique A is decided to be stored after modification.

The object chosen to be stored is adapted to the future need:

The Reading Technique chosen (Technique A) is modified into the company-specific representation and a training course is developed to enable training people to get better yield. The change made is documented in the Lessons Learned. Modification Approaches are also written describing how the reading can be adapted to changes in the project environment. The Lessons Learned and Modification Approaches are stored in a new version of an experience package together with the technique. [R4.3]

The object is characterised according to its Characterisation Scheme found in Table 2. *The characterisation of technique A is shown in Table 4* [R4.1].

Table 4. Characterisation of the Reading Technique to store (Technique A)

Attribute	Attribute value
Technique	Checklist-based reading
Document size	Large
Document Type	Code
Representation	Company-specific
Yield	70%

3.4 Repackaging of experience in the Experience Base

The need of objects in future projects, as exemplified in Section 3.3, suggests evolution of the Characterisation Schemes used:

If the programming language used varies between projects, it should be used as an attribute in the characterisation of the Reading Techniques. The Experience Base must allow a new attribute (programming language) to be added to (and also removed from) a Characterisation Scheme [R3.1, R3.2].

If a Characterisation Scheme is changed, the stored objects associated with the scheme must be examined and, for example, supplied with an extended characterisation or removed due to not fulfilling new requirements for objects in the Experience Base.

A Reading Technique in the Experience Base, developed for the application domain business software must be removed when the development organisation is aiming to develop software exclusively for the satellite industry in the future, due to a significant increase in the required reliability.

3.5 Summary

This section has presented a fictitious scenario of reuse. The next section summarises the technical requirements for an Experience Base derived as the implementable aspects of the concepts and necessary activities introduced previously.

4 Technical Requirements

The previous sections 2 and 3 have presented several concepts and activities involved in general reuse of software experience. Some of these concepts and activities are currently not possible to support by functionality implemented in an Experience Base. For example, the *Evaluation & Selection* of a set of existing candidates retrieved from an Experience Base or the *Modification* of the candidate selected from an Experience Base to make it fulfil the requirements stated in the current project. Such concepts and activities are in general too complex or too poorly understood by the software engineering community to allow the formalised definition required to implementing them. Several concepts and activities can, however, be implemented in an Experience Base, for example, the structure used for characterizing an object (representing experience) and the operation of retrieving objects similar to the object required in the current project.

The technical requirements for an Experience Base, presented in this section, are derived as the implementable aspects of the concepts and activities presented in the introduction to reuse of software experience (Section 2) and the reuse scenario (Section 3). The technical requirements for an Experience Base are logically grouped in the following subsections.

4.1 Modification effort measure

The formal Modification effort measure specified in this subsection is required by the similarity based retrieval carried out in the identification of existing objects similar to the desired one (See *"Identification"* in Section 3.2).

R1.1 The Experience Base should be capable of representing directed distance values $d_{i|k,l}$ for any pair of values k and l for an attribute a_i in the modification effort measure.

R1.2 The Experience Base should be capable of representing a creation distance $d_{i|\theta,l}$ for each value l of an attribute a_i in the modification effort measure.

R1.3 The Experience Base should be capable of representing a removal distance $d_{i|k,\theta}$ for each value k of an attribute a_i in the modification effort measure.

R1.4 The Experience Base should provide a modification effort measure with a weight (w_i) associated to each attribute.

R1.5 The Experience Base should provide a modification effort measure, whose modification effort is calculated as a weighted sum of the involved distances,

$$D = \sum_{\forall a_i} w_i \cdot d_{i|_{k,l}}$$

4.2 Retrieval of objects based on modification effort

The retrieval of objects specified in this subsection constitutes a significant part of the activity Identification, where objects similar to the object required in the current project are retrieved (See *"Identification"* in Section 3.2).

The retrieval of objects based on modification effort has the following input products:

- Target classification expressed as values for a set, A_{tc} of attributes, $\{v_1, v_2, ..., v_p\}$, where v_i is the value for attribute a_i in A_{tc} and p is the number of attributes contained in A_{tc}.
- Relations required to other objects.

Based on the input products, the retrieval based on modification effort should provide outputs according to requirements R2.1 to R2.4

R2.1 The retrieval based on modification effort should provide a list of objects sorted in descending order of their similarity to the target classification using a chosen modification effort measure.

R2.2 The retrieval based on modification effort should not only search the current sub-type of objects but also the sub-types derived as specializations of the current sub-type.

R2.3 The retrieval based on modification effort should supply the listed objects with their characterisations and Characterisation Schemes.

R2.4 The retrieval based on modification effort should supply each listed object with its similarity to the target classification.

4.3 Support for evolution of Characterisation Schemes

The evolution of Characterisation Schemes, as specified in this subsection, is in general required when maintaining the objects stored in an Experience Base (See Section 3.4).

R3.1   The Experience Base should allow new attributes to be added to a Characterisation Scheme.

R3.2   The Experience Base should allow attributes to be removed from a Characterisation Scheme.

4.4 An Experience Package

The information to be stored together with an object, collectively referred to as an Experience Package, is used when evaluating an object retrieved from an Experience Base (See *"Evaluation & Selection"* in Section 3.2).

R4.1   The Experience Base should associate every experience package with a characterisation of the object, i.e., a set of values $v_1, v_2, ..., v_j$ according to the j attributes in the Characterisation Scheme for the current sub-type of objects.

R4.2   The Experience Base should associate every experience package with any number of textual descriptions containing available Modification Approaches and Lessons Learned.

R4.3   The Experience Base should be able to store and manage versions of experience packages (See Section 3.3).

4.5 Informal description of objects needed in future projects

Guidance on what objects to store in an Experience Base is provided by the informal descriptions of objects needed in future projects. This type of information should in general be structured according to object subtypes (See Section 3.3).

R5.1   The Experience Base should enable storage of textual descriptions ordered in a hierarchical structure according to the sub-type of object described.

4.6 Structure of Experience Base

This subsection summarises the requirements on the structure organising experience packages in an Experience Base (See Section 2.3).

R6.1   The Experience Base should organise sub-types in a hierarchical structure. This structure should be allowed to be different and separated from the structure in R5.1.

R6.2   With every sub-type the Experience Base should associate a Characterisation Scheme.

R6.3   With every sub-type the Experience Base should associate a modification effort measure (D).

R6.4 The Experience Base should provide inheritance of Characterisation Schemes from a sub-type to its more specialised sub-types.

R6.5 The Experience Base should provide inheritance of modification effort measures from a sub-type to its more specialised sub-types.

R6.6 With every sub-type the Experience Base should associate a set of experience packages.

R6.7 The Experience Base should enable representation of relations between objects of any type.

4.7 General database requirements

Several characteristics that are desired in general database applications are applicable for an Experience Base as well. These aspects are mainly (more information on this subject can be found in any standard textbook on database technologies):

- The Experience Base should provide a *proper management of large objects* to enable storage of not only the characterisation of an experience, but also the experience itself (for example, a process model or a checklist for inspecting requirement documents).
- The Experience Base should manage *concurrent users* in a controlled fashion, for example, a situation when one user want to retrieve an item currently updated by another user.
- The Experience Base should provide *security* in terms of sufficient protection of confidential data to avoid unauthorized users accessing it.
- The Experience Base must provide *safety* in terms of reliable storage of its contents, i.e. no information lost at system failures.
- The Experience Base must possess a certain usability, i.e. the functionality as specified by requirements R1.1 to R6.7 should not only be *existing* but also *easily available* for the user of an Experience Base (user-friendly).
- The Experience Base must possess a certain *maintainability*, i.e. the contents in the Experience Base should be easy to update (some of these aspects are covered by requirements R3.1 and R3.2).

The fulfilment of *database requirements* described in this subsection are in general dependent on the specific application within a database technology or implementation approach (i.e., a certain tool), where as the fulfilment of *reuse related requirements* as given by R1.1 to R6.7 are common for different applications within a certain implementation approach. A third type of requirements is *organisation specific requirements* (for example, adaptation to an organisation specific quality management system or business processes used within an organisation). The general relation between the three kinds of requirements is shown in Fig. 4.

5 Implementation approaches

In order to evaluate the ability of available implementation approaches to fulfil the reuse related requirements from Section 4, a specific tool for each implementation

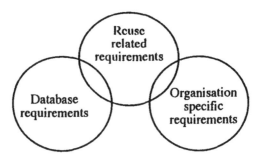

Fig. 4. Different kinds of requirements to be stated for an Experience Base

approach has been studied. The selected approaches and the tools representing the different approaches are examples, rather than an exhaustive evaluation of available techniques. Case-Based Reasoning originating from the field of artificial intelligence [1] is represented by CBR-Works, O_2 is representing Object-Oriented Databases and Informix Dynamic Server is an Object-Relational Database [7].

The fulfilment of the reuse related requirements for an Experience Base provided by the three implementation approaches is summarised in Table 5. None of the implementation approaches fulfils all requirements and each of the tools investigated must be supplemented with additional capabilities in order to be used as an Experience Base.

Table 5. Fulfilment of reuse related requirements by different representatives for implementation approaches.
Fulfilled requirement marked with •; Partly fulfilled requirements marked with o

Requirement	CBR-Works	O_2	Informix Dynamic Server	Requirement	CBR-Works	O_2	Informix Dynamic Server
R1.1	•			R4.1	•	•	•
R1.2	•			R4.2		•	•
R1.3	•			R4.3		•	•
R1.4	•			R5.1	•	•	•
R1.5	•			R6.1	•	•	•
R2.1	•			R6.2	•		
R2.2	•			R6.3	•	•	•
R2.3	•			R6.4	•	•	•
R2.4	•			R6.5	•		
R3.1	•	•	•	R6.6	•	•	•
R3.2	•	•	•	R6.7		o	o

Studying Table 5 might give the impression that: (1) "CBR-Works is most suitable to use as an Experience Base, since only three requirements have to be additionally fulfilled compared to twelve requirements for the two other tools" and (2) "O$_2$ and Informix Dynamic Server are equally suitable to be used as an Experience Base". But the requirements [R1.1] to [R2.4] constitute a group of requirements related to the similarity-based retrieval, either collectively implemented in an available implementation approach or not at all.

To fully evaluate the suitability to use a certain tool or implementation approach, database and organisation specific requirements (See Section 4.7) must also be taken into account. The intended use of the list of requirements is therefore to provide a basis for a general evaluation of an existing technology from a reuse viewpoint.

6 Summary and Future Work

This paper has elicited requirements for an Experience Base to be used as a repository for experience gained in software projects. These requirements are concerned with those aspects of reuse-related concepts and activities that are implementable and automatable. The requirements are further of a technical nature, leaving organisational issues out of account. The 22 requirements presented in Section 4 are mainly concerned with the retrieval of experience from an Experience Base and how experience is packaged and organised in an Experience Base. An Experience Base should be capable of retrieving not only those experiences identical to, but also those similar to the needs of a current project. The experience should be packaged together with information enabling a proper evaluation of its suitability for reuse in a certain project.

The different implementation approaches for an Experience Base investigated are case-based reasoning, object-oriented and object-relational databases. These are examples of implementation approaches, rather than an exhaustive survey of available techniques. Case-based reasoning is found to provide the similarity-based retrieval, but not the proper packaging and organisation of experience as required for an Experience Base. Both object-oriented and object-relational databases are found to provide a better packaging and organisation of experience than case-based reasoning, but no retrieval of experience based on similarity. Each of the studied implementation approaches thus lacks some functionality necessary for an Experience Base. To fully evaluate the suitability to use a certain tool or implementation approach, database and organisation specific requirements must also be taken into account.

One issue of future work is the extension of the available implementation approaches in order to obtain the required functionality for an Experience Base. Another issue of future work is concerned with increasing the understanding of the concepts and activities involved in reuse of software experience. If this understanding can be increased, more aspects of the concepts and activities can be implemented and supported by an Experience Base.

102

Acknowledgements

The authors would like to thank our colleagues Robert Storlind, Even-André Karlsson and Magnus C. Ohlsson who have given insightful comments on earlier versions of this paper. Thanks also to the anonymous referees and the editors for comments that have substantially improved the paper. This work was partly funded by The Swedish National Board for Industrial and Technical Development (NUTEK), grant 1K1P-97-09690.

References

1. A. Aamodt and E. Plaza, "Case-Based Reasoning: Foundational Issues, Methodological Variation, and Systems", *AI Communications*, 7(1), (1994) 39-49
2. V. R. Basili and H. D. Rombach, "Support for comprehensive reuse", *IEE Software Engineering Journal*, (1991) 303-316
3. V. R. Basili, G. Caldiera and H. D. Rombach, "Experience Factory", *Encyclopedia of Software Engineering*, John Wiley & Sons, Volume 1, (1994) 469-476
4. V. R. Basili and G. Caldiera, "Improve Software Quality by Reusing Knowledge and Experience", *Sloan Management Review*, (Fall 1995) 55-64
5. V. R. Basili, S. Green, O. Laitenberger, F. Shull, F. Lanubile, S. Sørumgård and M.V. Zelkowitz, "The Empirical Investigation of Perspective-Based Reading", *Journal of Empirical Software Engineering*, 1(2), (1996) 133-164
6. C. L. Braun, "Reuse", *Encyclopedia of Software Engineering*, John Wiley & Sons, Volume 2, (1994) 1055-1069
7. M. Broomé, "Requirements and Implementation Approaches for an Experience Base", Master Thesis, Department of Communication Systems, Lund University, CODEN: LUT-EDX(TETS-5326)/1-110/(1998)&LOCAL 13,(1998)
8. W. B. Frakes and T. P. Pole, "An Empirical Study of Representation Methods for Reusable Software Components", *IEEE Transactions on Software Engineering*, 20(8) (1994) 617-630
9. K. L. Heninger, "Specifying Software Requirements for Complex Systems: New Technologies and their Application", *IEEE Transactions on Software Engineering*, SE-6(1) (1980) 2-13
10. W. Kim, *Introduction to Object-Oriented Databases*, Computer Systems Series (1990)
11. R. C. Linger, H. D. Mills and B. I. Witt, *Structured Programming - Theory and Practice*, Addison-Wesley (1979)
12. M. Oivo, "Quantitative management of software production using object-oriented models", VTT Publications 169 (1994)
13. E. Ostertag, "A Classification System for Software Reuse", PhD dissertation, University of Maryland (1992)
14. A. A. Porter, L. Votta and V. R. Basili, "Comparing Detection Methods for Software Requirements Inspection: A Replicated Experiment" *IEEE Transactions on Software Engineering*, 21(6) (1995) 563-575
15. R. Prieto-Diaz, "Domain analysis for reusability", *Proceedings of the 11th International Computer Software and Applications Conference (COMPSAC'87)*, Tokyo, Japan (1987), 23-29

Proactive Knowledge Delivery for Enterprise Knowledge Management

Andreas Abecker, Ansgar Bernardi, and Michael Sintek

German Research Center for Artificial Intelligence (DFKI GmbH)
Knowledge Management Group
Postfach 2080, D-67608 Kaiserslautern, Germany
e-mail: {aabecker|bernardi|sintek}@dfki.uni-kl.de
http://www.dfki.uni-kl.de/frodo/knowmore.html

Abstract. An overview of the recent trends in modern enterprises motivates the central requirements for knowledge management and its support by information technology. We illustrate proactive knowledge delivery and context-sensitive information retrieval by presenting the KnowMore system. This prototype realizes active support by providing relevant information to current tasks in enterprises which are managed by a workflow system. We identify the key concepts which need to be represented in order to deal with the existing heterogeneity. We sketch the architecture of the system and highlight some implementation details.

1 Motivation: Enterprise Knowledge Management

The role of knowledge as an important, maybe the most important productive factor of modern enterprises is increasingly recognized. In today's highly dynamic environments the effective use of all available knowledge in an enterprise - be it documented, formally coded, or available in the heads of the employees - is indispensable for success. Knowledge Management (KM) tries to tackle this problem and develops tools and methods to support the acquisition, conservation, and effective use of knowledge in an enterprise. To this end, combinations of management sciences and information technology are investigated and developed towards support by business information systems and enterprise information infrastructures (see, e.g., [8] or [9]). In this endeavour, several difficulties keep reappearing: Expensive decisions in an enterprise are made without considering available knowledge. Experiences, especially costly ones, are made multiple times by independent people. Available information is contained in heterogeneous information sources, ranging from people over unstructured or semi-structured documents to databases and coded business rules. The heterogeneity of these sources makes timely access difficult, even if employees are aware of the existence of relevant information and knowledge - but typically they are not!

To tackle these difficulties, a promising approach is the integration of the various information sources which exist in an enterprise into a comprehensive enterprise information infrastructure. Together with the appropriate access services, this information infrastructure is often called Corporate Memory, Organizational Memory

Information System (OMIS), or shortly Organizational Memory (OM). Concluding the analysis of some industrial case studies, [7] argue that an Organizational Memory should exhibit several distinguishing properties, among them:

1. **INTEGRATIVE FUNCTIONS:** all real applications are characterized by a highly interwoven handling of data, formal knowledge (workflow steps, formal decision rules, mathematical formulae, etc.), informal representations (texts, memos, minutes of meetings, documentation, business letters, graphics and drawings) and knowledge embedded ("materialized") in artifacts/representations of work (e.g., a product design). Not only the conjoint view and usage of all these representations is important, but still more, the various interrelationships among them (a decision is grounded on a dossier which employs some formal calculations, it is negotiated in a meeting and documented in the minutes, and it leads to other decisions and effects on the final result of work). Furthermore, already at the technical level, there is a huge amount of heterogeneity since we have to build upon many legacy knowledge and information systems.

2. **ACTIVE SUPPORT:** In the rapidly changing business information world, users are often not aware that there is useful information in the system available. Even if they are, they do not necessarily know where and how to search for it (in an optimal way). Even if they know, searching costs time and effort. Thus, the OM should actively offer interesting knowledge.

An approach to the first issue is faced with the heterogeneity of more or less informal knowledge representations which are in use in real knowledge-work processes. Consequently it is necessary to design an OM system as, so to speak, a meta information system, which on the basis of a knowledge-rich retrieval component provides access to existing legacy knowledge and information systems.

A solution to the second issue lies in the close integration of an OM with the business processes of the enterprise and their IT enactment in workflow systems. As each task in an enterprise is part of some - probably explicitly known or even formalized - business process which in turn can be operationalized in workflow systems, the workflow engine can be employed to trigger active information support. The context of the process, on the other hand, can be used both for determining relevant information as well as for precise indexing when new information is entered into the OM.

Figure 1 illustrates these concepts: The OM comprises a variety of heterogeneous information sources. From this, decision support is offered automatically to specific tasks in various business processes. New information is captured and stored in the OM, taking into account the context of the business process where it was created.

In this paper we focus on the active support by workflow-embedded, precise-content information retrieval from various, heterogeneous sources. The embedding into the business workflows facilitates the active support, while the necessary integration issues are tackled by uniform meta descriptions of the various knowledge sources based on logic-based modeling and three relevant ontologies.

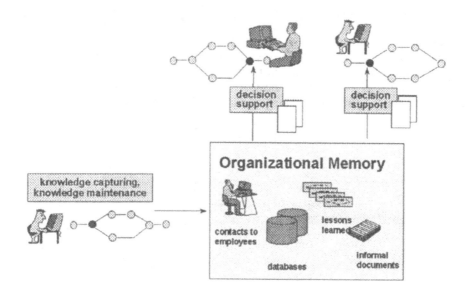

Fig. 1. An Organizational Memory in the context of business processes

In the following sections, we describe the basic functionality of our system prototype developed in the KnowMore (Knowledge Management for Learning Organizations) project and elaborate a bit on its realization principles and implementation issues. Furthermore we sketch the functionality of the supporting toolbox which is necessary to make the introduction of the KnowMore approach in an enterprise a feasible task. In the last section, we discuss some future work and open questions.

2 Proactive Knowledge Delivery With The KnowMore System

As an example consider a very simple process: a first contact to a potential customer at our research institute. Figure 2 gives an impression of the first steps of the formal workflow to be performed: After the initial contact (e.g., a telephone call), the relevant topics of interest are identified (for instance, specific technologies or tools potentially useful for the customer, or former projects dealing with similar issues as the customer's problems) and appropriate information material is selected (for example, a technology whitepaper, a brochure about a specific tool, or a project flyer). Having done this, a nice information package can be sent to the potential customer. After some time there will be a reply: *No interest* ends this particular process, a request for *More Information* loops to the identification of relevant information material, while *interest* leads to further steps, e.g., the arrangement of a meeting or the definition of an appropriate offer to the customer. Most of the activities in this process can be considered knowledge-intensive. Figure 2 also gives an idea about possible support for these activities: When selecting the information material to be sent active suggestions from the system would be helpful, supposed that the system takes into account the information from the activities done so far, e.g., the selected topics. An automatic, context-aware archiving of the results is useful when a similar process is started at a different time and / or location: The initial contact will then profit from information about earlier contacts to the same company or about similar cases.

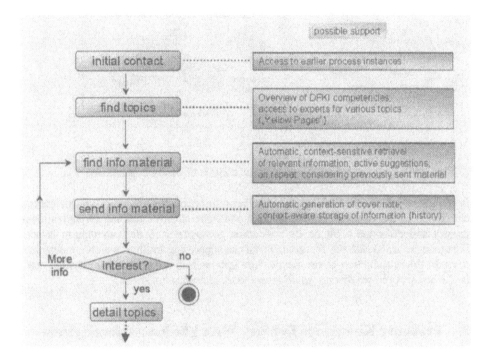

Fig. 2. A simple workflow with possible support for knowledge-intensive tasks

In order to provide such a service, the KnowMore approach proceeds with the following steps:

1   Model the overall business process with a conventional BPM or workflow tool.
2   For knowledge-intensive tasks (KIT) extend the respective workflow activity by generic queries to be posed to the OM, the answers of which would help to perform these tasks.
3   During workflow enactment instantiate the generic queries, try to answer them through the OM and actively deliver (or, offer) the answer to the user.

Figure 3 shows a screenshot of our experimental system prototype. On the left, in the background, we see an editor window of the workflow application used to indicate relevant information material. To do this it is necessary to fill the text fields in the input mask. The KnowMore system provides support in the following way:

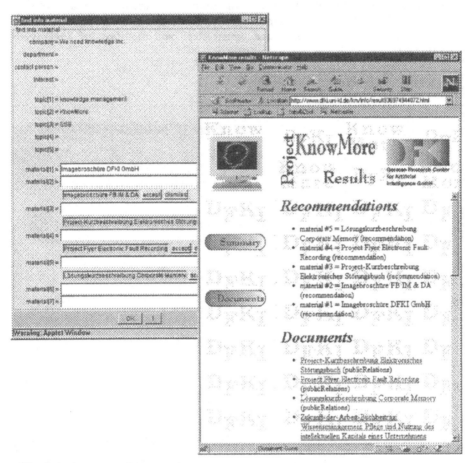

Fig. 3. Active support by suggesting relevant information material

When the workflow engine starts this activity, the system takes the information needs associated to the activity and finds out whether some element of the OM is relevant to this task (i.e., whether there is some material which is relevant wrt. the topics identified). This suggested decision value is inserted in the user input mask offering a proposed solution (in the example, the suggestion comprises documents about the DFKI, a paper about corporate memories, and some material on the ESB system which is an example of an organizational memory). The suggested information elements are ordered according to their relevance computed by the retrieval function as well as to a predefined order based upon their information type, and are offered to the user as hyperlinks in the KnowMore information browser (note that our system uses standard web browsers with Java applets for the user interface).

The user is free to accept or dismiss the suggestions or to select different material according to personal knowledge. Whatever the choice, the system keeps track of the solutions and the workflow, and records the results automatically together with the relevant context information. If, sometime later, further material is to be selected, the system remembers the results of the earlier steps and modifies the suggestions accordingly.

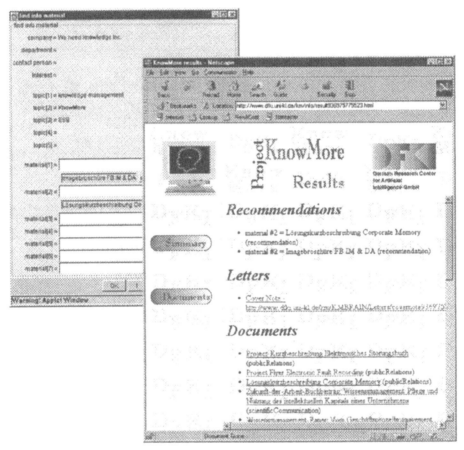

Fig. 4. Context-aware support: information from earlier activities is taken into account, resulting in modified suggestions

Figure 4 shows the support after some material has already been sent: Not only is the list of automatically computed suggestions shortened by the already-used elements, there is also an additional link to the letter which has been written earlier.

Thus the system actively offers supply to the user by providing context-specific relevant information.

3 Realization of the KnowMore System

For realizing the functionality described, the KnowMore system makes the following technical provisions:

- Each KIT in a business process model is equipped with a support specification describing the respective information needs as generic queries or query schemes to be instantiated at runtime, together with their appropriate preconditions and postprocessing rules for the results, which govern the activation triggers and the presentation of the results, respectively.

- In order to instantiate the query schemata at runtime thus exploiting situation-specific knowledge and context parameters, the retrieval process must have access to the workflow parameters. These parameters are represented in variables which are handled by the workflow environment. As they go typically beyond what is modeled in a conventional workflow specification we talk about KIT variables, although there is no conceptual difference between them and conventional work-flow variables. They simply describe the information flow between tasks in the workflow, and are the communication channel between workflow and information retrieval agents (in the above example, the product slot). To enable the necessary reasoning for intelligent retrieval, the KIT variables must be embedded into a domain ontology (essentially, this means that their values must be of a type defined as an ontology concept) which can also contain retrieval heuristics about them.

- For enabling precise-content retrieval from manifold heterogeneous sources in the OM, a powerful representation scheme for uniform knowledge description must be provided. We propose logic-based modeling of structure and metadata, information content and information context on the basis of formal ontologies.

3.1 Combining ontology-based information modeling and workflow integration

Figure 5 shows the basic architecture of the KnowMore system. It implements the OM architecture principles described in [1]. Active support is achieved by declarative support specifications attached to workflow models at process definition time: Each activity description is extended by the appropriate generalized queries, which in turn are formulated using variables refering to the (extended, where necessary) workflow environment and data flow among activities. When triggered at runtime, information agents instantiate the queries and perform the precise-content Information Retrieval (IR) on the various information sources. As both the content descriptions of the heterogeneous knowledge sources and the values used for the query instantiations are based on an comprehensive domain ontology, logic-based IR algorithms traverse the domain ontology to perform semantically sound query expansions. Appropriate retrieval heuristics control this use of the ontology. The resulting queries retrieve the information which offers relevant support for the particular activity. On the basis of an information ontology, declarative models of information sources and knowledge items realize a homogeneous description of the form of the available knowledge; the content of each knowledge item is described with respect to the domain ontology. Thus the necessary abstraction from technical and semantic heterogeneity is achieved by relying on ontologies and meta data.

It is important to note that the realization of the KnowMore system fits well into the standard architecture of workflow systems as promoted by the workflow management coalition. Figure 6 illustrates this fact: The KIT descriptions are an extension of the workflow relevant data handled by a WfMC-conform workflow engine. The worklist handlers start the relevant activities and trigger in addition the information agents specified in the KIT descriptions. These agents than access the context information in the extended workflow relevant data, evaluate parameters and search heuristics to find relevant information and offer the results to the user. In spite of the fact that the KnowMore prototype uses a self-developed workflow engine, the results are thus compatible with a vast amount of existing and commercially available workflow implementations.

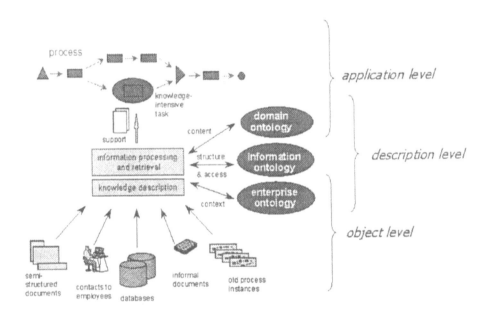

Fig. 5. The 3-layered OM architecture of KnowMore

3.2   Search heuristics specify the traversal of the ontologies

When an information agent is invoked by the worklist handler it takes two separate input elements from the current instantiation of the KIT description: the instantiated parameters which represent the actual context of the information request, and the search heuristics specified in the KIT description. Based on this, the information agent accesses and evaluates the various information sources, and retrieves and computes the relevant information (cf. Figure 7).

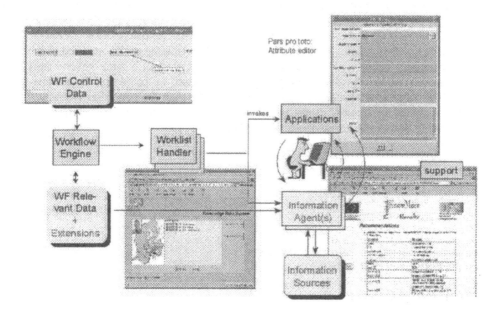

Fig. 6. The KnowMore extensions fit into the WfMC workflow architecture

In this scenario the specified search heuristics plays an important role: by traversing the ontologies accordingly, the information agent interprets the static structure of the ontologies to decide about the relevance of information in the actual context of the retrieval task at hand.

Example 1: Consider a part of a domain ontology describing the competences of the members of our DFKI research group shown in Figure 8. Suppose Tino to be our only employee, known as competent in the field of object-oriented databases. If we are now searching for a person competent in the field of databases, a simple keyword based search would fail. However, if we can use the subsumption relationships between competence fields shown in Figure 8, together with a general search heuristics stating that people knowledgeable in a specific area can also be considered competent in the more general topics, we can expand our scope of search, thus finding Tino who will certainly have some knowledge in general database questions.

Example 2: In order to exemplify the use of a slightly more complicated search heuristics consider the following scenario. One source of knowledge which is readily available in every company describes which person works (or worked) in which project(s). If we just represent which technologies were relevant in which projects (in addition to people and technologies, and direct links between both), we can easily infer that people working in a project that deals with some technology are of course competent in this technology.

In Figure 8, we show the complete scenario including people, technologies, projects, and *worksIn* as well as *usesTechnology* links. If we are now looking for an expert in deductive, object-oriented databases (DOODB), we find the ESB project[1], and, via the *worksIn* link, we find Mike who is supposed to be competent in DOODB. If we also had to our disposal another general heuristics (similar to the one used in the prior example) which would state that someone competent in a more general area could also be knowledgeable in its specializations, again, we could find Tino. However, this conclusion apparently is much more unsafe than the two other heuristics. Thus, it should be possible to formulate sort of a "cascading strategy" pursuing a sequence of search paths with decreasing certainty.

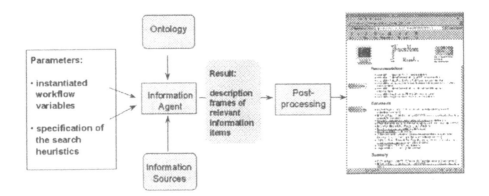

Fig. 7. The information agent uses the context parameters and a search heuristics

In this example, we exploited "sparse" indices with the help of intelligent traversal heuristics. Of course, the same effect could have been achieved with simple retrieval methods and a "complete indexing", putting all knowledge into the indices that is now heuristically inferred at runtime. At first hand, the reasons for choosing our approach were solely pragmatic: in a real-world enterprise, we will always have to live with incomplete information, maintenance problems, and partly out-dated data. Under such circumstances, relying on a minimal extension - which must be put in and maintained – together with powerful completion methods seems to be the preferable approach. But, there is also a more fundamental reason: at least retrieval heuristics referring to the actual query context parameters can by no means reasonably be put into the index

---

[1] A DFKI application project which employs DOODB technology for contextually-enriched recording of maintenance experiences for a complex coal mining machine [3].

database. If, for instance, I want to retrieve people competent in a given area or any more general area which is still more specific than my own knowledge, this information can hardly be put into the indices in advance (for each possible querying employee).

If we would do competence retrieval by hand, an intuitive way would be: take as input a graphical representation of the knowledge structures considered (illustrated as directed graphs in Figure 8), start with the given search items (i.e., marked nodes in the graph) and traverse this graph until a person is found which can be reached from the query items through a "reasonable" sequence of steps. In the examples of the previous section, the meaning of "reasonable sequence of steps" was illustrated by search heuristics describing graph traversal strategies which promise to lead from a competence field to a person which is supposed to know something about this field. Since we believe that such search heuristics are very much too domain and application specific to be formulated once forever and built into the system in a hard-wired manner, we propose a declarative heuristics specification formalism to be interpreted by the CKBS. A heuristics expression is a sequence of formulae of the following form:

$f_1 \circ f_2 \circ \ldots \circ f_n$ (denoting the functional composition of the f_i) with $f_i \equiv (\lambda)^{\gamma}$

where λ is a link or an inverse link (written as $link^{-1}$) and γ is a "partial closure specification", i.e., one of the following path length specifications:

n, $n..m$, $\geq n$, * (as abbreviation for ≥ 0), or + (as abbreviation for ≥ 1).

Such a formula takes as input a set of nodes of the directed graph under consideration and, for each node, follows the links specified in the formula in right-to-left order, in each step delivering an intermediary set of nodes as starting point for the next step. "Partial closure" means repeatedly following the same link type (in the case of γ $\equiv$ * generating the reflexive and transitive closure of the relation denoted by that link in the ontology). A heuristics formula makes sense if it delivers only person nodes as result set. A sequence of formulae is evaluated in its sequential order with the semantics in mind that less trustworthy heuristics should be denoted last.

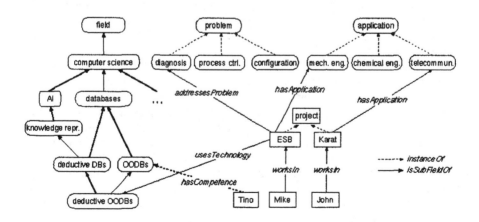

Fig. 8. People / technology ontology plus related project information

Example 1:
The first example of the previous section can then be specified as follows:
1. $(hasCompetence^{-1})^1$
   "First search for people directly linked to a search concept."
2. $(hasCompetence^{-1})^1 \circ (isSubFieldOf^{-1})^+$
   "Then look for people competent in some subfield."
For the sake of clarity, we have denoted two formulae here. An alternative formulation would have been: $(hasCompetence^{-1})^1 \circ (isSubFieldOf^{-1})^*$

Example 2:
The second example can be denoted as follows:
1. $(hasCompetence^{-1})^1$
   "First search for people directly linked to a search concept."
2. $(worksIn^{-1})^1 \circ (usesTechnology^{-1})^1$
   "Then search people working in a project applying the technology in quest."
3. $(hasCompetence^{-1})^1 \circ (isSubFieldOf)^1$
   "Finally look for people experienced in the direct superconcept of the topic in quest."

These examples show how heuristics expressions can provide a declarative means for tailoring and tuning the retrieval engine. The heuristics described should not be understood as prescriptive and valid in all environments. They shall just illustrate how ontology-based search heuristics could look like and how they can be written down in an intuitive, declarative, yet expressive way. Exactly the fact that heuristics may differ significantly from domain to domain, from company to company, or application situation to application situation makes such a declarative and easily adaptable formalism interesting and appropriate.

We illustrated the language constructs needed for formulating our sample heuristics. Of course, there are also boolean connectives useful; but only further work and experiments in a fielded application will show what expressiveness is really necessary in application examples. For a finalized, full-fledged search heuristics language, one could imagine, e.g., some kind of quantification, qualitative path length restrictions, or expressions over query context parameters.

Such a heuristics language is certainly more intuitive and flexible than directly coding search heuristics into the implementation of the retrieval machinery. It is necessary because in our opinion, practical applications cannot be sufficiently solved by few general search heuristics like the ones proposed in most papers on ontology-based IR. Of course, it is still not very easy to use such a language for an end-user, but (i) in practice it will be used by employees at the application programmer level, and (ii) it would be an interesting idea to provide both a graphical browser interface and an automatic retrieval engine and try to automatically derive (e.g., by explanation-based learning) search heuristics from user's manual interaction. It should also be noted that explicitly encoded factual knowledge about people's competences is superior - *if available*. What we propose is to enhance - in a cascading search strategy - the retrieval facilities of a system which must also be robust in a dynamic and incompletely modeled world.

3.3 Implementational aspects

Figure 9 gives an overview of our current implementation. The KnowMore prototype has been implemented in JAVA which allows it to be used on all JAVA-enabled platforms. The KnowMore server holds all relevant data, i.e., the business process model enriched by KIT variables and support specifications as well as the OM archive together with the respective knowledge descriptions and the underlying ontologies. Business process models can be designed using the ADONIS commercial BPM tool (the KnowMore specific extensions are modeled as comments in the activity descriptions) [4, 6], and are later parsed into the KnowMore representation formalism. The core part of all so-represented knowledge is an object-centered knowledge representation formalism. The basic language constructs of this formalism are mapped in turn onto conventional relational databases which are coupled with JAVA via JDBC.

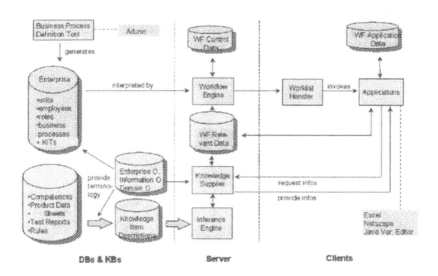

Fig. 9. The KnowMore system has a web-enabled client-server architecture

The KnowMore server hosts both the workflow engine and the knowledge-based retrieval machinery. Workflow enactment involves two parts: the server, implemented as a JAVA application, and client worklist handlers, implemented as JAVA applets which connect to the server via standard TCP/IP sockets. The architecture and communication protocols are designed in compliance with the Workflow Management Coalition standards such that later on, when the scenario is stable and proved, it should be possible to switch from our homemade KnowMore workflow engine to a commercial one.

4 Supporting OM Creation and Maintenance: The KnowMore Toolbox

As shown above, the realization of a comprehensive, active OM requires extended process models, several ontologies of different complexity, and a continuous integration of information entities, especially documents, into the system. Figure 10 gives an overview of the set of tools which has been created to facilitate these tasks. The extended business processes are defined using a commercial modeling tool (ADONIS by BOC GmbH) which has been extended by KIT modeling facilities - a set of forms supporting the description of the KIT information. In order to facilitate the definition of the various ontologies, a methodology of interactive thesaurus-based ontology construction has been defined and realized in an editor. Based on the analysis of domain-specific available texts, the cumbersome task of ontology construction is effectively supported by reference to automatically discovered term correlations and clusters. The description of the knowledge items is also supported by automatic tools: A learning text classification tool creates important parts of the meta data automatically. Details of these supporting tools are beyond the scope of this paper, but in summary a comprehensive environment for OM construction has been realized.

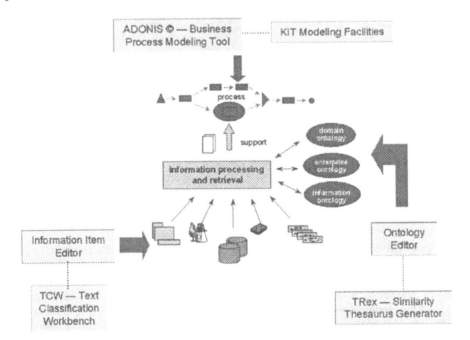

Fig. 10. A comprehensive toolbox supports the OM realization

5 Conclusion and Future Work

Knowledge management - storing, maintaining and distributing relevant knowledge - has been motivated as a crucial endeavor in modern enterprises. A suitable support by information technology asks for proactive, context-sensitive knowledge delivery. We demonstrated that these goals can be achieved by the integration of information retrieval agents with an extended workflow environment. The former require an encompassing uniform knowledge description to cover all relevant knowledge (and information) sources. The latter results in the introduction of support specifications in the representation of knowledge-intensive tasks in the workflow.

Our system architecture illustrates the components and their integration into a comprehensive client/server system. The prototype is currently expanded in several application examples. On the long run, we will generalize its principles into a generic framework for Organizational Memories (OMs). We will clarify central components in this scenario and their communication mechanisms. The objective of this research is a flexible, agent-based OM architecture [2]. Beyond this, our future work will focus on methodological aspects: How can the proposed OM approach systematically be introduced in a company, and which development support can be offered to this objective?

ACKNOWLEDGMENT: The work described in this paper has been done in the projects KNOWMORE funded by the German Federal Ministry for Education and Research (bmb+f) and KNOWNET funded by the European Commission.

References

1. A. Abecker, A. Bernardi, K. Hinkelmann, O. Kühn, and M. Sintek. Toward a technology for organizational memories. IEEE Intelligent Systems, May/June 1998.
2. A. Abecker, A. Bernardi, and M. Sintek. Developing a knowledge management technology - an encompassing view on KnowMore, Know-Net, and Enrich. In IEEE WET-ICE '99 Workshop on Knowledge Media Networking, Stanford, CA, 1999.
3. A. Bernardi, M. Sintek, and A. Abecker. Combining artificial intelligence, database technology, and hypermedia for intelligent fault recording. In ISOMA-98: 6th Int. Symposium on Manufacturing with Applications, Anchorage, Alaska, May 1998. TSI Press, Albuquerque, New Mexico, USA. This paper won the ISOMA-98 Best Paper Award.
4. BOC GmbH. The Business Process Management Toolkit ADONIS. URL http://www.cso.net/boc/english/index.htm, 1998.
5. U.M. Borghoff and R. Pareschi. Information Technology for Knowledge Management. Springer, Berlin, Heidelberg, New York, 1998. Some articles of this book also appeared in a special issue of the Journal of Universal Computer Science, vol. 3, no. 8, Springer, 1997.
6. D. Karagiannis, St. Junginger, and R. Strobl. Introduction to business process management systems concepts. In B. Scholz-Reuter and E. Stickel, editors, Business Process Management, Lecture Notes on Computer Science, LNCS. Springer-Verlag, 1996.
7. O. Kühn and A. Abecker. Corporate memories for knowledge management in industrial practice: Prospects and challenges. In [5], 1998.
8. I. Nonaka and H. Takeuchi. The Knowledge-Creating Company. Oxford University Press, 1995.
9. K.M. Wiig. Knowledge Management: Foundations. Schema Press, Arlington, 1993.

Goal-Oriented and Similarity-Based Retrieval of Software Engineering Experienceware

Christiane Gresse von Wangenheim[1], Klaus-Dieter Althoff[2], Ricardo M. Barcia[1]

Federal University of Santa Catarina, Production Engineering, 88049-00 Florianópolis, Brazil
{gresse,rbarcia}@eps.ufsc.br

Fraunhofer Institute for Experimental Software Engineering (IESE), Sauerwiesen 6,
D-67661 Kaiserslautern, Germany
althoff@iese.fhg.de

Abstract

For the successful reuse of software engineering know-how in practice, useful and appropriate experienceware has to be retrieved from a corporate memory. As support is required for different processes, purposes, and environments, the usefulness of retrieved experiences depends mainly on the particular reuse situation. Thus, a flexible retrieval method and similarity measure is required, which can continuously be tailored to specific situations based on feedback from its application in practice. This paper proposes a case-based approach for the retrieval of software engineering experienceware taking into account those specific characteristics of the software engineering domain, such as the lack of explicit domain models in practice, diversity of environments and software processes to be supported, incompleteness of data, and the consideration of «similarity» of experiences. The approach is illustrated through its application in the REMEX system, a prototypical Experience Base application for the experience-based support of the planning of software measurement programs.

Keywords: software engineering experienceware, similarity-based retrieval, similarity modeling and maintenance, goal-oriented retrieval, case-based reasoning, software process improvement

1 Introduction

The application of an Experience Factory (EF) is successful and beneficial, if the available knowledge is effectively and efficiently used organization-wide to support software process tasks. Essential for the usage and acceptance of an Experience Factory in practice is the usefulness of the Software Engineering (SE) experiences retrieved from the Experience Base (EB). Yet, the identification of «useful» experiences is complicated due to the specific requirements to an EF in the software domain.

Those requirements derived from our experiences on experience-based support of planning of measurement programs [18,23,24,26,29] and from other SE areas [3,17,10,28] include:

Goal-oriented retrieval. The possibilities to support software process tasks through the reuse of experiences from the EB are manifold. Some examples are:

- A project manager can reuse a quality model on effort distribution from a similar past project as a basis for the effort estimation of a new software project at the company IntelliCar, which produces embedded software for automobiles.
- A developer can reuse lessons learned regarding the development of Java applications to solve a specific problem, which occurred during the development of an e-commerce application at the company IntelliCommerce.
- A quality assurance team can reuse measures and data collection instruments from past measurement programs in network management projects while planning a new measurement program at the company IntelliPhone.
- A process engineer can reuse a process model on code inspections, which has been developed at his company IntelliMed, when introducing code inspections in a new project.
- A tester can reuse descriptions of problems that occurred in the past during testing to prevent the repetition of those failures during the current testing process.
- An experience engineer can reuse individual experiences gathered from several past projects to identify patterns and develop general domain knowledge during the maintenance of the EB.

To enable comprehensive support, the EF has to provide support for various reuse scenarios. Therefore, various types of experiences, denoted as experienceware [24], have to be retrieved from the EB for several software process tasks, viewpoints, environments addressing various purposes. This requires the explicit definition of *retrieval goals* based on the reuse scenarios and a parametric retrieval mechanism, which is tailorable to the particular retrieval goal and supplies useful experienceware wrt. the particular goal.

Similarity-based retrieval. As the usefulness of experiences can only be determined when it has been tried to reuse them in the current situation, the a posteriori criterion of usefulness is predicted through the criterion of similarity between the present situation and the one described in the experience, assuming that similar situations (or problems) require similar solutions (see Figure 1). For example, we assume, that measurement

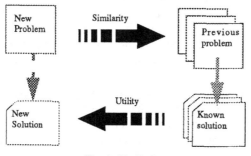

Fig. 1. Similarity

programs with similar goals use similar quality models and measures or that similar problems occurring during code inspections have corresponding solutions. In this context, an important issue is the notion of similarity. In the SE domain, it is very unlikely to find an artifact in the EB fulfilling completely the needs of the current situation, because each software product, project, or organization is different. We rather have to search for experiences that have been gathered in past situations and are similar to the current one. For example, assuming a project manager wants to reuse a quality model on effort distribution for the planning of a new software project, which is characterized as shown in Table 1 (Present Project).

Table 1. Example of project characterizations

Characteristics	Present Project		Past Project 1	Past Project 2	Past Project 3
application sector	automobile		automobile	aerospace	aerospace
programming language	C, Assembler		C, Assembler	C, Assembler	C, Assembler
project team size	3		2	20	15
experience level	medium		medium	high	low
complexity	high		high	high	medium
(estimated) product size	20K		15K	80K	50K

Based on a set of indexes[1] relevant for the retrieval of useful experiences, the current situation description is compared to the experiences stored in the EB. It is very unlikely that a project with the same characteristics has already been done in the company, yet, it is quite probable that in the past «similar» projects have been performed. For example, project 1 with 2 developers and a system size of 15K (and the other characteristics unchanged) as shown in Table 1. Although, not perfectly matching the characteristics of the present project, the effort model of the past project could still be used as a basis for the current estimation and adapted to fit the present situation completely.

Therefore, the retrieval of experiences with similar characteristics in relation to the present situation is required, rather than perfectly matching the given characteristics as, for instance, done in database management systems or information retrieval systems. This is a nontrivial task, as it considers the evaluation and comparison of complex knowledge representations to define similarity concerning the reuse of measurement experienceware.

The similarity of experienceware can be judged on two levels: global and local. *Global similarity* measures are based on the number of indexes that the past and present situation have in common. In the example shown in Table 1, project 1 would be considered more similar to the present project (four corresponding indexes) than project 2 (two corresponding indexes) or project 3 (one corresponding index).

---

1. As index we denote attributes of the case that predict the usefulness of the case concerning the given situation description and are used for retrieval and determination of the similarity value.

In addition, depending on the specific retrieval goal, the correspondence of certain indexes might be more important than others. For example, for the retrieval of lessons learned on the programming language C, the application sector may be unimportant, whereas the perfect match of the programming language is imperative and the experience level is considered as important. Therefore, depending on the retrieval goal the relevance of each index for the determination of the global similarity value has to be determined and is explicitly represented by *relevance factors*.

Considering only global similarity may often lead to the rejection of cases as reuse candidates in the SE domain, because only a few of their index values are identical to the given situation although two cases might be quite similar. For example, searching for lessons learned wrt. the programming language C, also experiences related to the use of C++ might be of interest. Thus, the determination of similarity has to be extended to regard also *local similarity* between the values of the indexes.

Incomplete information. The retrieval mechanism must also be able to cope with incomplete information, as it may be impossible or too resource-consuming to describe the current situation completely to search for relevant SE experienceware. For example, during the planning phase of a software project, information on which testing tools will be used may not yet be available. On the other hand, stored experiences might also be incomplete, for instance, some features were unknown in the past or new features have become relevant for the retrieval due to changes of the software environment. For example, when a company starts to use different inspection techniques, the feature «type of inspection» may become important to discriminate quality models on fault detection rates. This potential incompleteness of data has to be explicitly considered when determining the similarity of experiences.

Continuous evolution. While in one organization the type of inspection technique may influence the number of faults detected, the type has no influence in another one. Due to such a lack of common domain models in the SE domain and differences between software organizations, support for the continuous evolution of the retrieval mechanism is required. Initially, only hypotheses about correlations between SE experienceware, indexes, and retrieval goals can be set up. They have to be continuously tailored to the specific environment based on feedback from the application of the retrieval mechanism in practice. For example, new indexes have to be included, if necessary, or relevance factors of indexes have to be adapted, if their importance for the retrieval process changes.

Therefore, the EF has to provide comprehensive support for the explicit definition and maintenance of retrieval goals and a parametric and robust similarity measure that predicts the usefulness of experienceware based on a set of predefined indexes in relation to the specific retrieval goal.

In this context, Case-Based Reasoning (CBR) [6] plays a key role [16,23,24,34], as it provides a broad support for similarity-based retrieval for all kinds of experienceware and continuous incremental learning. Reuse candidates in a CBR system are retrieved by partially matching the given situation description with the cases in the case base and inducing a total order among the cases based on numerical similarity values assigned to each case through a similarity measure [4,33,38].

However, the definition of a retrieval method and similarity measure for the retrieval of SE experienceware is not trivial as tailored support for different objects, processes, purposes, viewpoints, and environments is required. And, what represents relevant software know-how differs among companies with respect to their context, needs, and business goals. This requires a flexible retrieval method and similarity measure that can be tailored to different reuse goals.

Some CBR approaches enable to increase the flexibility of the similarity measure for a specific application or class of application. Based on experiences on reusing software measurement experienceware in industrial projects (e.g., in the context of the projects CEMP [18] and SoftQuali [29]), we propose an approach that systematizes such CBR approaches for the goal-oriented retrieval of SE experienceware. Based on the similarity model applied in PATDEX [7], our approach deals explicitly in a tailorable and evolutionary manner with different retrieval goals as well as incompleteness of information and enables a comprehensive consideration of global and local similarity.

In Section 2, we outline the retrieval process and its principle steps. The generic similarity measure is described in detail in Section 3 and the continuous evolution of the retrieval mechanism in Section 4. An example application of our approach in the domain of software measurement is presented in Section 5. Section 6 provides a discussion of our approach in relation to other research work. Conclusions and future research directions are addressed in Section 7.

2 Retrieval of Software Engineering Experienceware

To provide experience-based support for software process tasks regarding the requirements described in Section 1, the retrieval process includes the following steps:

Step 1. Situation assessment. The objective of the retrieval is stated through a retrieval goal and the current situation is described by a pre-defined set of indexes related to the particular retrieval goal. The importance of each index with respect to the specific retrieval goal is expressed through a predefined numerical relevance factor assigned to each index (see Section 3.3). An index can also be used as a filter, requiring that it perfectly matches the ones in the situation assessment, when marked as «essential». Indexes described as «irrelevant» are not further considered for the retrieval. Unknown indexes are explicitly marked. Figure 2 illustrates a situation assessment with an exemplary set of indexes. The situation assessment can be done manually by the user or automatically, if the required values can be inferred from information available in the EB.

Step 2. Exact matching of indexes marked as essential. In a first step, the cases of the EB are matched with the given situation description with respect to the indexes marked as essential. By perfectly matching those indexes, a set of potential reuse candidates is determined. Figure 2 shows a simplified example: while comparing the cases of the EB with the situation assessment, Case_03 and Case_11 are considered as potential reuse

Situation Assessment

Reuse goal		
object	lesson learned	
purpose	guide solving of problem	
process	sw measurement	
viewpoint	quality assurance personnel	
environment	IntelliCar	
Indexes		
department	irrelevant	ABS
staff size	0.1	10
application domain	essential	automobile
improvement goal	0.4	sw system reliability improvement
programming language	irrelevant	Ada
dev. experience	0.1	high
sw system size	0.1	unknown
measurement maturity	0.3	initial
task	essential	measurement goal definition

Measurement -EB (excerpt)

CASE	Case_003	PS	Case_007	PS	Case_011	PS
organization	FuelInjection	--	FuelInjection	--	FuelInjection	--
staff size	15	E	100	W	50	W
application domain	automobile	--	automobile	--	automobile	--
improvement goal	sw system reliability improvement	E	sw system reliability improvement	E	development cost reduction	W
prog. language	Fortran	--	Ada	--	C	--
dev. experience	medium	E	low	W	low	W
sw system size	15 KLOC	U	80KLOC	U	60KLOC	U
msmt maturity	--	R	--	R	--	R
task	measurement goal definition	--	measurement plan development	--	measurement goal definition	--

Fig. 2. Simplified retrieval example

candidates, because the values of the indexes marked as essential are equal to the present ones. Case_07, which describes an experience regarding the development of the measurement plan, is not further considered as the value of the index «task» is different to the one of interest.

Step 3. Partial matching of cases. For all potential reuse candidates, a similarity value is computed by partially matching the indexes (except the ones marked as essential) using a specific similarity measure with respect to the retrieval goal (see Section 3). Cases with a higher similarity value than a given threshold are considered as sufficiently similar and the most similar cases are proposed to the user as reuse candidates. Continuing the example shown in Figure 2, Case_03 is considered more similar to the given situation than Case_11, as the values of the indexes of Case_03 are more similar to the current ones.

Step 4. Selection of reuse candidate(s). Based on the proposed reuse candidates associated with their similarity value, the user can explore the cases via browsing and navigation along their relationships, select the most appropriate case(s) for reuse and, if necessary, adapt them to fit the current needs. Additional information included in the cases concerning their reuse in the past, for instance, frequency of reuse, adaptations done, or reuse cost further guide the selection and adaptation process.

To identify useful experienceware based on similarity, we need a flexible similarity measure (see step 3), considering the specific requirements as described in Section 1

3 Similarity Measure for Retrieving Software Engineering Experienceware

In this section, we define a generic similarity measure (i.e., a parameterized set of similarity measures) for the identification of similar SE experienceware in the EB that can be tailored to a specific reuse goal.

In the EB, a $case_k = (E_k, e_k)$ represents an experience in an object-oriented frame-like representation through its features and (terminal and nonterminal) values (experience $E_k = \{(E_{k1}, e_{k1}), (E_{k2}, e_{k2}), ...\}$ with the features E_{ki} and their values $e_{ki} \in W_i$), describing the know-how gathered in a past software project, the context from which it originates, and its interdependencies with other products, processes, and resources. For further information on the representation of SE experienceware see [21].

The similarity measure is used to assign a similarity value (defined as a real number $\in$ [0,1]) to the stored cases by matching them partially to a given situation description (see Section 2). Basically, a similarity measure sim(x,y) can be defined by [4,33,38]:

A mapping sim: M x M $\rightarrow$ [0,1] on a set M is a similarity measure iff $(\forall x, y \in M)$:

- sim(x,x) = 1   (reflexivity)
- sim(x,y) = sim(y,x)   (symmetry)[1]
- sim(x,y) = 1 $\leftrightarrow$ x = y

3.1 Goal-Oriented Retrieval

Based on reuse scenarios, retrieval goals are determined. Retrieval goals explicitly state the object to be reused, the purpose of reuse, the related task, the specific viewpoint, and the particular environment (see Table 2).

Table 2. Retrieval goal template

Goal Template	Example 1	Example 2
Retrieve <object>	quality model	lesson learned
for the <purpose>	development of new product	guide problem solving
concerning <process>	project planning	software measurement
from the <viewpoint>	project manager	quality assurance personnel
in the context of <environment>	company IntelliPhone	company IntelliCar

Based on the retrieval goals, reusability factors are determined through interviews with domain experts. This includes the specification of related concepts, relevant indexes, and their relevancy. Objects defined in the retrieval goal, are explicitly described in a concept glossary [36] stating their intended purpose and users. Relevant characteristics for the input to the retrieval process, which will be used for the matching process (denoted as indexes) are identified, based on the following considerations with respect to the specific retrieval goal:

- What are characteristic attributes to describe the object?
- Which information is required for the execution of the task concerning the specific purpose?

---

1. For our purposes, we assume a similarity measure to be symmetrical, as it is used for the computation of a similarity value of a case of the EB in reference to a given situation assessment. However, in general, similarity measures need not to be symmetrical.

- Which information is required for the identification and selection of adequate objects?
- Which attributes enable to discriminate objects?
- Which minimal quality must the objects have?

For each of the identified indexes, its type, range, and cardinality are explicitly defined [36] to allow a consistent knowledge representation and to support the situation assessment.

As a result, each retrieval goal g is associated with a particular set of indexes, represented as a list of features $C_g=\{C_{g1}, C_{g2},...\}$. The range of the value c_{gi} of the feature C_{gi} is defined by W_i, its respective range definition stored in the EB (see Figure 3).

The present situation is assessed based on the pre-defined set of indexes with respect to the retrieval goal. The description of the present situation is represented as a list of feature-value pairs $Sit=\{(C_{g1}, s_1), (C_{g2}, s_2),...\}$ including the features $C_{gi} \in C_g$ and their values $s_i \in W_i$ (see Figure 3).

3.2   Dealing with Incomplete Data

As today SE domain models are usually not available in practice, we often have to deal with incomplete information, concerning the input as well as the cases stored in the case base. Our approach is based on Tversky´s contrast model [37] as applied in PATDEX [7]. This model expresses similarity of two objects through a linear contrast of weighted differences between their common and different features. Concerning the potential situations that can occur when comparing the given situation and a stored case the following feature sets are distinguished:

- E: Set of corresponding features. The value of the feature of the given situation corresponds with the one of the stored case. For example, if both, the situation assessment and the stored case state the feature «experience of developer» as high.
- W: Set of contradicting features. The value of the feature of the given situation does not correspond with the one of the stored case. For example, if in the past no effort reporting tools were available, but now in the given situation the feature «effort reporting tools» is stated as available.
- U: Set of unknown features. The feature is only contained in the stored case, but not stated in the actual situation description. For example, when initiating a software project certain information, such as «software system size» may be stated as unknown in the situation description, although available in the stored cases on past projects.
- R: Set of redundant features. The feature is stated in the given situation description, but not contained in the stored case. Cases may have been stated incompletely in the past for various reasons, for instance, time pressure or lack of domain knowledge. For example, during the continuous organizational learning process, the feature «developer experience» may not have been considered initially, but later become important for the identification of relevant cases.

Figure 2 shows an example on the feature sets (FS) of the cases of the EB for the given situation description. This subdivision into different feature sets allows the explicit handling of unknown information and corresponding/contradicting features during the retrieval process by associating with each of these feature sets a different weight (α, β,

Example Index Set		Type and Range Definition	Present Situation	
C_1	organization	Taxonomy	s_1	ABS
C_2	org. msmnt infrastructure	Binary symbol	s_2	yes
C_3	staff size	Interval of number [0,100]	s_3	[8,10]^a
C_4	improvement goal	String	s_4	"improvement of system reliability"
C_5	application domain	Unordered symbol: {automobile, airplane}	s_5	automobile
C_6	programming language	Unordered symbol: {Ada, C, C++, Fortran}	s_6	Ada, C
C_7	developer experience	Ordered symbol: {none, medium, high, expert}	s_7	high
C_8	sw system size (KLOC)	Number: [0,100]	s_8	unknown
C_9	project duration (month)	Number: [0,100]	s_9	12
C_{10}	measurement maturity	Ordered symbol: {initial, low, routine}	s_{10}	low
C_{11}	task	Unordered symbol: {msmnt goal def, msmnt plan dev, data collection}	s_{11}	msmnt goal definition

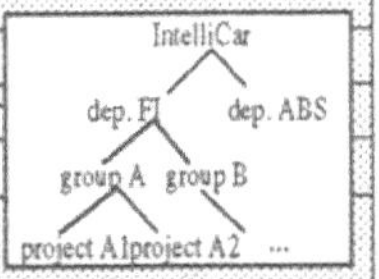

The tree shown for the Taxonomy type (IntelliCar): IntelliCar → dep. FI / dep. ABS → group A / group B → project A1 / project A2 ...

a.   The project team size varies from 8 to 10 developers during the software project.

Fig. 3. Exemplary index set

$\gamma, \delta \in [0,1]$). Depending on if we choose an optimistic or pessimistic strategy, we can weigh the corresponding features stronger than the contradicting ones or vice versa, respectively. In the software engineering domain, where companies are today beginning to build up EB´s and a rather small amount of experience available, we suggest an optimistic strategy with $\alpha > \beta$, weighting corresponding features stronger than non-corresponding ones. Unknown features are considered as less important for the identification of relevant cases ($\gamma=0$). Redundant features are believed to have an impact on the determination of relevant cases. But as the specific values are not available in the respective case in the case base, they are associated with a very small weight ($\delta \ll \beta$). The weights depend on the specific environment and may change during the life cycle of the EB, for instance, when the number of available experienceware cases increases a more pessimistic strategy might be more beneficial to avoid the retrieval of a too extensive amount of cases.

3.3   Relevance of Indexes for Similarity

The retrieval of experienceware from the EB is only useful, if the retrieved experienceware can actually be applied in the given situation. The problem here is to identify relevant features for the retrieval of appropriate cases, before trying to reuse this experience in the present situation. Based on PATDEX [7], relevance factors are defined, which determine the importance of a feature. However, in the SE context relevance factors have to be related to the specific retrieval goal. Thus, for each index $Cg_i \in$ index set C_g for a specific retrieval goal g, a relevance factor $\omega_{gi} \in [0,1]$ is defined. For each retrieval goal, those relevance factors are represented by means of a relevance vector $R_g = \{\omega_{g1}, \omega_{g2},...\}$ with $\sum \omega_{gi}=1$ normalized. The relevance factor represents a weight used for the calculation of the similarity value. The relevance factors can be learned over time by a pseudo connectionistic approach [4] based on an abstracted Hebb competition learning taken from pattern recognition. Setting initially all indexes equally relevant, during the learning process the weights of features receiving a positive feedback are strengthened or weakened in case of negative feedback. In addition, the user can manually overwrite the stored relevance factors, if necessary.

Systematically capturing feedback on manual modifications of relevance factors through the user enables the continuous learning and tailoring of the relevance vectors, e.g., by disregarding features frequently marked as irrelevant of the index set.

3.4 Local Similarity of Features

For the comprehensive examination of the similarity between a given situation and the cases in the EB, local similarity between the values of a feature has to be considered. Thus, specific local similarity measures have to be defined for each index type, e.g., numerical, symbolic, or textual in dependence on the specific organization. Here, generic local similarity measures $\upsilon'(v_i, v_j) \in [0,1]$ for basic value types $W(v)$ in the software engineering domain [24,36] are provided, which still have to be refined for the specific environment in practice.

Let v_i and v_j be two values of a feature: v_i represents the value of the given situation and v_j the respective value of a stored case in the EB. Besides representing features by atomic values, e.g., the value «high» of the feature «developer experience», it may be necessary to represent features by sets of values. For example, the usage of different programming languages may be described through the set {C, Fortran, Assembler} of symbolic values. Thus, feature values are interpreted as sets with their minimal and maximal number of elements defined by their cardinality. The local similarity value is computed based on the normalized sum of best matches for each element of the value set in the situation assessment with the case [36]:

$$\upsilon'(v_i, v_j) = \sum e_2 \in v_j \ (\max (\upsilon(e_1, e_2) \,|\, e_1 \in v_i)) / \ card(v_j) \quad \text{if } card(v_i) > 0 \text{ and } card(v_j) > 0, \text{ or}$$

$$\upsilon'(v_i, v_j) = 0 \qquad\qquad\qquad\qquad\qquad\qquad \text{otherwise}$$

In the following sections, local similarity measures $\upsilon(v_i, v_j)$ for the computation of a similarity value between two atomic feature values are described for basic types [22].

Number. Indexes can be described by numbers, e.g., the value *100* of the feature *size of software system in KLOC*. The similarity between two numeric values can be described as an asymptotic function [9]. The semantic of such a similarity function is that differences between the two values cause a asymptotic decrease of similarity. To tolerate differences between the two values until a defined distance x1 the following similarity function can be used:

$$\upsilon(v_i, v_j) = \exp\!\left((-a \cdot \left|v_i - v_j\right|)^3\right) with (a \in \Re)$$

Other possibilities are, e.g., a step-function if the value only may be useful or not, or linear functions, if the similarity increases linearly with the decrease of distance between the two values.

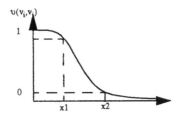

Fig. 4. Exemplary asymptotic similarity measure

Interval. In the software engineering domain it might be necessary to describe certain indexes by intervals of numbers, e.g., the interval [8,10] describing the feature «number of project personnel», which varied between 8-10 developers in the particular software project. The similarity of two features described by intervals can be calculated by regarding their borders [34].

Be $v_i=[low(v_i), high(v_i)]$ and $v_j=[low(v_j), high(v_j)]$ intervals:

$$\upsilon(i, v_i) = \begin{cases} \dfrac{low(v_j) - low(v_i) + low(v_j) - high(v_i)}{2} & \Leftrightarrow high(v_i) < low(v_j) \\[2mm] \dfrac{low(v_j) - low(v_i)}{2} & \Leftrightarrow low(v_i) < low(v_j) \le high(v_i) \le high(v_j) \\ & \Leftrightarrow low(v_j) \le low(v_i) \wedge high(v_i) \le high(v_j) \\[2mm] 1 & \\[2mm] \dfrac{high(v_i) - high(v_j)}{2} & \Leftrightarrow low(v_j) \le low(v_i) \le high(v_j) < high(v_i) \\[2mm] \dfrac{low(v_i) - high(v_j) + high(v_i) - high(v_j)}{2} & \Leftrightarrow high(v_j) < low(v_i) \\[2mm] \dfrac{low(v_j) - low(v_i) + high(v_i) - high(v_j)}{2} & \text{otherwise} \end{cases}$$

Binary Symbol. Binary symbols, representing the values *yes* and *no*, can, e.g., describe features like «*inspection used*» or «*effort reporting tool available*».The similarity measure for binary symbols is defined by:

$$\upsilon(v_i,v_j) = \begin{cases} 1 & v_i = v_j \\ 0 & v_i \neq v_j \end{cases}$$

For example, in case of the feature «inspections used» with the values (yes, no), the similarity measure $\upsilon(v_i,v_j)$ is 1 if in both cases inspections are performed or not, and 0 if they are performed in only one case.

Ordered Symbol. Ordered symbols represent symbolic values in a determined order, for instance, the values of the feature «*experience of the developers*» can be classified into the following categories *(expert- participated in complete system development; high - participated partly in development; medium-participated in training; none)* in decreasing order.

For this type the same similarity measures as defined for numerical values can be used by associating every symbol with its ranking number in the list of all possible symbols of this type. The distance between the values of the list can be expressed by associating the ranking numbers with each value, for instance, considering the feature «*experience of developer*» (none→1, medium→2, high→3, expert→4), assuming an equidistant order of the values. Another possibility is the association of user-defined numerical values, which allows to express a non-equidistant order of the values, e.g., (none→1, medium→3, high→5, expert→6). Here, a smaller difference between high and expert experience is assumed than as, for example, between none and medium experience. These transformation have to be made under careful consideration and preservation of the semantic meaningfulness regarding the manipulation of the data.

Based on the associated numerical values, the similarity functions as described for numbers can be utilized for the determination of the similarity value between ordered symbolic values.

Unordered Symbol. Unordered symbols represent symbolic values without any order, for instance, like the values *(C, C++, Smalltalk, Ada)* of the feature «*programming language*». For the determination of similarity between values of a finite unordered list of symbols, the similarity measure can be defined in form of a similarity matrix represented as a triangular matrix S_{ij} that assigns every combination of values v_i, $v_j \in W(v)$ a respective similarity value $\upsilon(v_i,v_j) \in [0,1]$ (see Table 3). If the values are identical, then $\upsilon(v_i,v_j) = 1$. If the values are different, the specific similarity value between two values is given in the similarity matrix explicitly defined in a specific environment. For example, the programming language C can be considered more similar to C++ ($\upsilon(C,C++) = 0.7$) than to Ada ($\upsilon(C,Ada) = 0.1$)).

Table 3. Exemplary similarity measure for the feature «programming language»

v_i/v_j	Fortran	C	C++	Smalltalk	Ada
Fortran	1	0.6	0.4	0.1	0.1
C	a	1	0.7	0.1	0.1
C++			1	0.4	0.4
Smalltalk				1	0.6
Ada					1

a.   *For symmetric similarity measures the values S_{ij} and S_{ji} are equal.*

Taxonomy. A taxonomy is a n-ary tree in which the nodes represent symbolic values, representing the relationship between the values through their position within the taxonomy. An example is an aggregation taxonomy, denoting the has_parts relationship between an object and one or more of its parts. Figure 5 depicts an example of a hierarchical taxonomy of organizational units.

For the definition of a similarity measure for taxonomies we follow the approach of [15] by assigning similarity values to the inner nodes of the taxonomy. Every inner node K_i of the taxonomy is annotated with a similarity value $SV_i \in [0,1]$, such that the following condition holds: if K_j is a successor of K_i then $SV_i < SV_j$. The deeper the nodes are located in the hierarchy, the higher the similarity value can become. This means that the value SV_i represents a lower bound for the similarity of two arbitrary objects from the taxonomy.

Be K_i, K_j nodes of the taxonomy, $<K_i, K_j>$ the node that is the nearest predecessor of K_i and K_j, and $SV_{<Ki, Kj>}$ the similarity value assigned to the node $<K_i, K_j>$. The similarity measure of the nodes K_i, K_j is then defined by:

$$\upsilon(K_i, K_j) = 1 \qquad \text{if } K_i = K_j \text{, or}$$
$$\upsilon(K_i, K_j) = SV_{<Ki, Kj>} \qquad \text{otherwise.}$$

For example, assuming a similarity value assignment as shown in Figure 5 for the organization taxonomy, the similarity value υ(projectA1, department ABS) is 0.4, whereas the similarity value υ(group A, group B) is 0.6. Other possible similarity measures for taxonomies are, for instance, the computation of the path distance between the nodes in the taxonomy tree utilizing a similarity measures for numerical values.

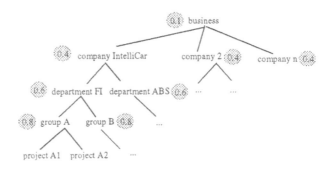

Fig. 5. Example of a taxonomy

String. Strings describe feature values in textual form, e.g., the feature «*improvement goal*» by *"reduce number of failures"*. Computing the similarity between text strings considering a reasonable semantic is quite difficult in general. As far as possible, text strings should be avoided and replaced by symbolic values. Yet, a basic approach to determine the similarity can be based on the greatest common substring-string ratio [9]: Here we compute the ratio of the sum of the length of common substrings to the total length of v_i. Small common substrings (length ≤ 3) are not considered in order to filter articles and propositions. For example, assuming the feature «improvement goal» is described in the current situation by v_i:*"reduction of effort"* and the case$_k$ by v_j:*"reduce*

$$
\upsilon(v_i,v_j) = \begin{cases} 0 & \text{if } (|v_i| = 0) \\[2mm] \dfrac{\sum |cv_j|}{\sum |w_i|} & else \end{cases} \qquad max|cv_j| \text{ length of common substring per word } w_i \text{ of } v_i
$$

$$
\text{and } (|cv_j| > 3) \text{ and } (|w_i| > 3)
$$

development effort", then the resulting similarity value is:

$$
\upsilon(v_i,v_j) = \frac{|reduc| + |effort|}{|reduction| + |effort|} = \frac{5 + 6}{15} = 0,73
$$

3.5 Similarity Threshold

When an EB only contains few cases, as probably in the beginning of building an EB, many cases with a very low similarity value may be retrieved due to the lack of more appropriate alternatives. To prevent overloading the user with less useful information, cases with a small similarity value are excluded by setting a threshold. The threshold explicitly states when cases are to be considered to be *sufficiently* similar. Here, we define different thresholds for local and global similarity values.

- **Global similarity threshold.** As part of the definition of retrieval goal g a threshold $\varepsilon_g \in [0,1]$ is explicitly stated. This threshold defines for the specific retrieval goal the lower border the global similarity value has to exceed to consider a case as a reuse candidate. The threshold is individually captured as part of the retrieval goal definition which allows an instantiation of the threshold specifically for a retrieval goal. For example, if cases suggested as reuse candidate have been rejected several times by the user with respect to the specific retrieval goal, the corresponding threshold can be increased. The increased threshold results into an acceptance of cases as reuse candidate only with higher similarity values in the future. The global similarity threshold can be dynamically updated based on the user feedback on the suggested reuse candidates.

- **Local similarity threshold.** Considering the local similarity between the values of a feature, we have to decide when those values are considered as (sufficient) similar. Here, we define a local threshold $\theta_i \in [0,1]$ for an index C_i which expresses when to consider two values of this index as (sufficient) similar. Depending on the specific environment and number of available experienceware in the EB this threshold can be dynamically adapted. For example, in the beginning, θ_i can be set to a low value, continuously increasing while the EB grows, to avoid the retrieval of a vast number of experiences.

3.6 Global Similarity Measure

Considering the specific requirements given in the software engineering domain as described in the previous sections, we define a generic similarity measure $sim(Sit',E_k')$. The similarity measure is based on the following assumptions:

- Set of indexes $C_g = \{C_{g1}, C_{g2}, ...\}$ wrt. the particular retrieval goal g,

- Sit′ = $\{(C_{gi}, s_i) \in$ Sit I relevance factor $(S_i) \neq$ essential$\}$,

- $case_k = (E_k, e_k)$ of the case base, with $E_k′ \subseteq E_k \wedge \forall\ E_{ki}′ \in Cg \wedge$ features $E_{ki}′ \in Cg$ and their respective values $e_{ki}′$,

- local similarity value $\upsilon′(s_i, e_{ki}′)$ of the indexes s_i and $e_{ki}′$,

- weight ω_{gi} of the relevance vector R_g wrt. the retrieval goal g,

- local threshold $\theta_i \in [0,1]$ for index C_{gi},

The feature sets E, W, U, R are defined as:

$$E = \{C_{gi} | (C_{gi} \in Sit′ \cap E_{ki}′) and (\upsilon′(s_i, e_{ki}′) \geq \theta_i)\}$$

$$W = \{C_{gi} | (C_{gi} \in Sit′ \cap E_{ki}′) and (\upsilon′(s_i, e_{ki}′) < \theta_i)\}$$

$$U = \{C_{gi} | (C_{gi} \in E_{ki}′ - Sit′)\}$$

$$R = \{C_{gi} | (C_{gi} \in Sit′ - E_{ki}′)\}$$

with the weights of the feature sets $\alpha, \beta, \gamma, \delta \in [0,1]$.

Then the similarity measure is defined as:

$$sim(Sit′, E_k′) =$$

$$\frac{\alpha \left(\sum_{s_i \in E} \omega_{gik} \cdot \upsilon′(s_i, e_{ki}′) \right)}{\alpha \left(\sum_{s_i \in E} \omega_{gik} \cdot \upsilon′(s_i, e_{ki}′) \right) + \beta \left(\sum_{s_i \in W} \omega_{gik} \cdot (1 - \upsilon′(s_i, e_{ki}′)) \right) + \gamma \left(\sum_{s_i \in U} \omega_{gik} \cdot (1 - \upsilon′(s_i, e_{ki}′)) \right) + \delta \left(\sum_{s_i \in R} \omega_{gik} \cdot (1 - \upsilon′(s_i, e_{ki}′)) \right)}$$

The similarity measure as defined above is used in the retrieval process for the identification of reuse candidates from the case base wrt. the given situation. Based on the similarity value calculated with the similarity measure, a $case_k$ is considered as reuse candidate, if all features marked as essential in the given situation exactly match the respective features of the case and $sim(Sit′, E_k′) \geq$ global similarity threshold ε_g of retrieval goal g.

4   Continuous Evolution of Retrieval Mechanism

Due to the fact, that the introduction of influential parameters for the retrieval mechanism depends on the specific environment and may change over time, the continuous tailoring of the retrieval mechanism needs to be supported during the whole life cycle of an EF. For example, supplemental context characteristics may become relevant for the discrimination of experiences. Assuming, for example, that the attribute «*experience of developer*» had not been considered as an index for the retrieval of lessons learned on JAVA applications in the past, as all available experiences were related to the same development team without variations in the level of experience. When, for example, other teams with a different level of experience also start to develop JAVA applications, the characteristic may become important for the distinction of experiences and, consequently, has to be added as a new index with respect to the retrieval goal.

Continuous learning has to be supported regarding all parameters of the similarity measure to improve and optimize its performance. Therefore, the retrieval and reuse process is supervised and, based on the feedback from the user, appropriately tailored to the specific environment through the experience engineer. This is done by recording user behavior during the retrieval process and user (re-)actions on the retrieval results. These protocols and additional user-provided critics and suggestions can serve as a basis for the maintenance through the experience engineer (see Table 4). For example, if during the situation assessment a new index is frequently added by the user as relevant for the retrieval, it may indicate the need for the integration of this attribute in the predefined indexing scheme with respect to the specific retrieval goal. Manual modifications of the relevance factors of the indexes can imply the adaptation of weights (see Section 3.3) or even the removal of indexes, if they are frequently considered as irrelevant by the user. Variations concerning the number of retrieved reuse candidates (e.g., too many or too few cases are retrieved) can imply a different retrieval strategy, changing, for instance, the weights related to the feature sets (see Section 3.2) or the thresholds (see Section 3.5). Observing the frequent rejection of suggested cases can point at needed modifications, for instance, the increase of the global threshold for the retrieval goal (see Section 3.5). Table 4 summarizes possible feedback and its implication for the update of the retrieval mechanism.

Table 4. Examples of retrieval feedback and its implications

Feedback	Implication for update
Index manually added for retrieval	• Addition of index to the indexing scheme
Relevance factor manually modified	• Modification of weight assigned to the index • Index frequently marked as irrelevant might be removed from the indexing scheme
Increasing number of retrieved reuse candidates	• Changing optimistic strategy for similarity measure into a more pessimistic one • Increase of thresholds
Frequent rejection of cases suggested as reuse candidates	• If a specific retrieval goal is affected: increase of global threshold of the retrieval goal • If different cases are affected: review of indexing scheme and similarity measure considering additional critics and suggestions of the user

Based on further critics and suggestions from the user, the indexing scheme and similarity measure can be carefully reviewed and tailored by the experience engineer.

5 Application: REMEX - Reuse of Software Measurement Experienceware

The retrieval method has been implemented in the REMEX system [21,25] focusing on the goal-oriented and similarity-based retrieval of software measurement experienceware to support the planning of GQM-based measurement programs in practice. The GQM (Goal/Question/Metric) Paradigm [11,14,27] is an innovative technology for goal-oriented software engineering measurement. GQM helps defining and implementing operational and measurable software improvement goals. It has been successfully applied in several companies, such as NASA-SEL, Bosch, Digital, and Schlumberger [12, 18].

GQM-Based Measurement: GQM Plan

A GQM plan is developed based on a measurement goal consisting of the following components [13]:
- a goal, defining the object, purpose, quality focus, viewpoint, and context of the measurement program,
- a set of questions, operationalizing the goal,
- a set of models, specifying how to answer the questions,
- a set of measures, operationally defining the data to be collected to feed the models.

GQM Goal: Analyze the software process to characterize reliability from the viewpoint of the software developer at the company IntelliCar.

Q_1 What is the overall number of failures reported before delivery?

  M_1.1 count of failure reports turned in before delivery {ratio: integer}[1]

Q_2 What is the distribution of failures reported before delivery by criticality level?

  Model: Distribution = (# critical failures/ total # failures, # uncritical failures/ total # failures)
  critical: complete breakdown of system; uncritical: unable to perform one or more of the functions F1-F6

  M_2.1 classification by criticality {ordinal:uncritical:critical}
  M_2.2 count of failure reports before delivery {ratio: integer}

Q_3 What is the distribution of faults by life cycle phase of detection before delivery?

  Model: Distribution = (# faults in REQ/ total # faults,# faults in HLD/ total # faults,
  # faults in LLD/IMP/ total # faults)

  M_3.1 count of fault per life cycle phase where the fault was introduced {nominal: REQ, HLD, LLD/IMP}

Q_4 What is the total rework effort?

  Model: rework effort = (effort to isolate fault + effort to correct fault)

  M_4.1 for all failures reported before delivery: effort to isolate the faults that caused the failures (person-hours) {ratio: integer}
  M_4.2 for each fault detected before delivery: effort to correct the fault (person-hours) {ratio:integer}

  1 {scale: range}

Fig. 6. Simplified example of a GQM plan

In GQM programs, the analysis task of measurement is specified precisely and explicitly by a detailed measurement goal, called GQM goal. Relevant measures are derived in a top-down fashion based on the goal via a set of questions and quality/resource models. This refinement is precisely documented in a GQM plan (see Figure 6), providing an explicit rationale for the selection of the underlying measures. For the measures derived, measurement procedures are defined, specifying when, how, and by whom the required data can be collected, and appropriate data collection instruments (e.g., questionnaires) are designed. The data collected are interpreted in a bottom-up fashion considering the limitations and assumptions underlying each measure. The resource-consuming and error-prone process of planning GQM programs can be substantially supported through the reuse of measurement experiences [25,26]. However, the complexity of GQM plans makes it difficult to understand and identify relevant and reusable measurement products developed in the company's context in the past. This is exacerbated by the complex net of interdependencies between GQM products and the variety of planning tasks to be supported. Therefore, sophisticated ways are required for the intelligent retrieval of relevant experiences in the EB.

REMEX is a tool for the reuse-based planning of GQM-based software measurement programs. It supports the editing of all related GQM products (e.g., GQM goal, questions, models, and measures) and their storage. Fully integrated into each step of the planning of a GQM program is the option to retrieve similar GQM products from past measurement programs and to reuse them as a basis for the development of the present products. In addition, REMEX enables the systematic collection of lessons learned on measurement planning in form of problem/solution statements, their storage, and the similarity-based retrieval of them for the user on demand. The access of all GQM experienceware is provided via a web interface. The system also supports the systematic maintenance of the GQM-EB including the acquisition of new experiences and the continuous tailoring of the retrieval mechanism.

The REMEX system is implemented in Smalltalk/VisualWorks enabling the connection with standard databases (for the representation of experienceware cases and general domain knowledge) and its integration via Intra- or Internet (see Figure 7).

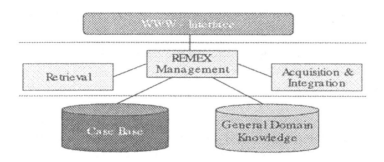

Fig. 7. System architecture

5.1 Retrieval Consultation

The retrieval of experienceware is intertwined into the GQM planning process. For example, when editing a GQM question, the user can request similar GQM questions from past measurement programs, without necessarily providing further input. In relation to the specific task for which support is asked, the system determines the requested retrieval goal and its current parameters defined in the system. For the formulation of the query, the system then automatically infers the required input information with respect to the specific retrieval goal based on the GQM products developed in the previous planning steps (which are stored as part of the present measurement program in the EB).

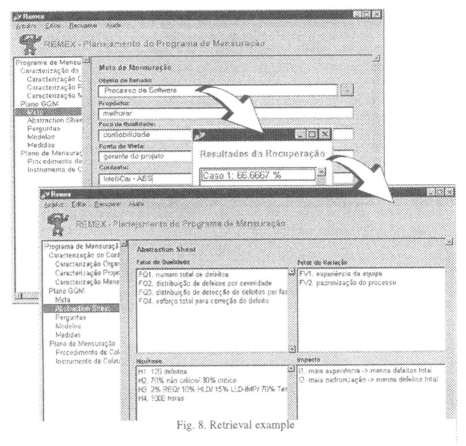

Fig. 8. Retrieval example

Figure 8 shows an example for the retrieval of an Abstraction Sheet (a GQM product that summarizes the complete GQM plan) based on the context characterization and the GQM goal determined in the previous steps of the planning process. As a result of the retrieval, REMEX supplies a list of similar abstraction sheets to the user ordered by their similarity value. Then the user can individually evaluate the suggested products and reuse them, if appropriate, in the present situation.

For an advanced retrieval, REMEX also offers the possibility to the user to manually change the indexes, their values, and their relevance factors, if necessary, in the specific situation.

Further support is provided through the possibility to retrieve problem/solution statements in each step of the planning process, for instance, to prevent the repetition of failures or to guide the solution of an occurred problem based on a solution strategy that has been adopted in the past.

5.2   Initialization and Maintenance of the Retrieval Parameters

Besides retrieving similar cases, the REMEX tool also supports the modeling and maintenance of the similarity relations. To focus on the organization-specific necessities and
characteristics, the retrieval goals and the corresponding parameters (e.g., indexes, relevance factors, etc.) can individually be adapted to the specific context (see Figure 9).
The knowledge acquisition and maintenance tasks are supported through graphical editors supporting the knowledge engineer to model complex organizational domain
knowledge and its relations.

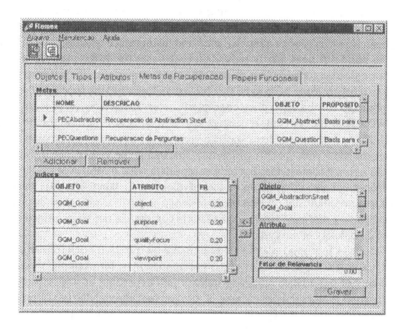

Fig. 9. Definition of retrieval goal parameters

6   Discussion

In the literature various approaches exist for experience-based support of the planning
and execution of software projects, primarily focusing on software code, for instance,
based on library and information science, knowledge-based systems, or database management technologies [19]. However, the majority of those approaches fails to recognize the complexity of SE experienceware in general, often requires a thorough classification of the domain, or does not provide any means for similarity-based retrieval. Recently, CBR has been recognized as a promising approach for the operationalization of
learning organizations in the SE domain [2,3,24,31,34]. Applications are developed in
different areas, like capturing best practices (e.g., [5,28]), effort prediction (e.g., [20]),
measurement [23,25], or change management [32]. The retrieval effectiveness of those
systems varies from simple browsing facilities to similarity-based retrieval methods.
However, the majority of those systems neither explicitly considers different reuse pur-

poses nor offers flexible retrieval methods and similarity measures tailorable to the specific goals.

In this context, an advanced CBR approach is PATDEX [7] that has been developed for the fault diagnosis of CNC machining centers, an analogous situation to the reuse of SE experienceware. PATDEX uses a flexible similarity measure explicitly dealing with unknown information, filter attributes, and local similarities, which forms the basis of a similarity model comparable to our approach. In PATDEX, the case-based test selection (focusing on "find the most relevant attribute for value determination") and case-based diagnosis (focusing on "find the most similar diagnosis") have been separated, by creating distinct case bases, one containing strategy cases for the selection of tests and a second one containing diagnosis cases. This can be seen in analogy to different retrieval goals. However, due to administration and maintenance reasons, it would be inefficient to build different, partly redundant case bases for different retrieval goals. Thus, as a single case (or parts) can be useful for several purposes, the retrieval method and the similarity measure have to be flexible and tailorable to the specific goal.

Some approaches involve an explicit concept of context in the retrieval process, for example, INRECA includes a context concept as a "similarity environment for the retrieval" [1,38]. Every context enables a specific view on the particular application domain and relates the view with specific properties. Enhancing the view concept from database technologies, a context does not only encapsulate static information for the definition of objects, but also information on their dynamic processing. Contexts can be defined and selected statically (during the knowledge acquisition phase) or dynamically (by the user during runtime). However, so far the concept has not been defined and implemented completely in the system.

Until now, only a few approaches enable to make the similarity determination more flexible for specific applications or classes of applications, for example, through dynamic ranking of importance ratings of indexes [30] depending on a specific retrieval context. ReMind enables the partitioning of the case base through the use of prototypes [8] and the assignment of a different set of importance values to each partition. However, if multiple retrieval goals have to be supported by a case base, then partitioning is not sufficient, because the cases potentially contribute to different retrieval goals (see argumentation above with respect to the maintenance and administration). Another approach is the association of one set of relevance criteria to each case, when cases are highly idiosyncratic. The set of importance values associated to a case emphasizes the combination of those dimensions of the cases that have been utilized in the past to judge the usefulness of a case. However, as in our application: if multiple retrieval goals have to be supported by a case base, the evaluation of the cases depends on the specific retrieval goal, i.e., in general the evaluation of a case differs for different retrieval goals. PATDEX models relevances of attributes with respect to a certain diagnosis, represented in a symptom-diagnosis matrix. As cases in PATDEX are classified diagnosis examples (each case represents a particular diagnosis), a specific relevance vector is assigned to each case, modeling the influence on the retrieval of the respective correct diagnosis. This enables the decomposition of the general retrieval goal "find diagnosis" into the subgoals "find/confirm diagnosis 1..n". However, SE experienceware cases represent unclassified examples. Only the introduction of retrieval goals, as in our approach that models the importance of particular attributes concerning a specific retrieval goal, allows the transfer of those techniques from PATDEX.

CBR-Works [35], one of the commercial successors of INRECA, offers a variety of possibilities to filter attributes of a query or to change weights dynamically. However, it does not explicitly model the concept of different retrieval goals.

Our approach systematizes the concept of goal-oriented retrieval through a flexible and tailorable retrieval method and similarity measure with respect to the specific goal. Different sets of indexes, their importance, and the similarity measure are associated concerning the specific goal, indicating how useful experienceware can be retrieved in the particular situation.

Many CBR systems evaluate similarity between cases only on the global case level. Based on the similarity model used in PATDEX, our approach also considers local similarities between single attribute values. Basic local similarity measures for different types of indexes in the SE domain have been developed, and the concept of a local threshold, defining similarity borders on the attribute level, has been integrated.

Another issue of essential importance in the SE domain is the continuous evolution of the retrieval process and the similarity measure based on feedback from its application in practice. Only a few systems offer learning possibilities regarding the similarity measure as, for instance, the tailoring of relevance factors (see [4] for an overview), which represent the basis for the learning possibilities of our approach.

7 Conclusions

For the successful reuse of software engineering know-how in practice, useful and appropriate experienceware has to be retrieved from a corporate memory. In this paper, we propose a flexible goal-oriented retrieval method and a tailorable similarity measure for the effective and efficient retrieval of software engineering experienceware based on our experiences on reuse of software measurement experienceware in industrial projects. The concept of goal-oriented retrieval is systematized that enables the retrieval of experienceware cases from one experience base for different goals. The approach shows how case-based reasoning systems, which can handle different retrieval goals, become more flexible and can deal with a broader class of problems.

Our approach is incorporated in the REMEX system, a prototypical experience base application for the experience-based support of the planning of software measurement programs. By now, REMEX can be seen as an advanced tool for the planning of software measurement programs providing significant support through the goal-oriented and similarity-based retrieval of experienceware. It further assists the modeling and maintenance of the experience base, the retrieval mechanism, and the generic similarity measure.

Further empirical research will be carried out to assess strengths and weaknesses of the approach. Based on the feedback from its application in practice we expect a basis for future research on methods for the guidance of tailoring the similarity model in industrial environments.

Acknowledgments

The authors would like to thank Marcos R. Rodrigues for his contribution concerning the implementation of the REMEX system.

References

1. Althoff, K.-D. et al.: Case-Based Reasoning for Decision Support and Diagnostic Problem Solving: The INRECA Approach. In Proc. 3rd German Workshop on Case-Based Reasoning (1995)
2. Althoff, K.-D. et al.: CBR for Experimental Software Engineering. In M. Lenz et al. (eds.), Case-Based Reasoning Technology - From Foundations to Applications, Springer Verlag (1998)
3. Althoff, K.-D., Bomarius, F., Tautz, C.: Using a Case-Based Reasoning Strategy to Build Learning Software Organizations. Accepted for the IEEE Journal on Intelligent Systems, special issue on „Knowledge Management and Knowledge Distribution over the Internet" (1999)
4. Althoff, K.-D.: Evaluating Case-Based Reasoning Systems. Springer Verlag, LNCS/LNAI series (to appear)
5. Althoff, K.-D., Nick, M., Tautz, C.: CBR-PEB: An Application Implementing Reuse Concepts of the Experience Factory for the Transfer of CBR System Know-How. Proc. 5th German Conference on Knowledge-Based Systems at German Workshop on Case-Based Reasoning (1999) (CBR-PEB is publicly accessible via http://demolab.iese.fhg.de:8080/)
6. Aamodt, A., Plaza, E.: Case-Based Reasoning: Foundational Issues, Methodological Variations, and System Approaches. AI Communications, 17(1) (1994)
7. Althoff, K.-D., Wess, S.: Case-based Knowledge Acquisition, Learning and Problem Solving in Diagnostic Real World Tasks. Proc. of the 5th European Knowledge Acquisition for Knowledge-Based Systems Workshop, Scotland/UK (1991)
8. Barletta, R.: A Hybrid Indexing and Retrieval Strategy for Advisory CBR Systems Built with ReMind. Proc. of the 2nd European Workshop on Case-Based Reasoning (1994)
9. Bergmann, R., et al.: Initial Methodology for Building and Maintaining a CBR Application. ESPRIT Project 22196 (1997)
10. Basili, V. R., Caldiera, G., Rombach, H. D.: Experience Factory. In J. J. Marciniak (ed.), Encyclopedia of Software Engineering, vol.1, John Wiley & Sons (1994)
11. Basili, V. R., Caldiera, G., Rombach, H. D.: Goal Question Metric Paradigm. In J. J. Marciniak (ed.), Encyclopedia of Software Engineering, John Wiley & Sons (1994)
12. Basili, V. R., et al.: The Software Engineering Laboratory - An Operational Software Experience Factory. ACM (1992)
13. Briand, L.C., Differding, C. M., Rombach, H. D.: Practical Guidelines for Measurement-Based Process Improvement. Software Process Improvement and Practice, vol. 2 (1997)
14. Basili, V. R., Weiss, D.M.: A Methodology for Collecting Valid Software Engineering Data. IEEE Transactions on Software Engineering, SE-10(6) (1984)
15. Bergmann, R.: On the Use of Taxonomies for Representing Case Features and Local Similarity Measures. Proc. of the 6th German Workshop on Case-Based Reasoning, Germany (1998)
16. Barr, J.M., Magaldi, R.V.: Corporate Knowledge Management for the Millennium. In I. Smith, B. Faltings (eds.), Advances in Case-Based Reasoning, Springer Verlag (1996)
17. Birk, A., Tautz, C.: Knowledge Management of Software Engineering Lessons Learned. Proc. of 10th Int. Conference of Software Engineering and Knowledge Engineering, San Francisco (1998)
18. CEMP Consortium: Customized Establishment of Measurement Programs. Final Report, ESSI Project Nr.10358 (1996)
19. Frakes, W. B., Gandel, P. B.: Representing Reusable Software. Information and Software Technology, 32(10) (1990)

20. Finnie, G. R., Wittig, G. W., Desharnais, J.-M.: Estimating Software Development Effort with Case-Based Reasoning. Proc. of the 2nd Int. Conference on Case-Based Reasoning, RI (1997)
21. Gresse von Wangenheim. C.: REMEX- A Case-Based Approach for Reuse of Software Measurement Experienceware. Proc. of 3rd Int. Conference on Case-Based Reasoning, Germany (1999) (http://c3.eps.ufsc.br/remex.html)
22. Gresse von Wangenheim, C., Althoff, K.-D., Barcia, R. M.: Intelligent Retrieval of Software Engineering Experienceware. In Proc. of the 11th International Conference on Software Engineering and Knowledge Engineering (SEKE'99) (1999); also: Technical Report PPGEP-C3001.99E, Graduate Program in Production Engineering, Federal University of Santa Catarina, Brazil (1999)
23. Gresse von Wangenheim, C., et al.: Case-Based Reasoning Approach to Reuse of Experiential Knowledge in Software Measurement Programs. Proc. of the 6th German Workshop on Case-Based Reasoning, Germany (1998)
24. Gresse von Wangenheim, C.: Knowledge Management in Experimental Software Engineering - Create, Renew, Build and Organize Knowledge Assets. Proc. of the 10th Int. Conference on Software Engineering and Knowledge Engineering, San Francisco (1998)
25. Gresse von Wangenheim, C., von Wangenheim, A., Barcia, R. M.: Case-Based Reuse of Software Engineering Measurement Plans. Proc. of the 10th Int. Conference on Software Engineering and Knowledge Engineering, San Francisco (1998)
26. Gresse, C., Briand, L. C.: Requirements for the Knowledge-Based Support of Software Engineering Measurement Plans. Journal of Knowledge-Based Systems, Elsevier, no. 11 (1998)
27. Gresse, C., Hoisl, B., Wüst, J.: A Process Model for GQM- Based Measurement. Technical Report STTI-95-04-E, Software Technology Transfer Initiative, University of Kaiserslautern, Germany (1995)
28. Henninger, S.: Capturing and Formalizing Best Practices in a Software Development Organization. Proc. 9th Int. Conference on Software Engineering and Knowledge Engineering, Spain (1997)
29. Kempter, H., Leippert, F.: Systematic Software Quality Improvement through Goal-oriented Measurement and Explicit Reuse of Software Development Know-How (in German). Proc. of the BMBF-Seminar Software Technology, Germany (1996)
30. Kolodner, J. L.: Case-Based Reasoning. Morgan Kaufmann, San Francisco, California (1993)
31. Kitano, H., Shimazu, H.: The Experience-Sharing Architecture. In D. Leake (ed.), Case-Based Reasoning Experiences: Lessons Learned & Future Directions (1996)
32. Lam, W., Shankararaman, V.: Managing Change During Software Development: An Incremental, Knowledge-Based Approach. Proc. of the 10th Int. Conference on Software Engineering and Knowledge Engineering, San Francisco (1998)
33. Richter, M.M.: On the Notion of Similarity in Case-Based Reasoning. In G. della Riccia et.al (eds.), Mathematical and Statistical Methods in Artificial Intelligence, Springer Verlag (1995)
34. Tautz, C., Althoff, K.-D.: Using Case-Based Reasoning for Reusing Software Knowledge. Proc. of the 2nd Int. Conference on Case-Based Reasoning, LNAI 1266, Springer (1997)
35. CBR-Works. tec:inno GmbH, Germany. (http://www.tecinno.com)
36. Tautz, C., Gresse von Wangenheim, C.: REFSENO: A Representation Formalism for Software Engineering Ontologies. Proc. 5th German Conference on Knowledge-Based Systems (1999)
37. Tversky, A.: Features of Similarity. Psychological Review, 84 (1977)
38. Wess, S.: Case-Based Solving of Problems in Knowledge-Based System for Decision Support and Diagnosis (in German). Ph.D. Thesis, University of Kaiserslautern, Germany, infix Verlag (1995)

A Knowledge Management Lifecycle for Experience Packages on Software Engineering Technologies

Andreas Birk[1], Felix Kröschel[2]

Fraunhofer Institut for Experimental Software Engineering, Sauerwiesen 6,
D-67661 Kaiserslautern, Germany
Andreas.Birk@iese.fhg.de

Andersen Consulting, Otto-Volger-Strasse 15,
D-65843 Sulzbach/Taunus, Germany
felix.kroeschel@ac.com

Abstract. Software engineering can benefit very much from customised knowledge management solutions. These should rely on reusable experience that is modelled explicitly and stored in central repositories. Few approaches exist yet that provide such knowledge management support to software engineering. Those that support it cover usually only part of the knowledge management lifecycle of the reusable artefacts.

This paper suggests a knowledge management lifecycle for experience about software engineering technologies and their application contexts. It primarily aims at supporting the planning of software projects and improvement programmes. The lifecycle model is substantiated by a tool implementation and evidence from an industrial trial application.

1 Introduction

Software engineering plays a key role in today's public life. Nearly every product of the manufacturing or service industries depends to a wide extent on software. The source of software engineering's impressive success is a tremendously fast progress in developing and deploying new technology. However, despite these achievements, stories about computing problems and failures are spread over the news quite frequently. These troubles seem not to fit into the picture of a successful new branch of engineering. A number of recent investigations have shown that the main cause of software engineering's failures is the same as for its successes: New technology–and, in the case of project failures, the inability to manage it successfully (cf. [17] and [12]).

The inherent risk of technology failure in software projects calls for a better management of our knowledge about technologies and their application contexts. Since the beginning of software engineering much effort has been put into the development of new technologies. Less attention has been paid to their application and empirical eval-

---

[1] This work was performed while Felix Kröschel was with Fraunhofer IESE.

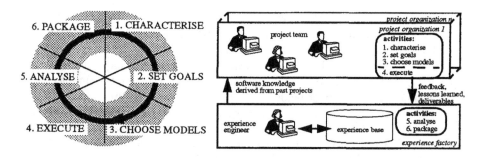

Fig. 1. The Quality Improvement
Paradigm (QIP) [4].

Fig. 2. The Experience Factory (EF) [4].

uation. We argue that this lack of information about when a certain technology can be applied most appropriately and when it should not be applied is the main reason for many technologies-caused project failures.

A knowledge management approach to the application of software engineering technologies has two basic requirements: (1) Precise and operational definition of software engineering technologies, and (2) the systematic investigation and documentation of the application contexts of technologies. While the first issue has already been subject to many research efforts, mainly in the area of process modelling (cf. [25], [9]), the application contexts of technologies have hardly been addressed, yet. For this reason, we have been focusing our research around the following questions: (1) How can technology application contexts can be modelled? (2) how can concrete context models be gained, used for supporting project planning, and evolved based on experience from technology application? This paper presents results from this work. It introduces so-called *technology experience packages (TEPs)* for modelling technologies and their application context. Further, a lifecycle model for developing, using, and maintaining TEPs is presented. For each lifecycle task possible support is illustrated using a prototypical tool implementation.

Our approach builds on the Quality Improvement Paradigm (QIP) / Experience Factory (EF) approach [4]. The QIP is a six-step cycle for continuous improvement in software engineering (see Figure 1). It serves also very well as a knowledge management paradigm for the software domain. The EF is the associated infrastructure for organisational learning (see Figure 2). It distinguishes the project organisation, whose main concern is software development, from the Experience Factory, whose main concern is to learn about software development and to support the project organisation with useful experience. Core component of the EF is the *Experience Base (EB)*, a repository of relevant software engineering experience. The EB contains a collection of *experience packages* that consist of a reusable artefact (e.g., a process model, an effort prediction model, or a code module) and information about when–i.e., in which situations–the reusable artefact can be applied.

Throughout this paper, emphasis is placed on software engineering technologies. Therefore, we refer to a specialised variant of experience bases: Technology experience bases (TEBs), that contain technology experience packages (TEPs). As software engineering technology we refer to every technique, method, or tool used for software engineering [4]. Special attention is paid to process technologies, such as inspection methods and methods for performing measurement programmes.

Section 2 addresses the interface between knowledge management and software engineering. It provides a survey of selected knowledge management solutions from software engineering and other fields. The concept of *technology experience bases* is introduced in Section 3. Sections 4 to 7 present a lifecycle for managing knowledge about software engineering technologies and their application domains. A project on the development of a TEB and its experiences are reported in Section 8. Section 9 presents the main conclusions from our work.

2 Knowledge Management and Software Engineering

Knowledge management can provide beneficial support to software engineering (cf. [7], [10]). This section explores the interface between these two areas. First, requirements on knowledge management of software engineering technologies are identified (Section 2.1). These are then used in Section 2.2 to survey and characterise relevant knowledge management tools. Finally, conclusions are derived from this survey that pin-point further needs for methodology and tool support.

Knowledge management is a term that is still widely discussed and that has no comprehensive and generally accepted definition yet. A concise definition that is widely appropriate for software engineering follows a definition proposed by O'Leary [22]:

Knowledge management is the formal management of knowledge for facilitating creation, access, reuse of knowledge, and learning from its application, typically using advanced technology.

This definition reflects the need of a learning organization for identifying knowledge, for storing it appropriately, for making it accessible, and for easing its reuse. Experience gained from reusing the stored knowledge items should be deployed to further evolve and extend the stored body of knowledge.

2.1 Requirements on Knowledge Management of Software Engineering Technologies

The need for knowledge management support in software engineering–in particular for the management of knowledge about software engineering technologies and their application contexts–can be specified in the form of requirements. In the following, a set of such requirements is provided. Some of these have been derived from the literature ([15], [3]). Others stem from an analysis of knowledge management needs concerning software engineering technologies (cf. [7]).

Support the entire lifecycle of reusable artefacts. A knowledge management system should support the entire lifecycle of the managed artefacts (or experiences or knowledge items), involving their creation, their retrieval and reuse, as well as the feedback of experience from using them.

Tab. 1. Comparison of selected knowledge management tools

	Support the entire lifecycle of reusable artefacts	Similarity-based retrieval	Retrieval based on incomplete information	Possibility to evolve the experience base	Support different types of knowledge	Precise representation of reusable artefacts	Intuitive characterisation of reusable artefacts	Links between reusable artefacts
Bore	●	●	●	◗	◗	●	◗	●
Msmt. Planning	◗	●	●	◗	◗	●	◗	●
KONTEXT	●	●	●	◗	◗	●	●	●
WebME	◗		◗	◗	◗	●	●	●
IDS		◗	◗	◗	●	●	◗	
Ontobroker		◗	●	◗	●	●	◗	◗
Kactus			●	◗	◗	●	◗	◗
Dedal		◗	●	◗	◗	●	◗	●
QuestMap	○			◗	●	●	◗	●
eule2	○		◗	◗	●			●
LotusNotes/ Domino	○	○	○	◗	●	○	○	○
LiveLink	○	◗	◗	◗	●			●
AnswerGarden	○			◗	◗			●

● = comprehensive support ◗ = support exists in part ○ = support is not explicit, but the tool offers means for developing it

Similarity-based retrieval . Retrieval of reusable artefacts should be based on appropriate similarity measures that do not require exact matches between a retrieval query (i.e., the specification of reuse requirements) and the retrieved reusable artefacts. This is necessary for knowledge reuse in software engineering, because the characteristics of software projects can differ quite much. So it is very likely that relevant reusable artefacts are characterised in a form that is not exactly matching a reuse situation.

Retrieval based on incomplete information. Retrieval of reusable artefacts should not require that for all attributes using which the artefacts are indexed information is provided in the retrieval query. This is necessary, because knowledge retrieval is usually performed at the beginning of a software project when some characteristics of the forthcoming project are not yet known. It should be possible to omit these characteristics when defining a retrieval query.

Possibility to evolve the experience base. The TEB should provide mechanisms for adding new knowledge artefacts, as well as for adding or removing attributes of existing objects. It should also be possible to generalise or specialise existing objects. This is necessary in order to support continuous learning and improvement in software engineering.

Support different types of knowledge. The experience base should support a variety of different knowledge types. They can have different representation structures, different access and usage processes, as well as different levels of maturity and reliability.

Precise representation of reusable artefacts. Reusable artefacts should be represented and stored–as far as possible–using a precise and sufficiently formal knowledge representation. This is needed for clarifying the semantics of the artefacts as well as for allowing for automated support of knowledge usage and maintenance.

Intuitive characterisation of reusable artefacts. Reusable artefacts–and in particular their application context–should be defined using terms that are intuitive to the knowledge users. This is important to assure that the experience base is accepted from its users and to allow for efficient usage processes.

Links between reusable artefacts. Explicit links should be established between related artefacts in the experience base. This is needed for being able to exploit relationships during maintenance and retrieval. For instance, technologies should be linked with the processes in which they can be applied.

There are also additional requirements that are important for the technical realisation of an experience base. Examples are access via the internet or intranet, view support, and information security. These are not addressed further, because the focus here is on the methodological concepts of knowledge management in software engineering.

2.2 A Survey of Knowledge Management Tools

Many knowledge management approaches rely mainly on the organisation of knowledge exchange between human agents (cf. [30] [22] [26]). However, our objectives for knowledge management in software engineering are to make knowledge assets explicit (e.g., in the form of technology experience packages), to store them in repositories that are widely accessible (i.e., technology experience bases), and to provide computer support for the management of this knowledge.

There is quite a number of tools available–either as research prototypes or as commercial tools–that address knowledge management. Some of these are specialised to knowledge management in software engineering. Abecker et al. [1] distinguish between process-oriented and product-oriented tools. Process-oriented tools aim at supporting or facilitating knowledge exchange between human agents during their work processes. Examples are groupware systems and intranet solutions. These tools are usually not particularly effective for supporting the management of knowledge about software engineering technologies and their application contexts. Product-oriented tools focus on the knowledge assets to be reused. These tools offer appropriate concepts for the knowledge management of software engineering technologies and application contexts.

Tab. 1 shows a collection of selected knowledge management tools and describes them with regard to the requirements stated in the previous section. The following tools have been included into the survey: *Bore* ([14] [15]) manages knowledge that supports the execution of corporate software development processes. It contains guidelines, lessons learnt, and frequently asked questions, following a case-based approach to knowledge representation and management. Gresse von Wangenheim et al. [13] are developing a tool for capturing experiences about GQM measurement planning (in the following denoted as *Measurement Planning*). *KONTEXT* [18] is a tool for managing the knowledge about software engineering technologies and their application contexts. It is described in more detail below, in Sections 4 to 7. *WebME*, a web-based tool for providing measurement data to project management has been developed at NASA's the Software Engineering Laboratory [29]. These four tools are all knowledge management solutions that are designed for specific software engineering tasks. The following tools are designed primarily for other domains, or they provide generic knowledge management infrastructures.

The expert system *IDS* [16] has been developed for the aircraft industry by making use of data-mining techniques for diagnosing purposes. *Ontobroker* [11] is an intelligent search tool (e.g. for searching the internet) based on ontologies. *KACTUS* [28] provides an interactive environment for browsing, editing and managing (libraries of) ontologies. A representation of a device model is used by the tool *Dedal* [8] for indexing and retrieving multimedia information about a designed device. The hypermedia groupware system *QuestMap* (cf. {27]) integrates different media and links the captured knowledge into a structure supporting the discussion process. *Eule2* [24] is a knowledge-based system for supporting office work in the life insurance domain. It integrates knowledge bases of different knowledge-based systems. The collaboration process in an organisation is supported by the widely used groupware tool *Lotus Notes/ Domino* [20]. For instance, it provides services for electronic mails, storing various types of documents and information, and it allows for annotating documents. The tool *LiveLink* [23] incorporates elements of collaborative work support and web agents on a document-centred knowledge base. By using *AnswerGarden* [2] two different types of knowledge are combined: recorded knowledge can be retrieved and individuals with knowledge of some kind are made known to the rest of the organization. Information access is organised through posing diagnosis questions.

The surveyed tools and their underlying methodologies represent quite different philosophies of knowledge management. It was a purpose of the survey to provide a broad overview and to place the four SE-specific tools into the context of other kinds of knowledge management tools. Please note that the classification schemes (i.e., the symbols in the table cells of Table 1) of different evaluation criteria (i.e., the table columns) can have slightly different semantics. The survey is not meant to rank the tools. Its objective is to illustrate that there exists a variety of technical solutions to common knowledge management requirements.

2.3 Observations from the Tools Survey

The knowledge management tools characterised in Table 1 can be evaluated using the requirements listed in Section 2.1. This evaluation provides an overview of the state of the art in knowledge management for software engineering applications. This section identifies the observations from the survey and briefly outlines needs for further tool support.

Support the entire lifecycle of reusable artefacts. The four tools that are specific to software engineering provide specialised support for more than one lifecycle phase. *Bore* and *KONTEXT* have a usage model that comprises all lifecycle phases from insertion of new knowledge via knowledge use to knowledge evolution. Other tools do either address only the core phase of knowledge use (then nothing is indicated in the table), or they support some kind of knowledge evolution without modifying specific artefacts. The latter is especially true for process-oriented knowledge management tools such as workgroup support systems.

Similarity-based retrieval . Similarity-based retrieval involving some kind of similarity function is realised in *Bore, Measurement Planning,* and *KONTEXT.* Other tools realise similarity-based retrieval using some other concepts such as heuristics. *Lotus Notes/Domino* offers the basic infrastructure for implementing similarity-based retrieval mechanisms.

Retrieval based on incomplete information. Again, *Bore, Measurement Planning,* and *KONTEXT* use explicit characterisation schemes for specifying queries and allow queries in which some characteristics are omitted (i.e., retrieval with incomplete information). This is also true for *Kactus* and *Dedal.* Other tools don't use characterisation schemes for knowledge representation and retrieval, but they allow for some kind of open retrieval.

Possibility to evolve the experience base. Dynamic extension and modification of the experience base is a standard feature that is provided by all surveyed tools in that new knowledge items can be added, removed, or modified. Specific support for automated generalisation or specialisation is not provided at all.

Support different types of knowledge. Every tool represents multiple types or dimensions of knowledge. But only some tools do also allow for extending the set of pre-defined knowledge types or are fully open with regard to the managed knowledge types.

Precise representation of reusable artefacts. Most tools apply some formal or at least well-defined structured knowledge or data representation. But some, mainly the hypertext-based ones, do not have a particularly well-organised, finer-grained representation scheme.

Intuitive characterisation of reusable artefacts. *KONTEXT* is different from the other tools in that it offers a specific representation concept for characterising the reusable artefacts in an intuitive manner. This is done using a redundant characterisation structure that has one view which models the intuitive terms used by decision makers, while the other view provides a precise and unambiguous definition of context characteristics. Most other tools allow for using intuitive identifiers of knowledge items, but only as far as object identity can be assured.

Links between reusable artefacts. Most tools have some kind of links between reusable artefacts thus that relations between associated kinds of knowledge can be explored by the user. These clusters of linked artefacts thus establish some new kind of "higher-order" object and allow the user to explore it interactively. Ontology-based systems (i.e., *Ontobroker* and *Kactus*) do of course also implement links between objects. But these objects are mostly of similar kind, and the linked entities do not establish a really complex new knowledge structure (i.e., other than the ontology itself).

Another knowledge management approach that focuses particularly on software engineering is the Quality Pattern approach [19]. It is a document-based approach that is not yet supported by specialised tools. Therefore most of the above evaluation criteria can not be applied to it appropriately. However, it demonstrates the importance of a semi-structured representation for different knowledge types that is combined with a system of typed links between the reusable artefacts.

As overall conclusion from the survey it can be noted that there exists a wide variety

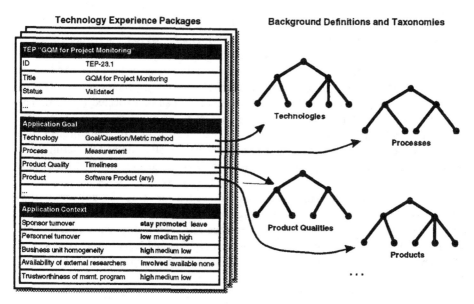

Fig. 3. Technology experience packages and their relations to background definitions and taxonomies.

of knowledge management solutions. Some have been designed specifically for use in software engineering, and these offer quite a wide spectrum of features. For several of the requirements, *KONTEXT* offers the most advanced support among these tools. *Lotus Notes/Domino* is potentially satisfying all requirements. But it would require some considerable implementation effort to actually establish these functions.

Future developments would be needed most in the areas of comprehensive lifecycle support (i.e., offering specific support for inserting new knowledge and evolving the already represented knowledge), support for automated generalisation and specialisation of artefacts[1], improved integration of multiple different knowledge types, and the definition of intuitive views on the stored knowledge, which can be tailored to the needs of certain user groups.

3 Technology Experience Bases

The technology experience base (TEB) is the basic repository of knowledge about software engineering technologies and their application contexts onto which our approach is based. It has been introduced briefly in Section 1. In the following, the structure of TEBs is explained in some more detail.

A TEB has basically two kinds of contents: (1) A collection of technology experience packages (TEPs) and (2) a collection of background definitions and taxonomies

---

[1] Basic technologies for this are provided for instance from the field of machine learning.

(see Figure 3). A TEP contains the definition of the respective technology (usually in the form of a process model) and specifies for which process (e.g., software design or measurement) it can be applied, which product quality (e.g., reliability or maintainability) of which product type (e.g., embedded control systems or medium-sized information systems) can be yielded using the technology, and in which context situation this application and quality impact of the technology can be expected (cf. [5]). The context situation is defined through a set of *context characteristics*. A context characteristic is an attribute/value pair that defines a characteristic of a software project such as team size or degree of management commitment. The attribute and its definition is referred to as *context factor*. A collection of associated context factors forms a *context model*.

Background definitions and taxonomies are needed for achieving uniform definitions of the contents of TEPs, for avoiding redundant storage of these TEP contents, and to provide an index structure for experience retrieval. Hence, each concept contained in a TEP has an associated background definition and is part of a taxonomy. A TEB contains–among others–taxonomies of technologies, processes, products, and product qualities.

4 A Knowledge Management Lifecycle for Technology Experience Packages

The tool survey in Section 2 has shown that most knowledge management approaches are lacking yet a comprehensive lifecycle support for the managed knowledge artefacts. In this section and the following ones we use the case of technology experience packages to illustrate how such a comprehensive lifecycle support can look like. The approach is substantiated by examples from a specialised knowledge management tool.

The knowledge management lifecycle for TEPs has three main phases (Figure 4):
- Gaining TEPs using *knowledge acquisition* and other techniques.
- Using TEPs to support software engineering, e.g., for *technology selection* during the planning of software projects or improvement programmes.
- Updating and evolving TEPs based on the *empirical evaluation* of software projects that have applied them.

In addition, we briefly address the build-up and installation of a TEB (Section 5).

For gaining TEPs, a particular emphasis is placed on knowledge acquisition techniques, because we claim that much knowledge about the application context of software engineering technologies exists already implicit in the minds of experienced software professionals, or it is distributed over a large number of different media throughout a software organisation (cf. [7]). Knowledge acquisition is considered to be the most beneficial source of knowledge when setting up a new TEB. The usage of TEPs and their empirical investigation are closely related to software projects or improvement programmes for which appropriate technologies are needed, and in which they are used.

A prototypical tool has been implemented for supporting the knowledge manage-

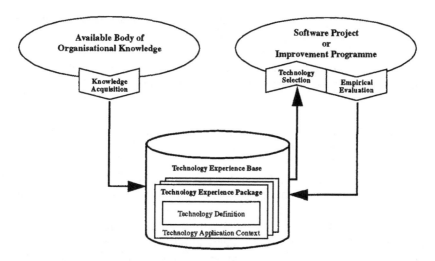

Fig. 4. The lifecycle model of technology experience packages.

ment lifecycle for TEPs. The tool is called *KONTEXT* (*KnOwledge maNagement based on the application conTEXt of software engineering Technologies*). It offers functions for the knowledge modelling tasks involved in knowledge acquisition and empirical evaluation of TEPs, as well as for the entire technology selection process. In the following sections, these functions of *KONTEXT* are explained in more detail.

5 Knowledge Acquisition of Technology Experience Packages

Most software organisations and experienced software professionals know much about the application contexts of software engineering technologies. However, this knowledge is often implicit or distributed over a large number of sources and hardly accessible. For this reason, knowledge acquisition is the preferred approach to quickly gain a large number of TEPs and to populate an initial TEB.

Alternative or additional information sources for developing TEPs are the software engineering literature, software measurement programmes, data mining and information research (using past project documentation, existing measurement data, or other organisational files), as well as empirical investigations such as surveys or case studies. However, all these techniques can also benefit from prior knowledge acquisition efforts that provide grounded hypotheses about the technologies and their application context.

The initial construction of TEBs, which should afterwards be extended and updated continuously, can in principle be done according to the following basic steps:

1. Identify and define the set of relevant technologies.
2. Determine the required target set of TEPs by specifying their processes, product types, and product qualities.

3. Conduct a pre-study of past projects in which the technologies have been used and collect relevant information from literature.
4. Develop background definitions and taxonomies of all relevant concepts that are to be represented in the TEB (e.g., precise operational technology definitions, process taxonomies, product quality definitions and taxonomies).
5. Conduct knowledge acquisition in order to gain context characteristics of the TEPs.
6. Model the TEPs based on the knowledge gained from knowledge acquisition.
7. Verify the modelled TEPs.
8. Validate the TEPs.

Figure 5 depicts the user interface of the TEP modelling component of *KONTEXT*. The leftmost part of the window guides the user through the process of modelling a collection of TEPs. It involves the insertion of a new technology, initialisation of a new TEP, modification of a selected or new TEP, as well as verification and validation of TEPs. The rightmost part of the window offers the functionality to perform the selected process step, in this case the modification of a selected TEP. The entire TEP is displayed and each component of it can be modified or extended.

Verification and validation of TEBs are very important. *KONTEXT* supports the automatic verification of TEPs such as completeness checks and some basic consistency checks. The extensive user guidance of *KONTEXT* avoids widely that wrong kinds of information could be inserted. Validation is currently supported through offering a well-structured report view on TEPs for inspection. Plans for future validation features involve several kinds of simulation-based and multi-expert checking.

6 Technology Selection Support Using Technology Experience Packages

A TEB can be beneficial for a multitude of tasks in software engineering, such as technology transfer and software risk management. As initial task to be supported, we focus on the selection of technologies during the planning of software projects and improvement programmes. We claim that this task is the one where decision support based on TEBs occurs most frequently and where it has the most direct impact on software development.

The selection of software engineering technologies during the planning of software projects and improvement programmes should follow the paradigm of informed decision making. There is a large variety of factors affecting the "right" decision, and the result of the decision can be highly critical to the success of a software organisation. Hence, tool support is required for supporting human decision making rather than for prescribing an "optimal solution".

We base the decision support process implemented in *KONTEXT* on the principles of comprehensive reuse as introduced by Basili and Rombach [3]. This results in the following multi-staged decision support and selection process:

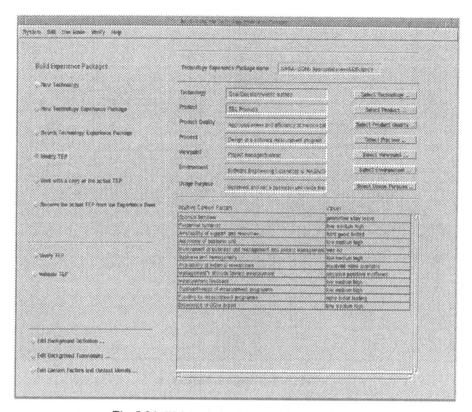

Fig. 5. Modifying a technology experience package.

1. Determine the candidate processes for which a new technology can be applied, the product type to be developed, and the product quality goal to be achieved. – This information allows to pre-select a set of candidate technologies and their TEPs. From the context characteristics of these TEPs, a customised characterisation questionnaire can be constructed. It will be used for characterising the forthcoming project or improvement programme in a form that is suitable to conduct similarity-based retrieval of those TEPs that are most appropriate for the given reuse situation.

2. Characterise the forthcoming software project or improvement programme using the customised characterisation questionnaire. – Using this characterisation, a similarity-based ranking of the candidate TEPs can be conducted. This ranking is expected to support the final selection decision to be drawn by the human decision maker (i.e., the planner of the project or improvement paradigm).

3. Select the most appropriate technology (or technologies) for the forthcoming project or improvement programme. – This selection should be justified explicitly in order to facilitate the achievement of commitment and as a basis for later evaluation of the decision.

In *KONTEXT*, we have implemented several features that we consider beneficial for informed decision making in software engineering. Our pilot implementation demon-

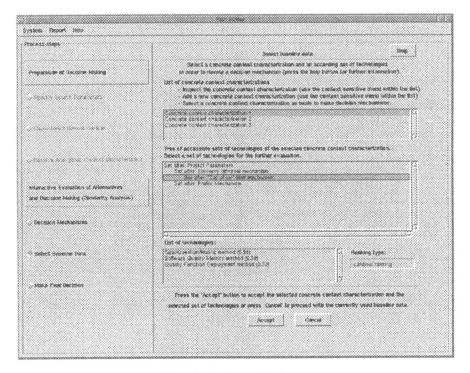

Fig. 6. Selecting a technology.

strates that these are practical solutions for advanced tool support for knowledge management in software engineering:

- Investigation of background information within the decision support process (e.g., technology definitions can be viewed before the final selection decision is drawn).
- Exploration of concurrent scenarios during the decision process. For instance, different characterisations of the forthcoming project can be used concurrently for similarity-based retrieval, and the results can be compared.
- Offering multiple different decision support mechanisms (e.g., multiple similarity functions or different multi-attribute decision making algorithms [21]; the decision maker can select the mechanism he/she regards most appropriate for the current type of selection).
- Backtracking and iteration of sub-steps of the decision process before the final decision is drawn. An example is the application of different decision support mechanisms using the same baseline information. Such a redundant decision process can increase the confidence in the results gained.
- Explicit justification of the final decision, in order to motivate the decision maker that he/she fully rationalises the decision.

The user interface of *KONTEXT* offers these features in its technology selection dialogue. It is shown in Figure 6. The rightmost column of the window guides the user through the multiple actions involved in technology selection. Among others, these are the preparation of the decision making by providing needed baseline information (e.g.,

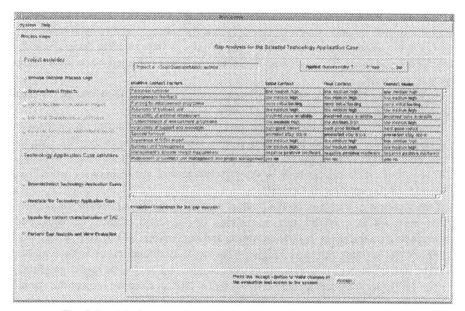

Fig. 7. Empirical post-project analysis of a technology application case.

characterisation of the forthcoming software project), the selection of a decision support method, and the drawing of the final decision and justifying it. The rightmost part of the window shows the dialogue for selecting baseline data for running a decision support algorithm that has been selected in a previous step. The baseline data involves one of possibly multiple alternative characterisations of the forthcoming project and a set of candidate TEPs. Since *KONTEXT* logs all activities of the decision process and their intermediate results, a hierarchy of gradually constrained sets of candidate technologies results from the iterative application of decision support algorithms. The second list in the window presents this hierarchical list of sets of candidate technologies and allows for selecting one of these sets. The technologies contained in the selected candidate set are depicted in the list at the bottom of the window.

For later evaluation of the application of the selected technology, the context characterisation and the entire trace of the decision support process are stored in the TEB. The following section explains how this information is used for refining and updating the TEB.

7 Empirical Evaluation of Technology Experience Packages

Objective of the empirical evaluation of technology experience packages is to possibly refine and update the contents of the TEB. When a technology is applied in a software project, this can be used as a case to investigate whether the information contained in a TEP is appropriate. The core question of empirical analysis is: Does the technology, when applied for the specified process and within the defined application context, really have an observable impact on the respective product quality? This question can be split into two separate investigations: (1) Has the product quality been achieved?, and (2) is the actual context situation of the project or improvement programme the same as defined in the TEP's context model and as it was expected when the technology was selected?

Depending on how the answers to these questions look like, there can be different consequences of empirical evaluation of TEPs:

- If the evaluation shows that the technology had significant impact on the product quality and that the actual application context was the same as in the TEP, then the contents of the TEB might be confirmed and provided with additional evidence. This would create deeper trust in the effectiveness of the technology when used later in similar application contexts.
- If the technology's impact on the product quality or the actual context characteristics were not as expected, then some kind of correction of the TEB is needed. Depending on the exact evaluation results and the contents of the TEB, the modifications can be quite different, ranging from small modifications of context models to the introduction of new variants of technologies and the partial re-design of multiple TEPs. For instance, it could turn out that a TEP on software inspections should better be split into two separate TEPs for variants of software inspections with and without inspection meeting. This would also require new, modified context models that clearly distinguish between the application contexts of the two inspections variants.

A detailed explanation of the analysis strategy for the empirical evaluation of TEPs is described in [6]. The main objective is to identify a causal link between application of the technology and the achieved product quality, under special consideration of the impact of the project context.

KONTEXT supports empirical evaluation by the following features:

- The trace of the technology selection process (cf. Section 6) including the initial characterisation of the project context (i.e., the expected characteristics of the forthcoming project) are stored in the TEB as a basis for future evaluation.
- The actual context situation at the end of the project can be supplied. It is then stored in the TEB.
- *KONTEXT* offers a user dialogue that guides through the process of analysing the deviations between initially expected context characteristics, actual project characteristics, and the TEP's context model (see Figure 7).

The object model of *KONTEXT*'s TEBs (see Figure 8) contains objects for representing information about projects and about the application of selected technologies in these projects (*technology application case*). This way, *KONTEXT* integrates abstract information about reusable artefacts (i.e., the TEPs) with concrete information about the actual reuse of these artefacts. This is not only beneficial for empirical analysis of technology application. It also provides information relevant for informed decision making during technology selection.

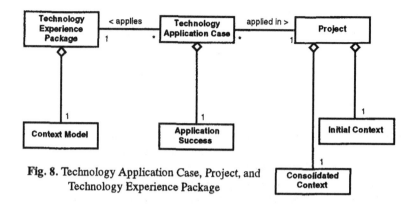

Fig. 8. Technology Application Case, Project, and Technology Experience Package

8 An Example Technology Experience Base

A technology experience base of the presented kind is currently being developed in ESPRIT project PROFES[1]. The objective of PROFES is to support industries that have strong product-related quality requirements, such as the embedded systems industry, with an improvement methodology that focuses improvement actions on those elements of the software development process that contribute most to the critical product quality factors. It places emphasis on the continuous learning about the impacts that software engineering technologies and the processes in which they are applied have on product quality. This information is modelled in the form of so-called product/process dependencies (PPDs) and stored for reuse in a central repository.

The PPD repository is widely analogous to the technology experience base introduced above. PPDs deploy the representation scheme of TEPs. The usage processes on the PROFES PPD repository are designed in accordance with the presented TEP lifecycle model.

The PROFES PPD repository contains information about software engineering technologies that has been collected from multiple literature sources and from three industrial software organisations that have participated in the PROFES project. It will be offered for public use via the internet. So other software organisations can use the PROFES PPD repository to support the identification of improvement actions (i.e., the selection of technologies that are to be applied in forthcoming software projects) in their improvement programmes. They also will be able to feed back their experience and thus help to evolve and extend the repository.

First experience from the industrial applications of PROFES substantiate core components of the presented TEP lifecycle model: The TEP representation schema has proven appropriate for representing the information needed within technology experi-

---

[1] ESPRIT project 23239, PROFES (PROduct Focused improvement of Embedded software Processes); funded by the European Commission. http:/www.iese.fhg.de/Profes

ence bases, knowledge acquisition has shown effective for gaining TEPs, and the importance of product quality goals, processes, and context factors has been demonstrated (cf. [6]).

9 Conclusions

The systematic management of knowledge about software engineering technologies and their application contexts is expected to reduce the risk of technologies-caused failure of software projects. Hence, knowledge management can be regarded an important means for further improvement of software engineering practices.

The Quality Improvement Paradigm (QIP) / Experience Factory (EF) approach ([4]) provides appropriate solution concepts for realising customised knowledge management of experience on software engineering technologies that is packaged for reuse during the planning of software projects and improvement programmes. This experience is modelled explicitly in the form of so-called *technology experience packages* (TEPs) that are stored in repositories called *technology experience bases* (TEBs).

We have suggested a structure for organising TEBs and a comprehensive lifecycle model (1) for gaining TEPs through knowledge acquisition techniques, (2) for using them to support technology selection during the planning of software projects and improvement programmes, as well as (3) for updating and evolving TEPs based on the empirical evaluation of software projects.

Our approach differs from existing ones in that it addresses all three phases of the lifecycle model at a considerably detailed technical level. It provides guidance for organising and running technology experience bases. A prototypical tool called *KON-TEXT* has been implemented in order to illustrate and substantiate the methodological concepts. An industrial trial application has provided first empirical evidence for the validity of the approach.

Acknowledgements

We want to thank our colleagues at the SLI department of Fraunhofer IESE for the many valuable discussions and the feedback they have provided to our work. Markus Nick has provided comments on an earlier version of this paper.

References

1. Andreas Abecker, Stefan Decker, and Otto Kühn. Organizational memory. In *"Das aktuelle Schlagwort" im Informatik Spektrum*, volume 21 of *4*, pages 213–214. Springer Verlag, August 1998.
2. M.S. Ackerman and T.W. Malone. Answergarden: A tool for growing organizational memory. In *Proc. of the ACM Conference on Office Information Systems*, pages 31–39, 1990.

3. Victor R. Basili and H. Dieter Rombach. Support for comprehensive reuse. *IEEE Software Engineering Journal*, 6(5):303–316, September 1991.

4. Victor R. Basili, Gianluigi Caldiera, and H. Dieter Rombach. Experience Factory. In John J. Marciniak, editor, *Encyclopedia of Software Engineering*, volume 1, pages 469–476. John Wiley & Sons, 1994.

5. Andreas Birk. Modelling the application domains of software engineering technologies. Technical Report 014.97/E, Fraunhofer IESE, August 1997.

6. Andreas Birk, Janne Järvinen, and Rini van Solingen. A validation approach for product-focused process improvement. Technical Report IESE-Report No. 005.99/E, Fraunhofer Institute for Experimental Software Engineering, Kaiserslautern, Germany, 1999.

7. Andreas Birk, Dagmar Surmann, and Klaus-Dieter Althoff. Applications of knowledge acquisition in experimental software engineering. In *Proceedings of the 11th European Workshop on Knowledge Acquisition, Modeling, and Management (EKAW'99)*, Berlin, 1999. Springer.

8. CDR, Center for Design Research. http://gummo.stanford.edu/html/gcdk/dedal/index.html, 1995.

9. Bill Curtis, Marc I. Kellner, and Jim Over. Process modeling. *Communications of the ACM*, 35(9):75–90, September 1992.

10. Henrik Eriksson. A survey of knowledge acquisition techniques and tools and their relationship to software engineering. *Journal of Systems and Software*, (19):97–107, 1992.

11. Dieter Fensel, Stefan Decker, Michael Erdmann, and Rudi Studer. Ontobroker: The very high idea. In *Proceedings of the 11th International Flairs Conference (FLAIRS-98)*, Sanibel Island, Florida, May 1998.

12. Robert Glass. *Software Runaways*. Prentice Hall, 1998.

13. C. Gresse von Wangenheim, A. von Wangenheim, and R. Barcia. Case-based reuse of software engineering measurement plans. In *Proc. of the 9th Int. Conference on Software Engineering and Knowledge Engineering (SEKE)*, 1998.

14. Scott Henninger. Capturing and formalizing best practices in a software development organization. In *Proc. of the 9th Int. Conference on Software Engineering and Knowledge Engineering (SEKE)*, 1997.

15. Scott Henninger. Case-based knowledge management tools for software development. In *Automated Software Engineering: An International Journal*, volume 4. Kluwer Academic Publishers, 1997.

16. IBM. http://www.software.ibm.com./data/ids/, 1998.

17. KPMG Ltd. Runaway projects–cause and effects. *Software World*, 26(3), 1995.

18. Felix Kröschel. A system for knowledge management of best software engineering practice. Master's thesis, University of Kaiserslautern, Kaiserslautern, Germany, November 1998.

19. Dieter Landes, Kurt Schneider, and Frank Houdek. Organizational learning and experience documentation in industrial software projects. In *Proceedings of the Workshop on Organizational Memories at the European Conference on Artificial Intelligence '98*, pages 47–63, Brighton, England, August 1998.

20. Lotus. http://www.lotus.com.

21. Mansooreh Mollaghasemi and Julia Pet-Edwards. *Making Multiple-Objective Decisions*. IEEE Comuter Society Press, 1996.

22. Daniel O'Leary. Using AI in knowledge management: Knowledge bases and ontologies. *IEEE Intelligent Systems*, pages 34–39, May/June 1998.

23. Open Text. http://www.opentext.com.

24. Ulrich Reimer. Knowledge acquisition for content selection. In *21st Annual German Conference on AI '97*, Freiburg, September 1997. http://www.dfki.uni-kl.de/km/ws-ki-97.html.

25. H. Dieter Rombach and Martin Verlage. Directions in software process research. In Marvin V. Zelkowitz, editor, *Advances in Computers, vol. 41*, pages 1–63. Academic Press, 1995.

26. Peter M. Senge. *The Fifth Discipline. The Art and Practice of The Learning Organization.* Bantam Doubleday Dell Publishing Group, Inc., New York, 1990.

27. S. Buckingham Shum. Negotiating the construction and reconstruction of organisational memories. *Journal of Universal Computer Science*, 3(8):899–928, 1997.

28. Department of Social Science Informatics Sociaal Wetenschappelijke Informatica. http://www.swi.psy.uva.nl/projects/newkactus/reports.html, 1997.

29. Roseanne Tesoriero and Marvin Zelkowitz. A web-based tool for data analysis and presentation. *IEEE Internet Computing*, 2(5):63–69, 1998.

30. Karl Wiig. Knowledge management methods. Practical approaches to managing knowledge. In *Knowledge Management: The Central Management Focus for Intelligent-Acting Organizations*, volume 3. Schema Press, Ltd, 1995.

Knowledge Management at a Software House:
An Experience Report

Peter Brössler

sd&m AG, Munich, Germany
Peter.Broessler@sdm.de
http://www.sdm.de

Abstract. This progress report describes the introduction of a knowledge management system at sd&m - a large software house in Germany. It explains the circumstances leading to the implementation of sd&m's knowledge management, the realization process as well as its pros and cons. Today, after nearly two years in operation, we would like to present a first evaluation and some thoughts and ideas for the future.

1 Introduction

Founded in 1982, sd&m has grown to employ nearly 700 employees, most of them software developers. The company specializes in designing and implementing large business information systems tailored to the specific needs of the client, while not restricting itself to a certain technology. Projects at sd&m may range in size and scope, involving from one to 100 team members.

2 Problems encountered

The company's rapid growth (more than 50% in some years) and its size (close to 700 employees today) made it increasingly difficult to maintain a consistently high quality standard for all projects. To remedy this problem, the company introduced an ISO-9001 certified quality management system in 1995. By the end of 1996, though this system helped avoid serious quality problems in our projects, it was felt that this form of quality improvement governed by rules and controls (audits) did not provide the necessary flexibility to really boost our projects.
Problems encountered:

- Acquiring the experience and skills needed in our projects (for instance, C++ programming or project management) takes a very long time.
- PCs, C/S, OO, Internet, etc. are great technologies compared to mainframes, but at the same time they are every project manager's worst nightmare. Just consider how many new versions of various Internet development tools are released within one year!

- Over a short period of time, a significant number of highly qualified and experienced people left the company. Some of them were the *only* experts in specific areas, leaving severe gaps in their projects and in the company.
- When using a technology (i.e. programming language, database system, middleware, CASE tool, operating system, ...) that was new to all team members of a given project, the engineers all too often resorted to the "learning by doing" approach. This approach sometimes led to serious time slips and/or quality problems.
- Often, the knowledge and insight gained with respect to tools, database systems, etc. were garnered in one project but not applied to others. So, instead of actually learning from mistakes, other projects using the same technology did not benefit from the existing experience. Consequently, they ran into the same problems over again, and in the end gathered the same, already available, experience.
- A large number of cases showed a lack of knowledge in the specific project, while this knowledge was actually available in the company! This problem usually occurred either because the project manager and the expert on the respective topic were not aware of each other, or the specialist was so involved in his or her own project that there was no time to support the other project.
- sd&m's projects are generally very challenging and sophisticated, both with respect to requirements and technology. Large corporations with their own extensive IT department (e.g. one of the major German banks) often contract sd&m to take over a particular project, mainly because they do not believe they will be able to successfully implement this project on their own. Thus, some of sd&m's projects could be considered "Red Adair projects". Unfortunately, such projects require the best resources, but not every employee in a company can be the best.
- Since the average timeframe for a typical sd&m project is quite long, a number of bids have been lost due to a proposed delivery date that was too late for the customer.

These problems led to many discussions among management and software development staff. The central question was how to improve the situation. The quality management system as a corrective measure can only detect the consequences of these problems, but is unable to prevent them in the first place.

3 Initial Ideas and Approaches

The first idea was to drastically limit the growth of the company, increase the average experience level and to prevent the worst case scenario, which is having few or no experienced software developers and project managers in a project team. Management eventually decided to limit the growth per year to a reasonable figure (around 25%). Although this decision was an important step in the right direction, it was not even close to solving all of the problems described above.

Another idea was to form an internal "Red Adair group" that could be called upon by troubled projects to help them tackle burning issues. The idea, however, was rejected because it was believed that this approach would not have actually solved the real problem.

It was then discussed to create the position of a "chief technologist", someone who could oversee all problems and offer possible solutions. It was quickly realized, though, that one individual could not possible fulfil such a complex and comprehensive task.

Many other ideas and solutions were offered, mostly directed at improving the educational situation at sd&m. Some of them have been successfully implemented and are still in place today, such as a lecture series on about twenty important topics given to newcomers by experienced sd&m staff. A better internal training program was an integral part of the solution, but it was felt still that more was needed.

In order to find the right solution, it was necessary to go back to company's roots, to the days when there was a staff size of about 50 employees. They all worked at the same location, the company's headquarters in Munich, and – most importantly – they all shared one single coffee room. And that was it. Sooner or later, every problem that could not be solved by the project team was discussed in the coffee room. It usually didn't take very long before the specialist for this topic was found and the problem was solved. When we compare the situation then with the situation today, the staff size of 50 versus 700 today is not the only difference: Instead of one coffee room, there are now ten, and while the 50staff had to deal with mainframe-based systems only, the number of technical topics today is not only higher, but the topics themselves are much more complex.

Eventually, we came up with the idea that would be successful in solving the sd&m's worst problems. The concept was to utilize as much of the company's knowledge as possible (which is mainly "produced" during project work) by identifying, collecting and spreading it. Furthermore, it was necessary to find a way to ensure that this knowledge was actually used in new projects (i.e. to fight the "not invented here syndrome") and also to promote the reuse of software components. Last but not least, it was crucial to supplement the knowledge and components developed in the course of projects for individual client solutions with more information and experience on a general level. All this was identified by the author as the need for a "knowledge management organization" [1],[3] to help the company to become a "learning organization" [2]. In mid 1997, the author was offered the position of "Technology Manager". The job description was roughly along the lines of a "chief knowledge officer", with a strong focus on technology.

4 Building a Knowledge Management Organization

In early 1997, when the management board of sd&m decided to ask the author to form a knowledge management group, a major difficulty had to be overcome. The company has a long tradition of avoiding unnecessary overhead activities, it believes in a lean organization that follows the development and the needs of the projects. With this in mind, it was obvious that not everybody welcomed the idea of a new central group – especially in middle management.

The author approached this challenge by developing a customized knowledge management concept for sd&m, which was then discussed with the entire management in great detail. He knew he could count on the approval of senior management, but also recognized that it was crucial to get as much support as possible from all managers. Many of the specific rules (see below) were developed during these discussions. The overall concept was described in a single overhead presentation, which the author then used to inform the whole company. In a series of about ten presentations, the knowledge management concept was introduced to all the different divisions and branch offices of the company. Besides informing everybody, these presentations also provided valuable additional input for the concept[1]. Last but not least, this was a first chance to attract interested colleagues to join the new group.

At that time, the group consisted of the author only. The goal was to have an operating group in place by early 1997.

What are the most important elements of sd&m's knowledge management[2]?

- The knowledge management group consists of so-called knowledge brokers. Most of them are employed as full-time knowledge brokers, so the group is not just a virtual organization.
- Each knowledge broker is responsible for one of sd&m's core topics[3]. The list of core topics was suggested in the initial concept and has been extended during the course of the following discussions.
- Knowledge brokers report to the technology manager. They work as knowledge brokers for a limited period of time, usually for one to two years. Then, they return back to their unit to work in projects as before.
- As a general rule, each unit contributes one knowledge broker. This eases the process of identifying candidates and also helps to generate a demanding attitude from all units: "We contributed an important consultant, what do we get back?".
- Knowledge brokers act as internal consultants, they support the projects with their knowledge and identify possible internal and external knowledge resources.
- Knowledge brokers also develop specific sd&m knowledge related to their topic. They describe best practice and maintain a knowledge store related to their specific area of expertise.
- The whole knowledge management group works as an internal service unit. Their clients are the projects themselves.
- The knowledge management group is also responsible for
  - ➤ the library,
  - ➤ education,
  - ➤ co-operation projects with partners (vendors, universities, ...),

---

[1] Many of the discussions took place via email or in newsgroups as follow-ups to the presentations.

[2] Because the important knowledge at sd&m is mainly technology-oriented, the terms "Knowledge Management" and "Technology Management" were and are used interchangeably.

[3] Current topics encompass: Requirements Engineering, Specification, Software Architecture, Database Systems, Quality Management, Testing, Internet Technology, Middleware Technology, Reengineering and Reuse.

> ➤ research enquiries,
> ➤ dealing with information providers (such as Gartner Group or Giga).
- Besides approximately 10 knowledge brokers, the technology manager, the secretary, and the librarian, a number of developers are needed to build and maintain technical elements of knowledge management.

5 Integrating the Processes

One of the greatest challenges for a successful introduction of a knowledge management system is its integration into the core processes. In our case, it is crucial that the knowledge management and the knowledge brokers are as closely related to the projects as possible.

Every project starts with a "kick-off" phase, which includes a kick-off meeting, and ends with a "touch-down" phase with a touch-down meeting. This is part of sd&m's quality management system. With the introduction of the knowledge management, a new rule was added to this standard procedure: a member of the knowledge management group has to take part in every kick-off and touch-down meeting. This ensures that a project learns about possible sources as early as possible and gets in touch with the knowledge management group, so the project team knows who to contact in case of problems. On the other hand, and most importantly, by attending the touch-down meetings the knowledge management itself learns about experience gathered during the project, including potentially reusable components. The results of these touch-down meetings become part of sd&m's knowledge base.

The support is needed most when a projects runs into a technical problem or when it needs general consulting support in technical matters. Furthermore, the group can also provide technical input for a bid during the acquisition phase of a project. In all these cases, it is vital to establish a common understanding of the actual problem and how the knowledge management group can support the project or the acquisition. For this purpose, a checklist has been developed.

6 Benefits for the Customer

As described so far, our knowledge management supports the projects. This also results in benefits for our customers:
- As more available experience is utilized by a project, fewer lessons have to be learned. For example, a project team does not have to evaluate the market of test tools itself, but can rely on the advice from a knowledge broker. This cuts down delivery time and sometimes even leads to a lower price for the customer.
- Leading edge technology in particular can introduce many risks to projects. By providing projects with the right technology and consulting service, these risks can be reduced.
- sd&m leaves technology and experience with the customer after completing a project. More often than not, project teams also consist of the client's staff. Therefore, sd&m shares its knowledge with its customers.
- By having knowledge brokers in place, customers can talk to subject matter experts during important project phases. Without knowledge brokers, this would hardly be possible.

7 Technology to Assist Knowledge Management

This is the most obvious part of sd&m's knowledge management system. Besides organization and processes, the storage and retrieval of knowledge must be supported by appropriate technology. Everybody in the company must be able to retrieve stored knowledge – not just the knowledge brokers.

What we have done (in brief):

- Each knowledge broker is responsible for one or more knowledge stores related to his or her specific topic. All knowledge stores share the same structure and presentational and navigational style. They are part of sd&m's Intranet.

- The technical quality and contents of our databases for employees, customers, partners, projects and acquisitions have been considerably improved. They are Lotus Notes databases.

- These databases have been integrated into our Intranet. Now, every employee has access to basic information on all customers, projects and employees. All relationships between customers, projects, employees and organizational units are hyperlinked in the Intranet.

- A skill database has been developed to store the skills of all employees. The skill database is an experiment in co-operation, because every employee assesses himself or herself and can introduce new skills as part of a skill tree.

- External resources have been integrated into the Intranet, such as reports from Gartner Group, Giga and Forrester.

- A central search engine makes it possible to search the whole Intranet to find all projects, people, documents, research results, books, etc. related to a specific subject[4].

- All of this is called the sd&m Knowledge Web (KWEB).

8 Cultural Aspects

As in probably all organizations that introduce knowledge management, cultural aspects proved to be the greatest challenge. Fortunately, sd&m had a good starting position: being asked something by a colleague is entirely welcomed – "all doors are open". To achieve and maintain a good knowledge management, however, much more is needed: people must be encouraged to behave proactively. This means they should share what they have learned with. Very often, though, this just doesn't happen. There are many reasons for this, the most prominent one being lack of time. Therefore, all traces of useful knowledge must be monitored very carefully and followed up accordingly. To this end, the touch-down meetings are an important source of information.

In terms of supporting and encouraging the reuse of software components we have developed specific procedures, which would require a separate report to describe.

---

[4] We are using technology from Verity for this, but have greatly enhanced the search engine with own extensions.

The most difficult job was (and to a lesser extent still is) finding knowledge brokers. People come to sd&m to work full-time on projects. The job of a knowledge broker is very different from that. Most notably, every knowledge broker has to be able to deal with many questions and topics at the same time. Not everybody is up to that challenge. As a knowledge broker, the fruits of labour are not as apparent as they are when working on projects. Last but not least, it's a personal change ... Nevertheless, we are happy to report that so far, all positions for knowledge brokers have eventually been filled.

9 Evaluation

In January 1998, was under full steam, with about 15 people actively working in this new group. Considering the staff at that time was around 550 people, this was quite a large number. A minority of these 15 people worked on systems to support the knowledge management (as described earlier). The management of sd&m set the evaluation date for the entire knowledge management for the end of 1998. At that time, there was no doubt that would continue to exist, as there was hardly anyone in the company who could imagine what sd&m would be like without . In the end, was proud to present a long list of satisfied projects.

Although it is very difficult to "prove" a financial pay-off, it can be seen very clearly that the problems described in Chapter 2 do not occur nearly as often as before – despite continuing double-digit growth. Additionally a huge majority (> 85 %) of all employees gave the answer "very satisfied" when being asked to rate sd&m´s knowledge management system. One year earlier this number has been below 40%!

It would certainly be nice to calculate an ROI (return on investment) for our knowledge management. But we have not yet found a way to accomplish this. There are even a number of arguments why it is hardly possible to do this. A few questions may be able to demonstrate this: How much is it worth to be able to apply new technology faster than your competitor? How much is it worth to have a library? How do you find out what share the knowledge management had on a successful acquisition?

10 Ideas for the Future

Here is a list of some plans and ideas for the future:
- Increase the number of situations for which a "self-service" from a knowledge store is sufficient and no knowledge broker is needed personally.
- Increase the number of useful documents in the Intranet.
- Move away from a pure cost-center by introducing charges.
- Further increase the willingness for sharing and reusing components.
- Offer more than just consulting to projects, e.g. training and even the full responsibility for software development environments.
- Carefully extend the consulting service to customers without neglecting the primary goal.
- Build knowledge management systems for customers.

11 References

[1]   **Davenport, Thomas H. and Laurence Prusak:** Working Knowledge: How Organizations Manage What They Know (Harvard Business School Press, 1998)

[2]   **Senge, P.** (1990). The Fifth Discipline: The Art and Practice of the Learning Organization, Doubleday Currency, New York NY

[3]   **Stewart, Thomas A. Intellectual Capital:** The New Wealth of Organizations (Currency/Doubleday, 1997)

"Talk to Paula and Peter – They Are Experienced" The Experience Engine in a Nutshell

Conny Johansson, Patrik Hall, Michael Coquard

Ericsson Software Technology AB
P. O. Box 518, SE-371 23 Karlskrona, Sweden
Conny.Johansson@epk.ericsson.se, Patrik.Hall@epk.ericsson.se,
Michael.Coquard@epk.ericsson.se

Abstract. People working in the Software Engineering field must solve problems every day to get their work done. For successful problem solving, they need to find others with specific experience. To help individuals with this, we created an 'Experience Broker' role in the organization. The broker must be officially recognized, and function as a facilitator for the internal human network in the organization. Our approach to the 'Experience Factory', what we call the 'Experience Engine', focuses on mediating referrals to sources holding the correct expertise—usually human sources. We claim that the most valuable experience is tacit and stored on the individual level. The most valuable experience transfer comes while on the job when the person holding the experience verbally relates to the learner directly. Getting the right context for this experience transfer is difficult without direct contact between the person with the experience and the recipient. Experience is transferred at the right time when the learner is actually working on something that concerns it. Values must be rooted in the organization, where individuals are willing to spend the necessary (most often short) time to spread valuable experiences to others in the organization. Our pilot project showed that a measurement and database approach is less valuable than individual face-to-face meetings, to transfer experience.

1 Introduction

The 'Experience Factory' [1] is an important approach for software companies in their struggle for survival. We felt it important to relate this approach to the current situation at the company, and to its organizational learning processes. We also believe that gradually integrating new ideas, concepts and approaches is the smoothest and best way for our company to apply such an extensive approach as the experience factory.

Ericsson Software Technology AB has several business centers to develop software products, called nodes, which establish product requirements and have primary customer interface as well as research and corporate functions. Each business center is divided into several business units, each normally working on one or up to three products. The business units have 20 to 30 employees each, for a company total of approximately 800 employees. Together, they develop a wide range of software applications, including several types of telephone switches, and mobile phone management systems.

This paper starts by describing the similarities and differences between the experience engine and the experience factory. The pilot run in 1998 is presented, followed by a section describing the narrower scope and focus of our measurements. The Experience Practice describes the basic values for experience transfer, then the role of experience broker and communicator are defined, and finally we describe the different experience occasions we identified.

2 The Experience Engine Vs. the Experience Factory

We believe that in applying the experience factory approach, the same applies with the software engineering discipline—these are laboratory sciences and we must experiment with techniques to see if they really work [2]. We realized rather quickly that we could not implement the entire approach, at least not directly. The name, 'Experience Factory' can lead to associations with industrial production. But software engineering is not about reproducing the same things—every product is different than all others [2]—so we renamed our application 'The Experience Engine'. We wanted to create an engine that would continuously work to recycle and transfer the collective experience within the company.

The experience factory focuses on process improvement. And it should not be part of any project organization, since its focus does not normally coincide with that of any other part of the organization. The experience factory should be an independent part of the organization that collects, analyzes, generalizes, formalizes, packages, stores, retrieves and reuses collective experience [1]. It can provide a project organization with two kinds of experience: one that hints at what to do and the other that guides in doing it. Further, it functions to investigate and introduce new technology to the company, is the skills center for software engineering, and has operative responsibility for process improvements.

In contrast, the experience engine does not take this broad approach. That would require a larger reorganization and defining a new separate group, so established concepts and groups at our company would need to be redefined. Relying on Hansen et al. [3], we feel it would be hard to integrate the experience engine if it were a separate functional department. The experience engine focuses on creating and managing experience transfer, integrating it with the existing organization, and the role of the individuals involved when this takes place. It does not focus on organizational structure—the roles are easily integrated with the existing organization.

The experience engine organization is, therefore, not as large as that of the experience factory. Our organization currently has one full-time and two half-time positions. The considerable difference in focus on measurements and quantification, is one reason for this. In our approach, generalization and customization are handled when the transfer occurs, face-to-face. This, as opposed to documenting the generalizations in writing, as required in the experience factory approach (as we have interpreted it). Hansen et al. [3] declares that companies that offer customized products should not focus on measurements and store this knowledge in a database.

This strongly supports the findings at our company and the characterization of our products. Furthermore, if the company has a business strategy that is based on innovative products and comprised of people who rely on tacit knowledge to solve problems, it can even quickly undermine the business, Hansen et al. [3].

Other activities also not included involve new technology infusion, skills management, and process improvement. They certainly exist in some form, but are organizationally considered on the business unit level, and so were excluded from the study. For example, process improvement activities are normally initiated by improvement proposals reported orally, or in intermediate or final reports. Our experience is that the best way to carry out process improvement is to include it as an activity in each project. These are coordinated and followed up at the business center level by a manager, with the results communicated to the rest of the organization primarily through informal channels.

One empirical study, related to our pilot, reports that the information system at our company is rather well developed. Formal communication channels such as electronic mail and documentation (written reports) have been well established for several years. But, this might be at the expense of verbal communication. Establishing a corporate culture that includes a coordinating mechanism for communication (to transfer knowledge and experience) is essential for employees' knowledge-creating activities [4].

Taking the entire experience factory approach would have been revolutionary at our company. We also thought it would not bring any improvement. First, it would require an extensive re-organization involving definition of an experience factory organization. Second, it would require unnecessary changes to work routines that are already perceived to work well. Finally, it would involve introducing a company-wide approach affecting all activities in the organization without any easily identifiable cost benefits. And, it would probably hinder the success of our other more important efforts where we did find shortcomings and a need for improvement.

3 The pilot project

The pilot project we set up was limited to a few business centers, and was designed to test our ideas and evaluate their cost benefits. We continuously refined, removed, and added new guidelines and working practices as we gained experience and feedback.

This pilot empirically covered over 100 experience transfer occasions in the organization. These involved a wide range of experience transfer related to management, technical, as well as business related issues. Management experiences were related to project management issues such as planning, progress reporting, and requirements change processing. Examples of technical experiences are design and code decisions, strategies, and solutions. Negotiations, agreements, and patent are examples of business issues addressed.

We felt it important to make a qualitative study. So instead of quickly analyzing a large number of occasions, we selected about 20% of the experience transfer occasions, and studied them in more detail. We felt the studies should be related to the context of the experience occasions. We generalized these experience occasions to determine common patterns, further developing our approach.

The project consisted of a core team with four persons working part time. All project members have a Software Engineering or Computer Science degree and several years of professional experience in software development.

The experience occasions were evaluated continuously using attitude surveys, both written questionnaires and oral interviews. During the evaluations, we identified problems with using written questionnaires. Without doing any quantitative analyses of the quality of the questionnaires—we identified several questionnaires that had been filled out in a hurry. In our view this produced unreliable results from the surveys. We have therefore started to use oral interviews, short occasions not planned in advance, where the interviewer orally goes through the questionnaire with the interviewee, who sometimes does not even see the questionnaire.

4 The measurement approach

Measurement is the process of assigning numbers or symbols to attributes of entities in the real world so they can be described using clearly defined rules [5]. Measurements in software engineering can be direct (as in cost or number of faults) or indirect, by combining different measurements (such as for productivity or fault density). The usefulness of a measurement depends largely on the control status of the process when it is collected [6]. This is the cause of variances observed during the process. The problem is that the causes of variance are rarely analyzed. The reasons we found for this are:

☐ When an organization starts measuring, its approach to measurement is too comprehensive, so too many measurements are defined,

☐ The necessary activities for analyzing the causes for variances are not completed,

☐ Feedback from analysis of the causes of variances is poor,

☐ Improvement activities initiated because of the measured variances are not followed.

Today, some companies still think they can put all their corporate knowledge on a server to form a kind of giant hyperlinked encyclopedia [7]. The real value of information systems is connecting people to people, so they can share their expertise and knowledge on the spot. We started with a significant effort to determine how measurements should be collected, packaged and stored. While the original purpose of the experience factory does not lend itself to creating a large database, this trap is easy to fall into. The trap is set by the descriptive illustrations of the experience factory, which often indicate storage using the now old-fashioned, disk storage device [8]—one easily visualizes physically storing experiences on a computer device. Our first approach included a large database, but after interviews, some research, and several work sessions, we concluded that this was not a good solution for the company.

In fact, we spent nearly 1000 hours on database specification before we realized this was not right for us. We determined this from the fact that over the last years we have gathered and stored large amounts of data in a large corporate database. This includes hundreds of measurements like lead time, planning vs. actual, productivity, and more. These data have rarely been analyzed for use in process improvement. Some of our time was even used to identify additional data to collect. When we presented yet another database specification, most everyone sighed at our approach. In the end, we found it more important for analysis and feedback efforts to gather a small number of different measurements. The time spent on these activities can at first be seen as wasted, but it was actually well worth finding the right direction to proceed.

We decided to narrow the scope of the measurement program. At the company level we focused on fault data and defining collection routines, storing principles, analysis methods (including statistical methods), activity definition (including responsibilities for monitoring the activities), and simple tips on how to provide feedback on the data and fault measurement results. We focused on fault data at the company level because this is the only general measurement we saw as worth collecting, now and in future. This approach is also supported by Demarco [9]. Additional measurements and local adaptations to the corporate approach were dealt with by the local organization.

The measurements are, to a greater extent, now used more as one of several indicators of a potential problem. We have de-emphasized measurements from being the 'only' basis for decision. Other indicators can be short verbal or written analysis sections for reports, but most often, involve communication within the group.

The measurements were designed to help develop a method for variance analysis and forecasting. These primarily concerned forecasting the number of faults in operations. We chose the standard method of correlation of metrics using simple linear regression technique [5]. We identified a few interesting correlations, but we now strongly doubt these can be of any practical use. This is mainly because:

☐ The measurements were collected during a five year period, when products, processes and people have changed significantly,

☐ There were several different 'unexpected' events, such as late requirement changes, resource reductions, and poor product usage during the measurement period, which resulted in the measurements becoming unreliable,

☐ Uniformity of the measuring methods also arose. These included different classification systems for faults and different definitions of measurement periods.

We are convinced that different projects cannot be comparable using measures only. The projects vary too widely in size, complexity, and project member's level of experience. We found it difficult to formalize the experience not only in pure numbers, but also in writing.

We also developed a process to support the measurement cause analysis. This simple process describes how to conduct the analysis of measurement deviations reported in a project. The process includes team member interviews and evaluation sessions to determine the cause(s) of the deviation. We noticed that even though a measurement deviates from the expected, this is not necessarily unacceptable. Special conditions in the project can cause deviations but these should not always be seen as indicators for action or other decision.

5 The Experience Practice

Our company values are based on a concept our senior management calls Guiding Lights. The five Guiding Lights, short phrases symbolized as lighthouses, show us the best course to follow and help us in our voyage into the future. One Guiding Light is 'We learn from each other'. This concept is emphasized to a greater extent in our organization since the ability to share knowledge and experience is most often an important aspect in salary negotiations between individual employees and their managers.

The goal of the experience engine is to transfer experiences efficiently through people building networks. To support this, we decided to define what an experience practice is. In doing so, we used the basic value contained in the concept 'We learn from each other':

The most useful experiences are stored in every individual's brain. This is the primary storing media, and verbal communication (preferably in face-to-face meetings) is by far the best way to communicate and spread these experiences.

Information and knowledge are sometimes distinguished [10]. Information expresses knowledge but is unreliable in transferring it. Knowledge should be transferred when the receiver is actually doing something related to the experience being transferred. Knowledge can be defined as: "a capacity to act" [10]. We consider experience as: "knowledge that has been perceived by acting". You can gain knowledge by reading specialist literature, but you can not gain experience without acting in practice. The main focus is to increase competency, and so transfer knowledge—a transfer mechanism which we consider equivalent to transferring experience.

This paper does not discuss in detail the difference between knowledge and experience. It is impossible to transfer knowledge precisely, but if the knowledge is merged with experience(s), it will most probably enhance competence. We use only the word 'experience' further, and do not consider the possible differences in the knowledge transfer and transferring experience.

Orr [11] states that experience is a socially distributed resource, stored and spread primarily through an oral culture. Interpreting raw measurement data is difficult without extensive routines to classify data and other context related definitions and restrictions. Written and stored information is barely recognizable to outsiders, so the author usually has to be contacted to understand the context of the experience [11]. In a face-to-face meeting with the source, the receiver can get immediate response to any questions and clarification concerning relevance, context and detail—whatever seems appropriate for the situation. In rank of importance, face-to-face meetings are the most valuable media for transferring experience—followed by telephone, video conferences, email, personally addressed mail, and finally impersonal mail such as formal reports [12].

Useful experiences are normally stored on the individual level. We can state, as Polanyi [13] and Nonaka and Takeuchi [4], that the most valuable experiences are tacit, and it is very hard to express these in words or numbers. The benefit and gain from spending time in trying to write down these experiences is hard to measure. The time it takes to transform this tacit experience into explicit experiences and write it down, is valuable and doing so often does not pay off.

Time must be taken by the author to interpret their experience, write everything down and then formulate the context. The person reading about this experience, in turn, has to spend the time to read and interpret the experience related. Several links must be performed in a uniform way to get the same result at both ends. We judge this unlikely in most cases—it is hard enough to express and transfer tacit experiences orally. But of course, we do not extend this concept into absurdity. Writing down specialist literature, documentation for standardized products or methods, and explicit (or apparently explicit) knowledge still serves a purpose.

Another important aspect is based on the axiom demonstrated by the postman game, which Swedes call the whispering game. If one person tells another an experience, who, in turn, tells it to another, and so on, the original experience related most probably differs greatly from the final version. Each individual adds, changes and subtracts their interpretations. This is analogous to the example of the written material described. Our finding in this case is that the most valuable and useful experience transfer comes when told by those who have actually gained the experienced themselves.

If experience is not stored in writing, it will disappear when the person who actually gained it leaves the company. This is, of course, negative, but we consider that:

☐ Experiences which can be unambiguously interpreted are (hopefully) stored in final reports,

☐ The life span of the experience in software engineering is short, and

☐ There is a fair chance that when our experience engine approach is established, the valuable experience has been communicated to another person, and it has been merged into their own experience, so it can be shared (in its new form).

To address this last point, we made a qualitative study of the company learning process. In order to understand the organizational learning process, the entire company must be considered, not just temporary projects [14]. We studied a number of projects in a limited part of the organization, but consider the findings applicable for at least the majority of projects at our company.

Our study indicated that individuals review and observe experiences from different perspectives, and so, reflect on it to a greater extent. Further, they interpret and use their observations for problem solving and decision-making. These are used as a base for acquiring more concrete experiences, which in turn forms the basis for more learning. These practical learning processes are similar to the cyclic learning process described by Kolb [15]. We think this indicates that experience is not as tied to specific individuals during its (longer) life span, as we initially thought. As well, people do not depend on older experiences since these are merged and refined into new, fresher understanding.

Strong management commitment is necessary to succeed with our approach. Senior and mid-level management must actively and continually support the experience engine and the principle it builds upon. Management support should not only include communicating information, but also action in continuously facilitating use of the experience engine.

6 Experience occasions

An important question was: 'When does experience transfer take place?' Our study indicates that much experience transfer takes place during informal communication. We believe common values can be developed to support such informal experience transferring. Shrivastava [14], among others, supports this. The transfer is dependent on the work environment, time, co-workers, and the type of transfer involved. We believe that direct communication is more suited for informal experience transfer than text.

What happens when two, or more, people meet and talk depends on their interpretations, language, personalities, and the context. The basic values for communicating experiences already exists in the organization and instances of experience transfer occur rather frequently. When introducing the experience engine, we saw that experience occasions could be identified in three categories, which we called 'Flashes', 'Learning Situations' and 'Education/Training' to more easily differentiate them. Flashes and Learning Situations are described in this section. Education/Training is when the learner lacks formal training and/or professional experience in a specific area. The experience engine is not designed for education/training situations.

Of course, whether an experience transfer belongs in one of these categories or the other is always debatable. We created these groups simply as practical guides to clarify them, but they are definitely not intended to formalize any relationships or be used as rules. In our pilot study we estimated there were 20 learning situations and 80 flashes in 1998. These are only estimates since we could not register some flashes and learning situations before being fully aware they had occurred.

6.1 Flashes

Flashes are the most common experience occasion. We identified two types of flashes: 'Broker Flashes', where the referral to an experience source is mediated; and 'Communicator Flashes', where experience is actually communicated. Most flashes were internal to the organization, involving employees. However, we see no limitation that others outside the organization can be involved in this type of experience occasion. We see this as a matter of mutual needs where there is no direct competition between the organizations. If we help you this time, you help us next.

Experiences are transferred most effectively when the receiver is performing in the process concerning the experience actually required [10]. Experiences are valuable only when they can be contextualized, decontextualized, and recontextualized at the proper time [16]. Broker Flashes do happen through written messages (mostly email), but occur more often in telephone or face-to-face meetings.

Face-to-face meetings are short occasions that usually happen by chance resulting from actual needs. In listening to people as they discussed everyday problems in corridors, on breaks, and at lunch, brokers can act as agents for those needing extra, experienced advice. It is at these short (usually only a few minutes), recurring occasions where we acted as middleman in the human network. However, to reduce relying on chance, we could create broker flashes by actively seeking them. The broker could create these flashes by:

☐ Walking around - dedicating time to just walking around specifically to talk and listen to others,

☐ Participating in reviews and inspections – these are designed for concrete active help to the receiver so this activity is therefore easy to adapt,

☐ Participating in project risk analyses,

☐ Participating in different kinds of cross-section teams and networks.

We defined communicator flashes as taking less than 10 minutes. They have sometimes occurred previously but only in limited sized groups, such as teams or units of less than 30. The conversion of the tacit experience to explicit experience— that is, interpreting and the opportunity to use the experience which is transferred, is occurs at the same time as the transfer. Explicit concepts can, for example, be created through dialogue using metaphors and analogies [4]. Communicator flashes do not cost the receiver anything. Examples are questions and problems regarding specific programming language constructs, product storage handling, and test case specifications.

6.2 Learning Situations

Learning situations are when the receiver has formal training but lacks professional experience. This situation normally requires planned time and takes more than 10 minutes. Learning situations involve on-the-job training where the receiver learns from doing in actual conditions, but in a session with an experienced communicator. This is also known as experience transfer by tradition. And is reported as being up to seven times more effective in transferring experience than the most common method– – the lecture [10]. The guidelines used for the conversion of tacit experiences to explicit experiences in communicator flashes also apply to learning situations.

Learning Situations can be when the communicator:

☐ Moderates a work-shop,

☐ Participates in developing a project plan with the receiver (for the receiver's project),

☐ Guides a quality coordinator in using company software quality assurance processes.

The best approach we found for calculating cost benefit was using simple attitude surveys on a case-by-case basis. These attitude surveys were done with either interviews or questionnaires. One example of a learning situation is where the communicator participated in a three-hour walk-through of a preliminary study. The receiver reported the walk-through (involving only the communicator and the receiver) as successful, estimating a savings of several hours and a considerable quality improvement gain.

This highlights our feeling that we are not only interested in actual cost benefits, but also other organizational and individual benefits. This is often difficult to measure in numbers so we felt the approach of estimating benefit using these attitude surveys could provide evidence of success. However, we do make a careful attempt to transform this 'tacit' understanding into explicit numbers. Each learning situation and communicator flash is, where possible, graded by value in a 10 point ordinal scale (1 to 10), and by estimated cost benefit (estimated number of hours earned).

Regarding another aspect, when companies pay for a service, they have to evaluate the results of the work performed. They should be keen to optimize the use of the time paid for, whether they buy it internally or externally. This argues strongly for the receiver to want to pay for the learning situations. Also, from the perspective of the communicator (and the financial unit they belong to), it is important that the learning situation does not affect their budget negatively. Follow-up for both costs and benefit would therefore be simplified if these situations are budgeted.

Again, we do not see any limitation for involving external personnel in learning situations. With the learning situation financed by the receiver, this is easier done than for flashes. However, the problem of allocating the necessary time for experienced communicators remains, whether this is acquired internally or externally to the learning situation. This kind of resource is scarce, especially in software engineering, so these busy people have difficulty allocating the necessary time.

7 Experience Broker and Experience Communicator

People in organizations must solve problems to get their work done every day. For this, they must often find expertise with this experience. We use the term expertise as the embodiment of experiences within individuals [17]. Individuals have different levels of expertise in different topics and in different contexts. To solve the problem of identifying the expertise required and selecting who to acquire it from, two new roles were created in the organization, that of 'Experience Broker' and 'Experience Communicator'. The experience broker has a visible, appointed role within the organization. This role is similar to the expertise concierge described by McDonald and Ackerman [17] and the contact broker role described by Paepcke [18]. Brokers must be visible and accessible to facilitate helping individuals looking for expertise, when they need an experience transfer. Experience communicators, on the other hand, have a more informal role in the organization.

Those lacking the necessary experience just contact the experience broker, who helps them find the right expertise, or experience communicators, with the necessary experience. Justification of the possibility to use the transferred experiences must be done at, or closely after, the time of transfer. If the conversion does not add any value or is not enough to be able to generalize and adapt it to one's own context, you need to seek other or more expertise.

The problem with expertise selection is well studied and described by McDonald and Ackerman [17]. People are often faced with choosing from among several possible experts. Additionally, if they have a complex problem they will most likely seek more expertise in order to achieve a higher probability of quality in selecting experience communicators, and/or generalization of the experience [17]. There will be many experience communicators but only a handful of specifically appointed experience brokers, connecting them all in the experience engine.

7.1 The Experience Broker

Experience brokers add some extra power to the engine to make it run better. They function as the hub of the experience engine network. Their primary responsibility is to maintain, extend, and facilitate using the experience engine network and its experience communicators. These are generalist with wider experience in using tools and methods–both within and outside the company. So they know a little about many different things, but can easily understand the company structure (products) and its processes.

In this sense, the experience broker is a loaf about—someone who listens, sometimes even eavesdropping, but who also talks with many people, referring those who need it to the right experience communicator(s). This is not to say they spy on employees, but they invest their time trying to find out what others' needs really are. This can be thought of as taking the organization's temperature, finding out what is going on, and solving networking problems. The broker therefore knows the projects currently running, even participating in formal activities for selected projects (including meetings) to extract what experience is needed.

The broker knows the arenas where people interact and should also try to find or create additional arenas for transferring experience [4]. This role is essential in creating a company learning climate.

The experience broker's role is to:

- Identify several experience communicators who can provide others with help/experience,
- Facilitate contacts with experience communicators,
- Strive to connect people across organizational boundaries,
- Be perceived as always available,
- Follow up on the benefits from flashes and learning situations.

This role must be fully recognized in the company for it to succeed. This means that it is both well known, and appreciated. The person acting as a broker must have a large contact network, and be respected as a generalist in the company. This can be achieved by communicating the concept as well as success stories through both informal and formal communication, including departmental and project presentations. An important consideration for such presentations is to have advance information about the current status of the projects or units the (potential) receivers represent. This way, the broker can find concrete applications for flashes and learning situations.

The restaurant is a useful arena for mediating referrals to experience sources. In the extreme case, the broker should always try to have lunch with different people, take breaks at different locations, and participate in activities with employees outside work. In these situations the broker always works when others have breaks, lunch or spare time. This may not be fully attainable from the broker's social perspective, but these arenas for mediation and experience transfer present good opportunities.

The experience broker must have good communication and interactive skills with others. Some people are naturally this way, but these skills can also be learned. Experience brokers must have a good sense of when to interact with a project or a person, and when not to. They should not, for example, disturb a person who is deeply occupied, and they have to know where to find the right person with the necessary experience to then mediate the contact. And even more important, project members and others must see their needs met when using the experience broker.

The length of time for anyone to be experience broker was also discussed. Though we have not come to any final determination, we believe this depends largely on the individual involved. While some should stay brokers for shorter periods, others have the qualities necessary to hold this role longer. Some are suited to do this full time, while others are more suitable as part-time brokers. One benefit with part-time brokers is that they can maintain their role as a generalist by participating in different projects with their remaining time. It is, however, of utmost importance that the organization has full confidence and trust in the individuals acting as brokers.

There are too many specialists and too few generalists at the company today. To ensure that the experience broker stays a generalist, they must be known to the various parts of the organization and different projects. One way to achieve this, is known as walk around management, which has been successfully used by great companies around the world. We feel this principle can be used for experience brokers, though they are not managers. This should be an independent position that is not assigned to any one branch or specialty.

As time passes, an increasing number of experience occasions will occur without any broker having knowledge of them. There are already examples of mediations where one communicator, shortly after an experience transfer, is asked for additional, or related, experience. In this case, an experience transfer occurs that no brokers know of—the contact is most probably taken directly with the communicator. This can result in a problem with following up experience occasions, but can also show progress towards the goal of the experience engine—getting people to build human networks.

7.2 The Experience Communicator

Experience communicators are those with the experience who are willing to share it with others. They should have some pedagogical skills in addition to their willingness. We do not think everyone with vast experience can act as a communicator, rather it is equally important, as with brokers, to have human understanding and social skills.

We found it important for experience communicators to try to give educational answers. These answers are focused on teaching receivers how to solve related issues by themselves in future. Lao Tzu is credited with coining a useful proverb: "Give the man a fish and you feed him for a day, teach the man how to fish and you will feed him for a life time". Providing educational answers means placing the answer in a broader context, or even just hinting at where to find the answer. For example, an answer may be easily available on the web or in a report. Otherwise, providing receivers with clues on how to solve the question themselves may be the best approach without further describing the detailed context.

Experience communicators should not do others' work. Rather, the communicator's main task is to help others solve their own problems. This is different than the role of a regular project resource. While using the communicator as a resource in a project may help the project in the short-term, it would damage the entire idea behind the experience engine. Little or no experience transferring would take place in such situations.

The role of experience communicator was an informal role in the organization. And we are strongly convinced that the role should remain so. The company already has a lot of positions and roles, and attitude surveys show low acceptance to introducing yet another role. However, we are considering how this informal role should be made more visible in the organization. The benefit to the communicators would be that they are perceived as valuable, attaining a degree of recognition in the company. We believe that an important factor would be to high-light the company value behind 'we learn from each other', and include it as an issue in salary negotiations.

It is also important for the experience communicator to give feedback to the experience broker. This not only ensures that processes can be reviewed, but also that the communicator actively takes part in the experience engine. It is equally important for the broker to know which communicators add value to the experience engine. For example, feedback from the communicator to the broker could be: "I have had many people calling me about the same type of problem. I think we need some courses in this field," or "I was asked a difficult problem that I could not resolve. I referred them to another person I know who is good in that field." This fits the goal of the experience engine: to get people to build human networks.

It is important to realize that everyone is not suited to be an experience communicator. Everyone does not have the aptitude and the social skills necessary to transfer their experience pedagogically. On rare occasions, we have had problems with evaluating an individual's suitability to be communicator, but we believe this can be handled in normal procedures within the organization.

8 For the Future

We will continue to refine our successful approach, focusing on mediating referrals to others as a source of collective experience. A five-fold increase in the number of mediations during a three-month period gives an indication. We plan to consider integrating more of the key features described in the 'Experience Factory' approach into our experience engine. In particular, process improvements will be a key issue for this. The extension of our approach will also most probably mean the organization will grow by one or two persons in the near future.

The five-phase model of organizational knowledge-creation process described by Nonaka and Takeuchi [4] will be studied. So far, we have only studied justification of experiences at the individual level. However, the need for an organization to conduct a justification on the organizational level [4] will be considered, to perhaps be introduced for some experience occasions.

Currently, we are incrementally extending use of the experience engine in the organization. Some spontaneous mediation and experience transfer takes place throughout the company, of course. But we plan to introduce it step-by-step. Experience engine implementation issues are currently being discussed—for example, is it necessary to formally define the role of the experience broker and will we still be able to reach the goals of the experience engine? We plan to allocate more resources.

The (informal) list of communicators has weekly additions. We also need to define and resolve the issue of recognizing the experience communicators.

As well, we need more success stories focusing on cost or lead time improvements. Success stories are one of the most important incentives to apply any approach. For our part, we want more stories that emphasize using project managers and team members, as well as success stories useful for senior management.

We found that the best solution to calculate cost benefit was to determine the benefit through attitude surveys, while not concentrating on cost only. We will continue to evaluate the communicator flashes and learning situations for perceived value, and estimated cost benefit using estimated number of hours earned. We strongly believe that these evaluations should be used with great care. They can be used as indicators but most probably should only rarely be used alone in making decisions on direction. These measurements are, however, necessary to provide indicators of benefit for the company, especially to senior management, from using our approach.

9 Conclusions

Using our 'Experience Engine' approach, we aim to eliminate the attitude that managing collective company experience involves huge databases and processing large amounts of measurements. Our approach favors verbally communicating valuable experience and de-emphasizes the practice of collecting too much data. This relies heavily on values of willingness to share experiences and to mediate referrals to others who hold the necessary experiences. It also relies on two important roles, experience brokers to mediate the referrals, the 'broker flashes', and experience communicators to transfer the actual experience. We use the terms 'communicator flashes', 'learning situations' and 'education/training' for experience occasions. The experience engine handles communicator flashes—short experience transfer occasions which take only a few minutes, and learning situations—longer sessions with experienced people, when the receiver has formal training but lacks professional experience.

The experience broker is a generalist who helps others in finding the right expertise with valuable experience. The broker is visible within the organization, and has a wide, general knowledge of methods and tools. The broker is active in arenas for mediating referrals to sources holding experience, and also tries to find and create new similar arenas.

The main task of the experience communicator is to help other people to solve problems. The communicator focuses on giving pedagogical (educational) answers to teach the receiver how to solve related issues on their own. The broker and the communicator must have an aptitude for interacting, and knowing how and when to interact, with others.

One drawback with our approach is its heavy reliance on senior, highly experienced and respected individuals, to act as brokers and communicators. These individuals are the most attractive ones on the market today increasing the difficulty in keeping them as brokers or communicators— or even keeping them in the organization at all. But, knowing that old experience is not as valuable as new, and that previous experiences are, to some extent, retained and combined with new experiences, we feel that reasonable staff turnover will not have a significant negative affect.

We have a vision that a formal experience broker role will not be needed in an optimal learning organization. When the practices outlined in this paper mature and reach higher company levels, many individuals will be able to act as brokers without being assigned the role of experience broker. Everyone can adopt the company values, and obtain the skills needed to act as communicators. Experience occasions will occur often, simply when people meet in the corridors, at the copier, or in the lunch queue. So before they buy their meal, they will have been served either an experience they need or the name of a human source with that experience.

10 References

[1] V. R. Basili, G. Caldiera, H. D. Rombach, *"Experience Factory"*, Encyclopedia of Software Engineering Vol. 2 Editor: J. Marciniak, John Wiley and Sons Inc., 1994, pp 528-532

[2] V. R. Basili, *"The Role of Experimentation in Software Engineering: Past, Current, and Future"*, Proceedings of ICSE '96, 1996, pp 442-449

[3] M. T. Hansen, N. Nohria, T. Tierney, *"What's Your Strategy For Managing Knowledge?"* Harvard Business Review March-April 1999, pp 106-116

[4] I. Nonaka, H. Takeuchi, *"The Knowledge-Creating Company"*, Oxford University Press, 1995

[5] N. E. Fenton, S. L. Pfleeger, *"Software Metrics, A Rigorous & Practical Approach Second Edition"*, International Thomson Computer Press, 1997

[6] A. Burr, M. Owen, *"Statistical Methods for Software Quality"*, International Thomson Computer Press, 1996

[7] T. A. Stewart, *"Intellectual Capital: The New Wealth of Organizations"*, Brealey Publishing, 1998

[8] PERFECT Consortium, *"The PERFECT Experience Factory Model"*, PERFECT Esprit-III Project 9090, 1996

[9] T. Demarco, *"Why does Software Cost so Much? And Other Puzzles of the Information Age"*, Dorset House, 1995

[10] K. E. Sveiby, *"The New Organizational Wealth"*, Berrett-Koehler Publishers Inc., 1997

[11] J. E. Orr, *"Talking about Machines - an Ethnography of a Modern Job"*, IRL Cornell Press, 1996

[12] R. L. Daft, G. P. Huber, *"How Organisations Learn: A Communication Framework"*, Research in the Sociology of Organizations Vol. 5, pp 1-36

[13] M. Polanyi, *"The Tacit Dimension"*, Routledge and Kegan Paul, 1966

[14] P. Shrivastava, *"A Typology of Organizational Learning Systems"*, Journal of Management Studies Vol. 20 No 1, 1983, pp 7-28

[15] D. A. Kolb, J. Osland, I. M. Rubin, *"Organizational Behavior: An Experiential Approach"*, Prentice Hall, 1995

[16] M. S. Ackerman, C. Halverson, *"Considering an Organization's Memory"*, Proceedings CSCW 98, 1998, pp 39-48

[17] D. W. McDonald, M. S. Ackerman, *"Just Talk to Me: A Field Study of Expertise Location"*, Proceedings CSCW 98, 1998, pp 315-324

[18] A. Paepcke, *"Information Needs in Technical Work Settings and Their Implications for the Design of Computer Tools"*, CSCW 1996, pp 63-92

Push or Pull: Two Cognitive Modes of Systematic Experience Transfer at DaimlerChrysler

Eva Wieser, Frank Houdek, and Kurt Schneider

DaimlerChrysler AG, Reseach and Technology,
Dept. Software Engineering, P.O. Box 23 60, D-89075 Ulm, Germany
{eva.wieser, frank.houdek, kurt.schneider}@daimlerchrysler.com,

Abstract. Individuals learn from experience no matter what they do.
But what is natural for an individual is far less straight-forward in groups
or companies. There are some suggestions in literature how this hurdle
can be overcome: The experience factory is a concept tailored to the
software domain. In the tradition of this domain, however, the concepts
are generally activity- or organization-focused and only rarely address
cognitive issues.
At DaimlerChrysler, we were called in to establish experience transfer
at the organizational levels in three business units. In three case studies,
we saw a recurring pattern of cognitive tasks. While these tasks were
carried out quite differently, there is a core to each of them that should
not be neglected.

1   INTRODUCTION

In general, reuse is seen as a key to increasing quality or decreasing time-to-
market or development costs [5, 25]. The spectrum of reusable components can
range from some lines of code and software architectures to project control metrics and complete development processes.

In particular, the idea of reusing *own* experience at the group or company
level is fascinating, as it helps us avoid making the same mistakes over and
over again. This kind of knowledge is related to the own environment, therefore
adoption is less complicated due to the same constraints. Reusing experience
means relying on insights rather than theoretical models or textbooks. In this
context, we define experience as a 'collection of observations and insights. Insights are conclusions reached by a human being with respect to the world or to
that human being' (a definition taken from [6] and slightly adapted). Strictly,
this implies that not experience itself (tuple of witnessing and insight) but experience knowledge (the insight) can be transferred. For the sake of simplicity,
we use the term 'experience' instead of 'experience knowledge'.

Reusing experience in the own software engineering environment implies being able to capture experience in one project and to transfer and use it in another
one. Since this activity usually exceeds the scope of the two projects, an additional organization is required to take care of it.

This idea founds the core concept of the experience factory approach proposed by Basili and co-workers [3]: Every time a new project (or activity) starts, processes, control metrics, products, etc. are selected from a collection of already-finished projects and tailored according to the new project's demands. After the new project has been finished, the gained experiences are added to the collection of experience (in the experience base). In this approach, a strong emphasis is put on the idea of measurement-based experience (e.g. error models, effort distribution models or quality models).

But from a cognitive point of view, this model makes some assumptions which do not necessarily hold in practice: (1) all relevant experience can be collected, and (2) there is real need for experience knowledge, i.e. there are people willing to reuse it.

In our work at DaimlerChrysler AG, we observed experience collection and reuse in real projects where we learned to pay significant attention to the cognitive issues, i.e. how to transfer experience from a human-oriented point of view. In this paper, we analyze and reframe three projects as case studies for this cognitive task. By doing so, we demonstrate how experience transfer can take different forms.

The most important findings of our observation can be summarized as follows:

- There is a great variety of methods for learning and experience transfer. The measurement-based one is only one alternative among others.
- Experience transfer can happen by pull or push, i.e. it can be driven by concrete demands or by offering the available elements. In the second case, continuous encouragement and motivation is essential.
- At the beginning of a systematic experience transfer initiative, the role of external knowledge can become important for the achievement of first improvements.

1.1 Structure of this Paper

In Section 2, we shortly describe the organizational and cognitive frameworks used for experience transfer, the experience factory paradigm, and the cognitive experience transfer cycle. Section 3 presents our case studies on experience transfer. In Section 4, we discuss our observations and give conclusions for future activities. A discussion of related work (Section 5) and our future steps (Section 6) end this paper.

2 EXPERIENCE TRANSFER

Experience has always been seen as one of the assets of an organization. The software business is often characterized as depending on rapidly changing technologies and a high turnover in the workforce. Thus, an organization has to be able to learn from a small number of examples within a short time. This constellation requires a systematic approach to experience handling.

2.1 Experience Factory Approach

With the advent of the learning organization, growing attention has been drawn to the learning software organization [15, 21, 31]. The primary approach that was inspired by software engineering (rather than business or economics, as in [7, 33]) is the so-called experience factory (EF). The EF approach was first introduced by Basili at NASA-SEL [2]. Despite the fact that it gained new attention as an instantiation of a learning organization, the EF was initially a reply to the concept of a software factory [9]. Basili claimed that the software as such should not be the focus for reuse in a factory, but instead the experience behind the software. A thorough treatment of the experience factory paradigm and its conceptual foundation, the quality improvement paradigm (QIP, see [3, 4], can be found in chapter 1 of this book.

The QIP proposes following a cycle of six steps. From characterizing the environment, setting goals, and choosing an appropriate process to carrying out this process, analyzing the outcome, and packaging what has been learned. These steps are described at a more abstract level and are not further detailed [4]. In order to understand what makes QIP — and, consequently, the EF — special, it is helpful to look at the underlying concepts:

- Model building is applied as a basis for understanding.
- Specific models need to be custom-built for each environment.
- Focus on improvement and interests are identified and prioritized with the emphasis on goal-orientedness.
- Process improvement is measurement-based.
- An explicit experience packaging phase/activity is scheduled.
- Feedback loops lead to continuous improvement.

The EF is seen as an instance of an organization that wants to follow the QIP [16]. From an *activity-oriented point of view*, the EF is basically a mechanism for the institutionalization of feedback loops and the steps of the QIP. In publications, the *organizational view* of an EF is often emphasized [2, 3, 18] (see Figure 1). It shows a distinct EF unit facing several project units and a strategic planning unit. Whereas this clear distinction indicates EF independence of any project, arrows symbolize communication, interaction, and the back and forth of information. In this way, all of the units interact to carry out the QIP steps. In several cases, we have seen how important it is to keep the balance between involvement and distance from project concerns [18].

The aspects of activity (what to do) and organization (where to do it) need to be taken into account when one establishes and runs an EF. Furthermore, we argue that it is essential to pay significantly more attention to the *cognitive view* of an EF (how to do it from a human-oriented point of view). In this respect, our model provides an additional dimension that we have found crucial in our EF projects. This dimension helps us to better understand what is going on around an EF, and it helps prepare us for aspects that could slip through the fingers in both organizational and activity views.

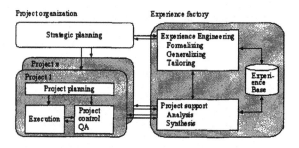

Fig. 1. Experience Factory (EF).

In a sense, we are most interested in the interplay of project organization and the experience factory organization when we recognize that this interaction is carried out by humans with their own interests, barriers, and motivations: What are the cognitive constraints on the arrows of Figure 1, and what needs to be done to keep experience and information flowing? We have seen in the case studies that a good answer to this question may be the most essential prerequisite for acquiring systematic learning from experience.

2.2 Cognitive Experience Transfer Cycle

We see the EF concept as a means to implementing systematic learning from experiences. Learning, however, is always influenced by cognitive factors [12, 36]. It takes place in a situational context that may dominate the importance of the contents to be learned: Depending on the learner's time pressure through work duties, for instance, and motivation in general, learning may face stiff challenges. Independent of content and the soundness of experience, poor motivation can be a reason for a stalled experience transfer. And motivation is nurtured more by the way people feel about information transfer than whether it is their task to carry it out or not. In other words, how and where experiences and derived advice is presented and the details of what is actually presented may be equally important. The same holds for eliciting experiences. When we neglected the cognitive dimension, we often failed to either solicit or to reuse experiences [18].

In order to cover the cognitive tasks, we adopted and adapted a model of organizational learning in the workplace [15]. Its origin lies in the field of Computer Supported Cooperative Work (CSCW). It has also been extended to bridge the gap between collaborative working and learning [23]. We agree that systematic learning shares several characteristics with group processes, so that the model can be applied analogously.

Four tasks are placed in a cycle (see Figure 2). They all describe how experience (or, as in the original, design knowledge [15]) can flow from one place to another. All four tasks are crucial, and a poor job in carrying out only one of them can stall all of the other efforts, as well. This may seem obvious at the superficial level of task interpretation. However, when we take a slightly closer look, challenges and pitfalls become more interesting.

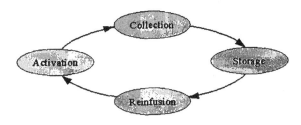

Fig. 2. Cognitive Experience Transfer Cycle.

- *Activating experience:* This task deals with a problem that is known in the field knowledge engineering [19,30]: Even people who have expert knowledge of a subject may be unable to convey their knowledge or experience. One typical reason is that people do not know what kind of information others need or what they consider to be experience. Another typical reason is that people often do not even know what they know. Polanyi calls this tacit knowledge [29]. Unconscious experiences of this kind need active help to become surfaced and voiced.
- *Collecting experience:* Depending on where and how experience is activated, there are different opportunities to capture it as it surfaces. In the easiest case, experience knowledge may be verbalized or written down by the person who has the experience. In more complex cases, experiences may be activated in daily work, but then there must be an easy way of capturing it [27,31]. This requires some means of storing it, means of communicating it to the EF, and the motivation of the participating people to use both [35]. When activation of experience is planned, the chance to be there when it happens is also improved.
- *Processing and storing experience:* Theoretically, storage is not an issue. Everything from databases to the Internet is available to store data in. In practice, however, storing becomes a problem of prioritization and decision. Not everything can be stored electronically. Limited resources, and more especially limited motivation, force any EF to develop a pragmatic and feasible concept of what and how to document and store - completeness is inachievable [1].
- *Making information relevant to the task at hand (reinfusion):* This task is most often neglected. We found that many people consider it to be merely a technical problem of making results available. Nowadays, the Internet or Intranet seems to be the solution. From a cognitive perspective, however, pure delivery of results is far from sufficient [15]. Much more emphasis must be

put on making this information helpful or relevant. An experience or experience derivative is rarely helpful in general. It only can be helpful for carrying out a certain task. Knowing what task needs to be worked on is, therefore, a prerequisite to collecting and processing gained results into something useful [21].

The four tasks form a cycle, and there is no indication of which one is the first. Activation seems to be a candidate, but, as the case studies will show, there are other options. The cognitive tasks shed a different light on issues that are often reduced to their technical dimensions. Each task depends on all of the others. All of the tasks are based on the same conviction that learning is so deeply engrained in human cognition that the cognitive aspects must not be abstracted out.

Unlike the QIP steps, for example, the cognitive tasks do not have to be strictly separated. On the contrary, it may be most advantageous to activate experiences by confronting someone with a previous solution when he needs advice. The reaction to this previous solution combines activation and reinfusion, and can be extended towards collection, as the work by Fischer et al. [13] has long shown in the domain of design environments.

In the case studies below, we have collected how three different EFs tried to cope with the cognitive challenges.

3 CASE STUDIES

3.1 Structure of the Case Studies

The case studies took place in real projects within Daimler-Benz AG (nowadays DaimlerChrysler AG). In each study, we start with a description of the context in which experience transfer should be established and why. Then, we describe the experience transfer related activities in that environment and their impacts. A review of the activities with respect to the experience transfer cycle ends each study.

The topics which were the focal point of experience transfer were (1) defect detection, i.e. experience about the effectiveness of early defect detection techniques in the software lifecycle, (2) project management, i.e. experience about project control and project tracking, and (3) software contracts, i.e. experience about writing contracts for outsourcing software development activities.

3.2 Case Study Defect Detection

In this case study, we deal with measurement-based experience, which is most closely related to experience transfer as intended by the experience factory approach. Unlike the other two studies, the result of the activation-collection-storing activities are abstract models rather than concrete advice for software development.

Context. The observed project is concerned with the development of embedded software for automotive systems. Software is developed in increments, where each increment can be seen as a small project of its own.

Since these kinds of systems have to meet the highest quality demands, much effort is spent on defect detection activities. In this environment, the mission of the experience factory was to establish more efficient defect detection processes in order to reduce the effort required for rework on errors recognized too late in the process chain.

This mission was broken down into the following rough steps: Introducing software inspections for program code for all of the increments, assessing the quality of the inspections, and reusing the findings on the efficiency of the inspection in order to improve not just the inspection process but also the development process. To assess the quality of the inspections, we measured the inspection data (i.e. effort, preparation time, number of defects found, etc.) and the amount of errors found in field testing. The experience factory implementation used here is, therefore, based on measurement programs and follows the QIP.

Experience transfer. As is usual in measurement initiatives according to GQM (which was the selected approach, see [4]), we carried out interviews with the project leader and various developers in order to be able to identify those not so obvious facts to look for, such as particular error classes. By establishing the measurement program, e.g. forms or measurement processes, the people involved became more sensitive with respect to the topic observed.

The data on the defined metrics was collected both during inspections (e.g. effort, preparation time, number of defects) and in the later field-testing activities (e.g. number of defects and related modules). This data was validated through discussions with the developers involved and afterwards processed in charts and figures. Figure 3 depicts one of these charts. It shows the relationship between defect detection intensity and preparation time. The numbers inside the graph denote the sizes of the documents in terms of number of pages.[1]

This figure illustrates that larger documents were read less intensively than smaller ones and, therefore, fewer defects were detected in these documents. The main reason for this was the enormous time pressure which made it impossible for the inspectors to spend more time on their preparation.

Another finding which was gained by measuring testing activities is depicted in Figure 4. This graph shows that more field-errors were reported in larger modules than in smaller ones. A more detailed analysis (i.e. comparing inspection intensity and field-errors for each module) confirmed this trend.

The experience gained in inspection intensity and its influence on field-errors was reported to the project manager. On the basis of these findings, he decided to expend one additional week of effort solely for inspection activities. Further measurement will show whether the proposed hypothesis 'more preparation time will reduce the number of field-errors' will hold or not.

---

[1] The real numbers, however, are re-scaled to protect company internal information.

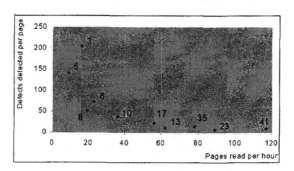

Fig. 3. Relationship between preparation time (pages per hour) and efficiency (defects found per page).

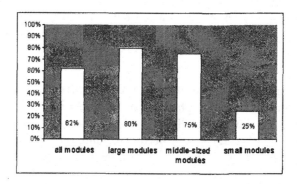

Fig. 4. Distribution of field-errors with respect to module size.

Cognitive perspective. As the underlying mechanism of experience collection used here — the QIP — is well defined, the cognitive tasks were also performed in an orderly fashion. Activating, collecting, and processing the experience correlated with goal identification, data collection, and data analysis, respectively. But there is no one-to-one correspondence. Goal and metric identification (primarily activation) has a great deal to do with collection (e.g. deployment of abstraction sheets [10]) and storage (e.g. documentation of the results of the interviews and discussions).

The outcome of this measurement-based experience collection was a quantitative model rather than concrete advice upon a specific problem. This makes the reinfusion step much harder since there is no task at hand for which the created experience package is immediately relevant. It is the duty of the experience manager to advertise the findings hoping that someone will be interested in them (in our case, this was the project manager, who was willing to reuse the experience by modifying his process). This makes the risk of 'push' obvious; the produced experience packages might not be reused.

3.3 Case Study 'Project Management'

This example of experience reuse started with external knowledge infusion. Its activities were initiated by a 'pull' effect, a request for information. Later, 'push' actions dominated, as the detailed tracking of projects must be carried out continuously and thoroughly.

Context. The experience reused in this case is about how to plan and track projects so that the current state of work is well recognized at any time, including any reasons for delays. Process improvement activities served as the source of the experience gained. They were carried out beforehand and were continued interweavingly. In the projects, highly complex embedded real-time systems were developed that range from middle-sized to large.

Improvement activities. The results of an extensive characterization of the organization identified project planning as a primary field for improvement. Methods of project planning in literature were examined and tailored to the concrete needs. First results were a better planning template and several metrics to track project progress and planned vs. unplanned activities. For the data analysis, two procedures were written that allowed automatic evaluation. Feedback on the measurement program lead to minor changes and enhancements of the evaluation procedures.

Creating experience packages. Processing the gathered information resulted in several experience packages describing the best practice of project planning and tracking as well as effort estimation and tracking. Their basic structure is depicted in Figure 5.

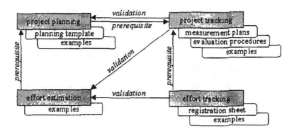

Fig. 5. Structure of experience package system.

The packages (gray shaded boxes) were put into HTML pages following the Quality Pattern structure [17], which, together, form a Quality Pattern System [22]. The white boxes sketch attached, but not further processed documents.

Experience transfer. The experience packages were reused in another project for which planning also turned out to offer a chance for improvement. The first exchange was carried out through an interview where both the leader of the old and the leader of the new project took part. They exchanged information about their projects, discussed commonalties and differences.

The meeting served as a starting point for active project support which the leader of the old project rendered to the new one. In our role as mediators, we had the chance to capture characterizations of the projects that would serve as a basis for future tailoring, i.e. how to deal with different project lengths, different phases in the development process, different strategies in changing requirements, different test strategies, etc.

Cognitive perspective. The experience cycle started with the step 'make experience relevant to the task at hand' based on the need for information that can be characterized as a 'pull' effect. External experience, i.e. literature, had to be made relevant by adjustment.

Despite the automated evaluation procedures, the awareness that tracking projects better helps to keep the schedule (as you are able to recognize delays earlier) and to build a profound basis for future estimations and planning had to be upheld through many discussions and continuous training, which indicates a clear 'push' situation.

Without personal coaching, the transfer between the two projects might easily have failed: the access to the information and a one-time explanation are simply not enough for a successful transfer, as some earlier efforts within the first project proved. A second advantage of personal coaching was given by the fact, that the information to be exchanged cannot always be prepared in time, despite the usefulness of a nice form.

Transferring the information about project planning activated implicit knowledge, as the project leaders, upon their turn to talk about project planning, came to exchange tips and tricks about how to lead projects.

We also found the acceptance of our initiative on planning and tracking quite dependent on the personality of the people concerned. If the mission contradicts the interests of someone, she will not carry out the mandatory tasks thoroughly enough.

3.4 Case Study 'Contracts'

In this case study, we encountered a 'pull' situation in which experience is requested for reuse before it has been collected and stored. The qualitative techniques deployed show quite different perspectives on the cognitive tasks as in the first two cases.

Context. Software development is not considered a core competence in all of the DaimlerChrysler business units. As a consequence, software development is often out-sourced, leaving DaimlerChrysler with the task of carrying out acceptance tests. When the experience factory started in this part of the company, a one-day workshop was devoted to finding goals and defining topics of interest. Acceptance processes were selected as the primary target. This area was identified as one in which there was room for improvement.

We started to activate experiences about acceptance processes by a series of interviews in order to gain a better understanding for the concrete problems and possible solutions that had been tried. For this purpose, open interviews seemed most appropriate. An interviewer was equipped with about a dozen rather general questions. During the interview, the respondent was encouraged to answer beyond the strict limits of the questions put. No sequence was imposed, and the interview should flow and be more like a conversation.

Another technique for opening up a business unit for experience transfer, a half-day workshop, was also implemented. People who had been carrying out actual acceptance processes were brought together to discuss questions on these issues (some of which had been raised in the interviews).

Experience transfer. Two of the people involved in the interviews or the workshop mentioned contracts and their influence on their acceptance efforts. One respondent reported a negative experience during acceptance due to a bad contract, while the other was proud to be able to tell that some contractual agreements helped them tremendously during acceptance testing. Those statements were documented but not immediately pursued. The main topic of interest was still the late phase of acceptance testing in the narrow sense.

Some weeks later, there was a request by someone else in the same business unit who had heard about the experience factory. Being in the phase just before signing a contract, he felt uneasy and wanted to make sure there were no known flaws in the draft contract. Even though all contracts are thoroughly checked by lawyers and business people, software engineering concerns had sometimes been neglected in the past. When this person asked the experience factory for assistance, he found that there had so far not been much experience or knowledge collected on the subject.

Nevertheless, this situation provided a unique opportunity: to demonstrate how the early phases (such as requirements and contracts) determined the success of late phases such as acceptance testing. Therefore, we started with immediate research on the topic, and the following steps were taken within fewer than two weeks as the contract had to be signed by a certain date:

1. Review interview protocols in which contracts were mentioned.
2. Carry out follow-up interviews with these people that were now focused on contractual issues.
3. Copy interesting parts of contracts and agreements that had been referenced in the interviews.
4. Check company standards and literature.
5. Carefully read through draft contract and comment on it.
6. Summarize three top recommendations, including a passage taken from one of the other contracts. We urged the problem owner to consider these issues even if there should not be enough time left to work through all of the other findings.
7. Institute a short follow-up meeting with the problem owner and discuss what we consider important and why.
8. After a few months, the problem owner reported on the project again, supporting many of our recommendations.

This process was not ideal, and we do not claim complete results for this kind of ad-hoc research. Some interesting results were achieved:

− The result helped where and when it was needed.
− The topic was recognized as an important area for experiences that have since then grown.
− We encountered several analogous situations in which a marginal topic was addressed and had to be dealt with within a few weeks.

Consequently, these kinds of situations must be taken seriously from a pragmatic point of view.

Impacts. Contractual agreements have since been turned into one of the most active experience exchange issues in that experience factory. It could start from a reasonable seed [12] of material:

− the response to our advice as well as some later feedback,
− a neutralized experience package that dealt with the most important questions raised during the interviews,
− a list of known pitfalls, such as blind reliance on ISO 9000 certification.

Several projects have received the experience package in the meantime. There was generally a personal meeting afterwards to explain the experiences and gather new input.

Cognitive perspective. The topic area of contract review was not approached using QIP. The experience on this topic was neither intentionally pursued nor *activated*, but an anchor remained in the interviewers' minds. Only later was there a need to reuse experiences that someone believed we had collected. How to make the findings *relevant to the task at hand* was not a concern: the task was perfectly clear, and the request ('pull') proved that there would be no motivational problems. The cognitive experience transfer cycle started at the *make relevant ...* part which then triggered one fast turn of the cycle:

- fast activation with focused interviews
- straightforward collection in interview protocols and written recommendations
- storing the data was not a high priority. Almost immediately this was tailored to be delivered. Intermediate storage happened in brains and on scrap paper. Afterwards, the findings and results were neutralized and documented.

There is always the temptation to quickly satisfy pull requests but to never document them. If this happens, one operates in the (usually well-known) firefighter mode. It is mandatory for any unit that wants to learn from experiences systematically to solicit feedback on what the advice did and then to go through all of the cognitive steps — even if it happens after the pull activities.

4   CONCLUSIONS AND DISCUSSION

Learning from experience at the group or company level is a complex and multifaceted task. This is true both for activity- and organization-based issues as well as for cognitive ones. Table 1 summarizes our activities in the three projects with respect to the cognitive experience transfer cycle.

Cognitive task	Defects	Project management	Contracts
Activate	GQM goal identification, Interviews, abstraction sheets; Feedback	Interviews; GQM goal identification; External knowledge acquisition	By chance: mentioned in different context; Later by focused interviews
Collect	Measurement; Protocols; Feedback meetings	Measurement program documents; Meetings with involved people	By interviewers, using question-lists; Copying contracts
Process and store	Statistical data analysis; Feedback with participants; Store in database	Store in a web-base; Presentation and feedback sessions with all potential users	Excerpt, compare from contracts; Neutralize and abstract; Write three-page sheet with hints and 'recommended wording'
Make relevant and reinfuse	Presentation for project manager in his planing phase	Meeting for direct exchange; Personal coaching	Simple, since reuse was requested (pull); phone call or short meeting

Table 1. Implementation of the cognitive tasks in the case studies.

Beyond the differences in the concrete actions (e.g. holding a feedback session or copying contracts), there are also superficial differences. In the defect detection study, the situation can be characterized as a push situation, where the 'contract' study shows a clear pull situation. The 'project management' study shows a combination of both.

In general, when a new topic area is established, both push and pull types of information acquisition can be observed. While QIP seems to assume that someone wants to push a topic into the experience factory, pull is often important in practice.

Another major difference is the source of experience. In theory, when following the concept of reusing (own) experience, external knowledge might be ignored, since it is not derived from witnessings in the own environment. In practice, there will be always a combination of internal and external knowledge. In the project management study, external knowledge was used for first improvements.

The two characteristics (pull/push, internal/external) have a great impact on the cognitive tasks, as well. Figure 6 illustrates this graphically for the pull/push characteristic. There, the numbers denotes the order of tasks and the width of the arrows indicates intensity and clarity assigned with the corresponding tasks (e.g. in an pull situation, it is clear how to reinfuse the gained experience, whereas in a push situation this task is most uncertain).

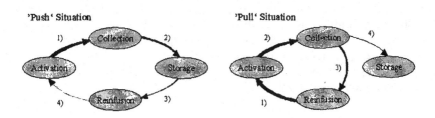

Fig. 6. Instantiation of the cognitive cycle in push and pull situations.

There are some implications of these cognition-based observations with respect to other experience transfer activities:

- As a rule, experience is not available as is. It has to be activated (tacit knowledge) or even exposed (e.g. by measurement activities). In particular, using only the QIP in a measurement-oriented sense as the driving paradigm is not enough.
- The delivery of experience packages is a necessary prerequisite for reuse, but it alone is not sufficient. Experience packages must be offered at the right time for the right task in the right form.
- Reuse depends not only on organizational issues but also on the attitude of the people involved. In particular in push situations, you have to motivate and encourage them until they are with you.

- The presented cognitive experience transfer tasks (Figure 2) describe a mental model rather than a fixed sequence of steps. Their concrete implementation (both at the individual level and across different activities) can look very different.
- Especially in pull situations there is always the temptation to neglect the storage task, as this task competes with reinfusion activities as, for example, making presentations. For sure, providing automated support for processing and storing lowers this temptation.

5 RELATED WORK

5.1 Reuse

In general, there are quite a few commonalties between traditional reuse (i.e. reuse focused on software components, designs, frameworks, etc.) and experience reuse. Both approaches face the same kinds of problems (e.g. reduction in development time, quality improvement, cost reduction) [2, 3, 20, 25].

Used informally, both approaches have the same deficits, e.g. non-repeatable success. Therefore, developers do not like to support reusability [25]. To overcome these deficits, reuse (i.e. both traditional reuse and experience reuse) must be a well-planned activity; its benefit is long-term [25].

But there are some differences, as well. Depending on the observed objects, experience reuse can have much larger impacts on the software development activities than traditional reuse. In theory, each project uses different development processes, since they are tailored upon experience to the actual project's demands [5, 2, 3]. Traditional reuse is bound solely to one (reuse-focused) process, e.g. a waterfall-like development process including activities for component identification and incorporation [25].

5.2 Experience Packaging

As laid out before, the existing work on experience transfer in general and experience factory in particular is mainly activity- or organization-oriented. Therefore, the task of the cognitive experience transfer cycle that most attention was paid to is packaging as a classic activity, i.e. an activity consuming inputs and producing outputs.

McGarry claims 'packaging [to be] a key element of successful reuse' [26, p. 214]. More general work on experience packaging was done in the ESPRIT-project PERFECT [28]. There, they have defined a general structure for experience packages consisting of a process model, quality models related to this process model, and lessons learned about this process.

Another experience packaging approach consists of quality patterns [16, 17]. Here, experience is documented in problem -solution patterns. This static view of experience is supplemented by a dynamic one [22] which describes the evolution of experience using observations to build best-practice descriptions.

5.3   Cognitive aspects

There is a long tradition of cognitive research around professional knowledge workers [11, 29, 32].

Several researchers work in organizational memory systems (see [1, 23, 35]). Their focus is in the storing task of our model, but all authors also consider the other tasks. All of this work, however, is centered around a tool, whereas our model does not prerequisite a tool (the experience base could be a folder on the shelf). Winograd and Flores [37] do not assume specific tools but focus on the interplay between people and computers in general. In our environment, computers and software development are the domain in which we operate, but so far they play only a marginal role as a tool in this process.

Fischer et al. [14] talk about software objects and how to reuse them from a cognitive point of view. Many of the concepts are similar to ours. However, we do not talk about only software objects (in particular not in the narrow, code meaning of the word) but about experiences that can take many shapes and forms — from interview notes to databases. There is a completely different emphasis.

6   FUTURE WORK

We have shown three different case studies that shed light on the cognitive dimension of running an experience factory.

The cognitive experience transfer cycle presented in Figure 2 and used as a reference throughout the rest of the paper also has implications for our future work. Among other things, such as building decision tables to select appropriate activation strategies in different situations, we are interested in tool support.

As a rule, an EF will have an electronic storing component. Up to now, we have experimented with the Intranet as an ubiquitous medium for information exchange. Not surprisingly, one single way of putting in experience is seldom an adequate way of activating experience. As the case studies have shown, different approaches from measurement to interviews to workshops can be applied. When a tool is involved, there may be even more options [8, 14, 31, 35]. Fischer [12] talks about 'reflection-in-action' as the mode in which a knowledge-worker can reach previously tacit knowledge. The same is true for experience. Fischer argues that we need to create 'breakdowns' intentionally to stimulate such a reflection act [12]. Either a person or a tool has to activate knowledge: Both will use approaches that are most suitable for their kind of contact to the problem owner.

Along the same line, the role of a tool in experience distribution is far more ambitious than a mere database query. The challenge is to say the right thing at the right time in the right way [34]. When we try to embed experience delivery into a tool that is used to carry out the task at hand, we have a much better chance of making it relevant to that task.

The above observations will shape the tools that we wish to develop in the future: tools that reach from interview experience collection forms to sophisticated

Intranet components. Analyzing the cognitive aspect of systematic learning from experience has reminded us of the final goal: better helping man to avoid making the same mistakes over and over again!

ACKNOWLEDGEMENTS

The authors wish to thank our colleagues involved in the EF initiatives, especially Heike Frank. Their contribution is gratefully acknowledged. Comments by Stefanie Lindstaedt helped to improve the presentation of this paper.

References

1. M.S. Ackermanm. Augmenting the organizational memory: A field study of Answer Garden. In *Proceedings of the Conference on Computer Supported Collaborative Work (CSWS)*, 1994.

2. V. Basili, G. Caldiera, F. McGarry, R. Pajerski, and G. Page. The Software Engineering Laboratory — An operational software experience factory. In *Proceedings of the 14th International Conference on Software Engineering (ICSE)*, pages 370–381, May 1992.

3. V.R. Basili, G. Caldiera, and H.D. Rombach. Experience factory. In Marciniak [24], pages 469–476.

4. V.R. Basili, G. Caldiera, and H.D. Rombach. Goal question metric paradigm. In Marciniak [24], pages 528–532.

5. V.R. Basili and H.D. Rombach. Support for comprehensive reuse. *Software Engineering Journal*, pages 303–316, 1991.

6. *Gro"ses Handlexikon in Farbe*, Gütersloh, 1979. Bertelsmann Verlagsgruppe.

7. J.S. Brown and P. Duguid. Organizational learning and communities-of-practice: Toward a unified view of working, learning, and innovation. *Organization Science*, 1(2):40–57, 1991.

8. P. Conklin and M. Begeman. gIBIS: A hypertext tool for exploratory policy discussion. *Transactions of Office Information Systems*, 6(4):303–331, 1988.

9. M.A. Cusumano. *Japan's software factories: A challenge to U.S. management*. Oxford University Press, New York, 1991.

10. C. Differding, B. Hoisl, and C.M. Lott. Technology package for the goal question metric paradigm. Technical Report 281/96, Universität Kaiserslautern, 1996.

11. G. Fischer. Supporting learning on demand with design environments. In *Proceedings of the International Conference on Learning Sciences (ICLS)*, pages 165–172, 1991.

12. G. Fischer. Turning breakdowns into opportunities for creativity. *Knowledge-Based Systems*, 7(4):221–232, 1994.

13. G. Fischer, A. Girgensohn, K. Nakakoji, and D.F. Redmiles. Supporting software designers with integrated domain-oriented design environments. *IEEE Transactions on Software Engineering*, 18(6):511–522, 1992.

14. G. Fischer, S.R. Henninger, and D.F. Redmiles. Cognitive tools for locating and comprehending software objects for reuse. In *Proceedings of the 13th International Conference on Software Engineering (ICSE)*, pages 318–328, 1991.

15. G. Fischer, S. Lindstaedt, J. Ostwald, K. Schneider, and J. Smith. Informaing system design through organizational learning. In *Proceedings on the 2nd International Conference on the Learning Society (ICLS)*, pages 52–59, Northwestern University, Evanston, 1996.

16. F. Houdek. Software quality improvement by using an experience factory. In R. Dumke, F. Lehner, and A. Abran, editors, *Software Metrics — Research and Practice in Software Measurement*, pages 167–182. Deutscher Universitätsverlag, Wiesbaden, 1997.

17. F. Houdek and H. Kempter. Quality patterns — An approach to packaging software engineering experience. *ACM Software Engineering Notes*, 22(3):81–88, May 1997. M. Harandi (ed.), Proceedings of the 1997 Symposium on Software Reusability (SSR).

18. F. Houdek, K. Schneider, and E. Wieser. Establishing experience factories at Daimler-Benz — An experience report. In *Proceedings of the 20th International Conference on Software Engineering (ICSE)*, pages 443–447. IEEE Computer Society Press, 1998.

19. A.L. Kidd, editor. *Knowledge Acquisition for Expert Systems*. Plenum Press, New York, 1987.

20. C.W. Krueger. Software reuse. *ACM Computing Surveys*, 24(2):131–183, 1992.

21. D. Landes and K. Schneider. Systematic analysis and use of experiences from software projects at Daimler-Benz. In A. Oberweis and H.M. Sneed, editors, *Software Management '97*, pages 63–73. Teubner Verlag, Stuttgart, 1997. (In German).

22. D. Landes, K. Schneider, and F. Houdek. Organizational learning and experience documentation in industrial software projects. *International Journal on Human-Computer Studies*, 51:643–661, 1999.

23. S. Lindstaedt. *Group memories: A knowledge medium for communities of interest*. PhD thesis, University of Colorado, Boulder, 1998.

24. J.J. Marciniak, editor. *Encyclopedia of Software Engineering*, volume 1. John Wiley & Sons, New York, 1994.

25. C. McClure. Extending the software process to include reuse. Symposium on Software Reusability, May 1997. Tutorial.

26. F. McGarry. Experimental software engineering; packaging for reuse. In H.D. Rombach, V.R. Basili, and R.W. Selby, editors, *Experimental software engineering issues: critical assessment and future directions*, number 706 in Lecture Notes in Computer Science, pages 213–215. Springer Verlag, Berlin, 1993.

27. J. Ostwald. *The evolving artifact approach: Knowledge construction in collaborative software development*. PhD thesis, University of Colorado, Boulder, 1995.

28. Perfect Consortium. Part 9: The PEF model. In *Perfect Project Documentation*. ESPRIT Project 9090, 1997.

29. M. Polanyi. *The tacit dimension*. Doubleday, Garden City, New York, 1966.

30. F. Puppe. *Systematic introduction to expert systems: Knowledge representation and problem-solving methods*. Springer Verlag, Heidelberg, 1993.

31. K. Schneider. Prototypes as assets, not toys. why and how to extract knowledge from prototypes. In *Proceedings of the 18th International Conference on Software Engineering (ICSE)*, pages 522–531, 1996.

32. D.A. Schön. *The reflective practitioner: How professionals think in action*. Basic Books, New York, 1983.

33. P. Senge. *The fifth discipline: The art and practice of the learning organization*. Doubleday Currency, N.Y., 1990.

34. M. Stolze. Visual critiquing in domain oriented design environments: Showing the right thing at the right place. In J.S. Gero and F. Sudweeks, editors, *Artificial Intelligence in Design '94*, pages 467–482. Kluwer Academic Publishers, 1994.

35. L.G. Terveen, P.G. Selfridge, and M.D. Long. From folklore to living design memory — human factors in computing systems. In *Proceedings of INTERCHI '93*, pages 15–22, 1993.

36. K.E. Watkins and V.J. Marsick. *Sculpting the learning organization — Lessons in the art and science of systematic change.* Jossey-Bass, San Francisco, 1993.

37. T. Winograd and F. Flores. *Understanding computers and cognition: A new foundation for design.* Ablex Publishing Corporation, Norwood, 1986.

Collecting, Storing and Utilizing Information about Improvement Opportunities: A Discussion of the Non-technological Barriers to Success

Henrik M. Giæver

Det Norske Veritas, Veritasveien 1, N-1322 Høvik, Norway.

http://www.dnv.com

Abstract. Total Quality Management (TQM) in various forms has for decades proved successful in improving productivity; continuous improvement and learning being essential tools also in Det Norske Veritas (DNV). Our suggestion for any improvement system is 1) Adjust ambitions to the socio-psychological climate in a unit before embarking on the explicit improvement road. 2) Without the backing of other managers, solutions may create harm rather than improvements 3) In a small unit, sophistication of the information technology will have insignificant effects 4) Align the reward mechanisms closely with what is to be achieved. 5) First analyse information that is collected for other primary purposes; then consider creating supplementing systems. This is based on our experience as a Quality System Advisor and Lead Auditor as well as with the Total Quality Management (TQM) practice of Det Norske Veritas (DNV). An improvement process was created and used for 9 months in a small unit in 1995-1996. No sophisticated technology was used. Many improvements took place in the 9 month period the system was operated, however it is questionable whether the success matched the expense (time, frustration, interpersonal friction, unrest). In this paper we describe the life and death of a small scale experience-database.

1 Introduction

Det Norske Veritas (DNV) is a knowledge intensive organisation that serves the international marketplace with a broad range risk management services. DNV has committed itself to TQM as its management philosophy, and is presently also working to provide the concepts, methods and tools for managing its Intellectual Capital. With the capability of TQM in producing efficiency and results for a wide range of very different organisations, and the present awareness of the importance of knowledge for the survival and success of organisations, there is a need to reflect on how organisational learning can be accelerated.

Within the framework of TQM and Knowledge Management (KM) it may be tempting to create costly information systems to record, analyse and take decisions about non-conformities and other improvement opportunities

In the maritime marketplace DNV has for more than 10 years systematically gathered information about incidents and accidents with the goal of improving our knowledge and providing improved services to our customers.

The internal improvement efforts in DNV vary and depend to a great degree on local initiatives.

In 1995 one unit took various TQM initiatives; a range of learning activities (courses) were initiated for the team alongside developing a process oriented and customer focused quality system. In this paper we will concentrate on the improvementsystem that was created (see figure 1).

2 The improvement system

The unit employed 14 persons involved in development and operational tasks; primarily serving internal customers.

Each employee was encouraged to identify and report (2) improvement opportunities (IO) (non-conformities, complaints; anything that could be improved in any way). Information was also collected directly from customers and via customer feedback forms that were used in larger deliveries.

The dominant reporting tool was MS e-mail (3). IO's were indiscriminately added to a MS Word file; open for all (4). Acute problems should be taken care of immediately, chronic problems should be reviewed by management every three weeks (6). A point was made of not rushing to conclusions; issues should be considered as a whole, some of them possibly having a common cause. A particular form was designed such reported issues could be grouped under one "problem".

One example of an actual "problem": "The standard of our premises" This was based on a number of observations, e.g. "950622: some of the white-boards seem dry; how often are they waxed?" "950824: The shelves are messy, and the standard varies", "950616: It would be beneficial if every room has a box for stuff that people leave behind", "Week 39: "many of our clients are unable to find the right room", "951208: We should all be able to operate the essential technical equipment in the rooms", "950616 What equipment should actually be in each room? Do we have a clear standard?".

The consequences of these undesired conditions should be elaborated; "There will be a waste of time, danger of misunderstandings and dissatisfaction for all parties involved, and the reputation of the unit and DNV will suffer", and a problem definition established: "The risk that our premises give a messy and unprofessional impression is unacceptable".

The form encouraged identification of causes as well as root causes, and the preparation of an action plan with allocated resources, calendar time and responsible (7). After implementation of the chosen solution (8), the effect would periodically be reviewed(9).

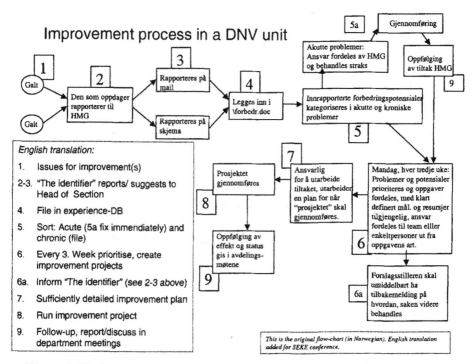

Figure 1 The improvement process in a DNV unit 1995-1996

3 Well, how did it go?

In retrospect, substantial improvements were made in the period, and our customers reported improved satisfaction and increased interest in buying our services.

After 9 months, other issues in the department demanded the better part of the attention, the unit merged with another, there was a management reshuffle and the improvement system quietly died.

It is highly questionable whether the success matched the "expense"; time, frustration, interpersonal friction, unrest.

4 Some Lessons Learned

1. The time needed (calendar as well as man-hours) in creating, agreeing upon and getting used to the system was considerably underestimated.
2. The attention of the system competes with day-to-day operation and is uncritically given a lower priority.
3. 9 months proved to be a to short period to create enduring new habits.
4. The lack of similar initiatives in surrounding environment made the system vulnerable to organisational changes.
5. The system fuelled insecurity and suspicion if already present.
6. Such a system requires a rare combination of abstraction and down-to-earth attitudes in order to work well.
7. "Involvement" and responsibility are far less sought after bu the employees than "modern" managers like to think.
8. "Explicit knowledge" (e.g. a statement in an e-mail or in an open file) has a high potential for misunderstanding and unproductive conflict.
9. The (lack of) use of information technology had no impact on the effect of the system.

5 Conclusions and recommendation

Our assistance to other companies in developing or assessing their quality systems confirms the experience in a unit in DNV. ISO 9001, 4. 13 (non-conformities) and 4.14 (corrective/ preventive actions) always create questions, tension frustration and unrest.

That is no reason to take lightly on these topics; together with innovation and explorative learning they represent a gold-mine for the organisations that succeeds. The main obstacles are not technical; they are human.

Consider:

1. Adjusting ambitions to the socio-psychological climate in a unit before embarking on the explicit improvement road.
2. Whether there is support and commitment from higher management; without their backing solutions may harm more than improve.
3. How to stay in step with the rest of the organisation. If you want to pioneer; make sure the rest of the team agrees.
4. How well is desirable behaviour rewarded and undesirable behaviour discouraged?
5. First analysing information that is already collected for other (primary) purposes. This may be of great value in the chase for improvement opportunities. Can the existing system be moderated to capture more?

6. ... whether the creation of dedicated IT systems are worth the expense, in a small unit, sophistication of the information technology will have insignificant effects compared to the other items in this list.

References

1. Argyris, Chris, 1991: "Teaching Smart People How to Learn". Becoming a learning organization, Harvard Business Review Reprint 1997, Boston.
2. Argyris, Chris, 1994: "Good Communication That Blocks Learning. What is a Learning Organization?", Harvard Business Review Reprint 1997, Boston.
3. Buene, Leif & Moen, Anne Sigrun 1996: Organisational Learning. Tech. Report. DNV 97-2011.
4. Deming, Edwards W., 1986: "Out of the crisis". Cambridge University Press. Cambridge.
5. Det Norske Veritas, CMS 110 1997: Total Quality Management in DNV, rev 0, 1997-04-24.
6. European Foundation for Quality Management, 1996: Assessor Manual/ Training binder. EFQM, Bruxelles.
7. Giæver, Henrik, 1998: "Does Total Quality Management Restrain Innovation?", Sociology Thesis, University of Oslo.
8. Hackman, J.Richard, 1995: "Total Quality Management: Empirical, Conceptual, and Practical Issues". Administrative Science Quarterly, no 40.
9. Giæver, Henrik, 1999: "Knowledge Management in DNV" http://research.dnv.no/Knowman/
10. March, James G. 1991: "Exploration and Exploitation in organizational Learning". Organization Science, No. 1, February 1991.
11. Nonaka, Ikujiro, 1991: "The Knowledge-Creating Company". Harvard Business Review Reprint 1997. "What is a Learning Organization?" Boston.
12. Thomsen Jan 1998: The Virtual Team Alliance (VTA): Modeling the Effects of Goal Incongruency in Semi-routine, Fast-paced Project Organizations. PhD dissertation, DNV report 98-2024, 1998.

Transferring and Evolving Experience: A Practical Approach and Its Application on Software Inspections

Frank Houdek[1] and Christian Bunse[2]

DaimlerCrysler AG, Research and Technology, P.O. Box 23 60, D-89013 Ulm, Germany
frank.houdek@daimlerchrysler.com
Fraunhofer Institute for Experimental Software Engineering (IESE), Sauerwiesen 6, D-67661
Kaiserslautern, Germany
christian.bunse@iese.fhg.de

Abstract. Experience and knowledge management are seen as key capabilities for systematic software development and process improvement. However, it is still not quite clear, how to get this vision to work. In this paper, a process for systematic experience transfer is presented. It covers the activities of experience acquisition, experience documentation and evolution, and experience reuse. This process is a result of the German publicly-funded project SoftQuali, and its practical use is demonstrated by two real project examples, dealing with experience transfer for software inspections. In general it is described how experience can be packaged, both to transfer the technique and to improve it.

1 Introduction

Software is becoming more and more important. This importance leads to an increase in the demand for high quality software products. Software as well as its development processes have to be improved continuously. To do so, best practices have to be identified, maintained, and transferred systematically from one project to another. A continuous, company-wide learning cycle must be established to transfer knowledge, avoid mistakes, and thereby improve both processes and products.

Everyone is willing to accept this high level view. But what does this mean? Up to now, it is not quite clear yet how to make this vision work. What are experiences? Humans always use this word intuitively without defining its meaning. However, there are several possible definitions. But each definition will have a different impact on the derived activities. In the context of this paper experience is understood as 'collection of witnessing and insights gained by a human' [1]. Strictly speaking, this implies that not experience itself (tuple of witnessing and insight) but experience knowledge (the insight) can be transferred. For the sake of simplicity the term 'experience' is used instead of 'experience knowledge' throughout this paper.

The next question will be 'How can experience be captured, documented, stored?' Experience has to be externalized to go beyond individual and towards organizational learning. To do so, a set of interacting mechanisms for experience acquisition, experience packaging, experience evolution, and experience reuse is needed.

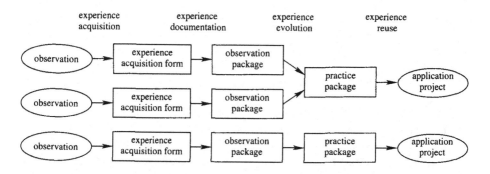

Fig. 1. Process of experience acquisition, documentation, evolution, and reuse.

In this paper, an implementation of these activities originating from the project Soft-Quali is presented. Its main idea is an aggregation of knowledge from concrete descriptive observations to generalized prescriptive descriptions. We start the experience transfer process by capturing real-life observations in observation packages. An observation packages contains the description of a real-life fact together with a description of the context the observation was made in. In a subsequent step, we can use these observation packages to build more mature practice packages. Unlike observation packages, practice packages provide constructive descriptions of processes (e.g. how to perform inspections) or products (e.g. software architecture for ATMs). These descriptions are build upon the concrete observations provided by the observation packages and (potential) external knowledge. By this, the descriptions are tailored towards one environments needs and restrictions. On request, practice packages are provided with or without experts help to all advice-searching people in one enterprise. Figure 1 depicts the entire process graphically.

To document experience itself, we applied the Quality Pattern approach [2]. Quality Pattern support structuring and documenting of experience. Its main idea is a presentation of experience in pairs of problem and solution assuming the following experts' behavior: Every time an expert has to solve a new problem, she remembers similar, previously solved problems and adapts and combines those solutions to a new one.[1]

In the subsequent sections, the elements of this process are described in more detail. To make the process more comprehensible, two real-life examples are presented, too. Both examples are concerned with process improvement in the domain of software inspections. In the first one, documented experience was used to transfer this technology from one environment to another. In the second example, documented experience was used to improve inspections across several sites.

The main findings of the work presented here can be summarized as follows:

---

[1] This way of finding solutions to problems is also used in case-based approaches (see, e.g. [3]). Case-based approaches retrieve upon a given problem description the most similar solutions (=cases) out of a set of know solutions and combine them to a new solution. But there are difference between Quality Patterns and case-based approaches with respect to their priorities. The Quality Pattern approach puts its emphasis on describing experience. Case-based approaches emphasize the operationalization of retrieval using formal models.

- Quality Patterns and their subtypes are suitable for documenting various types of experience (observations, lessons learned, proposed best practice)
- The evolutionary quality pattern model (which is the maturation from observations to practice packages) supports the evolution of knowledge over time. It helps make the complex area of experience management both more understandable and more usable.
- The approach is applicable in real-life, as shown in the two application examples.
- Knowledge and experience are increasingly becoming the main assets of software developing companies. In order to keep or improve competitive advantage, establishment of successful experience transfer mechanisms is becoming crucial. The approach presented in this paper is the first step in this direction

The remainder of this paper is structured as follows. In Section 2, the quality improvement paradigm (QIP) and the results of the PERFECT project are briefly introduced as basis for the work presented in this paper. Additionally the project SoftQuali, its objectives, structure, and partners are described. In Section 3, the question of how to structure and document experience to make it reusable is emphasized. Section 4 describes the task of experience acquisition. Section 5 gives a short glance at tool support for these activities. In Section 6, the application of the approach, in the domain of software inspections, is presented. Finally, we conclude in Section 7.

2 Context

This section gives an brief overview on related work providing the basics the presented framework is using.

2.1 QIP and PERFECT

Reuse of experience is a key element of the quality improvement paradigm (QIP) of Basili et al. [4]. In their work, Basili et al. describe a high-level process performed continuously. There are several steps in this process: First, an organization is characterized to determined their strengths and weaknesses. Based on these findings, improvement goals are defined and augmented by improvement procedures. During project work, these procedures are performed and measured. At the end of one cycle, the measured data is analyzed according to the defined goal and the findings are packaged for future usage. In their work, Basili et al. emphasize the importance of experience packaging. But they do not give any concrete guidelines for this task. Instead, they give some ideas on what experience packages should look like. For instance, they emphasize the importance of context descriptions, or introduce several types of experience packages, like process packages (experience packages providing experience on processes), product packages (e.g. software architectures), or data packages (providing quantitative materials, like fault distributions or cost estimation models).

The project PERFECT, founded by the European community, tried to make the idea of QIP more concrete [5]. Therefore, they were also concerned with the activities of experience documentation, evolution, and reuse. One result of the PERFECT project was a structure for experience packages consisting of the following parts:

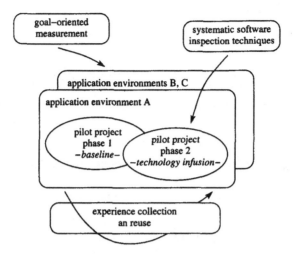

Fig. 2. Structure of the SoftQuali project.

- a process model, describing a process for a particular task,
- process quality models, providing quantitative models on, e.g., effort, fault density, or size, and
- process experiences, providing lessons learned regarding the proposed process.

The main deficit of this structure is that it is limited to process experience only and there exist no reports on its application. So it is unclear whether this approach really works.

2.2 The SoftQuali Project

The experience transfer approach presented in this paper is embedded in a larger framework within the SoftQuali project [6, 7]. However, there are interdependencies between the various elements of this project. To make the presentation more understandable, first a short overview on SoftQuali is given.

The SoftQuali project (full title: systematic software quality improvement by goal-oriented measurement and explicit reuse of experience knowledge) aims to apply the experimental paradigm (see, e.g., [8]) in the domain of software development and improvement. Figure 2 gives a graphical overview of this idea.

In each of the three involved application environments (depicted as A, B, C) the first activity was to build a baseline of the actual situation using goal-oriented measurement (GQM, [9]). On top of this baseline systematic software inspection techniques were tailored towards the needs of each application environment and introduced. Then, the new situation was measured as well. This whole process is augmented by experience collection and reuse to make the findings persistent and applicable both for new application environments within one partner and across the partners. This is done by the experience transfer approach presented in this paper.

Research partner	Application partner
DaimlerChrysler AG	ALSTOM Energy Technology
Fraunhofer Institute for Experimental Software Engineering (IESE)	Allianz Life AG
Siemens AG	Siemens AG (Logistic systems)

Table 1. SoftQuali project partners: Research partners and application partners.

Six partners participated in the SoftQuali project; three of them acted as research partners, three as application partners (see Table 1). More information on the project can be found on the projects web-page[2] or in the final project report [6].

3 Experience Documentation and Evolution

This Section first identifies several types of experience to be dealt with. Then, a mechanisms of experience evolution is given. A structure which fits in this framework, the so-called quality patterns, is presented.

3.1 Types of Experience

Documentation is essential to externalize knowledge and experience in order to enable people-independent transfer of experience. Especially in environments with a high turnover-rate (as in the software business, see, e.g., [10]) or in distributed development, documenting experience becomes a crucial activity.

Using the definition of experience given in the introduction, we can package experience in pairs of observations and conclusions. But this can be unsatisfyingly, as the subsequent example shows.

Example: To document the requirements for ATM switches, company XYZ uses the SA/RT according to Harel [11]. The project manager of this project observes, that this method is not successful in her project.

Here the question arises, whether the observations and conclusions should be described (e.g., 'SA/RT according to Harel is not suitable for analyzing ATM switches in company XZY because ...') or the proposals for improvement (e.g., 'I suggest to document requirements for ATM switches in company XYZ by ...'). Both alternatives are, in a way, problematic: In the first case, they document 'real' experiences, which may be of little use for future users ('Ok, I know what to avoid, but not, what to do'). In the second case, the proposed solution has not been experienced. We observed this dilemma quite often in our early work on documenting experiences. To deal with this problem, we build an evolutionary model of experience documentation including several types of experience packages:

– Observation packages are used to package experience originating from real-life observations. They may, but need not, include conclusions on these observations.

---

[2] http://www.iese.fhg.de/SOFTQUALI/

By this, observation packages are not necessarily useful for someone looking for a solution for his or her problem. But they are valuable input for subsequent activities, in which more mature experience packages are build.

- Practice packages provide applicable solutions for particular problems. These solutions must not necessarily have been experienced. They may originate from subjective conclusions or are derived from positive observations. The described solution is tailored for a particular environment, reflecting its situation, limitations, and special needs. The mission of a practice package is to provide the best[3] available solution for a problem in the given environment at a given point in time.

Another aspect which cannot be handled sufficiently using these experience packages concerns external experience. External experience is defined as knowledge that was gained in external environments and that is often generalized. Typical examples for external knowledge are the SA/RT technique and inspection guidebooks. These documents provide valuable information, but it is unclear what results the application of these descriptions will cause in a particular environment. To cope with this issue, theory packages are introduced.

- Theory packages provide external knowledge (i.e., experience gained in other environments). Typically, the information provided is very general and not adopted to the given environment.

3.2 Evolution of Documented Experience

Using these types of experience packages, the evolution of documented experience can be illustrated quite easily (see Figure 3). Often, experience transfer and evolution starts with external knowledge, e.g. from textbooks, seminars or consulting activities. This kind of knowledge can be packaged in theory packages. Typically, this knowledge have to be tailored towards the spcific characteristics, constraints, and demands of the environment. This may happen in working groups or via coaching of a consultant. The result of the tailoring activities is a first practice package documenting the best solution according to the current understanding. The application of this 'best practice' description will result in observations, which are packaged in observation packages. These observations may provide both positive and negative experience. If deficits are found in the described solution, new insights can be used to improve practice, building a new, more mature practice package. This evolution of practice packages is going on continuously, using new observation packages as well as new theory packages.

3.3 Quality Pattern

Given the model of evolution of documented experience, the question of documentation has to be dealt with. However, plain documentation is not sufficient enough.

---

[3] It is important to see that *best* is time-dependent here, i.e., a solution is not globally optimal, but optimal with respect to the current understanding. At a later point in time, another solution may be the best available solution.

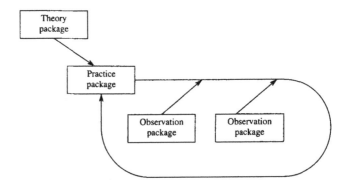

Fig. 3. Evolution of documented experience.

Documented experience must be processed to be easily accessible, readable, and understandable. Aiming towards those requirements, the Quality Pattern approach [2, 12] was developed. The main concepts of a Quality Pattern are problem-solution patterns, domain descriptions, explicit rationales, and the pyramid thinking principle.

The idea of problem-solution patterns was first published by C. Alexander [13] and has found wide adaptation in the area of design patterns. It is based on the observation that experts, who have to solve a new problem, remember similar problems and adapt and adopt their solutions to the new situation. They do not start from scratch every time. Quality Patterns use this idea by structuring information in a problem-oriented way. By this, the content of a Quality Pattern is aimed to fit a problem an experience-searching person will probably have (e.g., performing an inspection meeting, starting a new project, estimating project costs).

The description of the domain the experience was gained from is another crucial element in each Quality Pattern. The main reason for this is the understanding that no solution can be universally valid but is limited to a particular domain. The assumption is that applying a solution that worked for a similar problem in a similar domain will produce similar results.

By providing a rationale for the described problem-solution pattern, the reader can understand the why of the proposed solution and relate it to its own situation.

The application of the pyramid thinking principle [14] produces documents which are structured in several layers. In the top layer, only the most important information is presented. The layers below cover more and more details without providing totally different information than the layers above. The advantage of this principle is that the main content of a document can be understood quite fast. There is no need to read a whole document to see that is does not provide any interesting information. Figure 4 gives a graphical overview of the different parts of a Quality Pattern.

The upper part contains summary information which help a reader to get a first impression of the Quality Pattern's content. Then follows the main part providing problem, solution, and context (domain description). The lower part contains more detailed information like an example, the rationales, and administrative information.

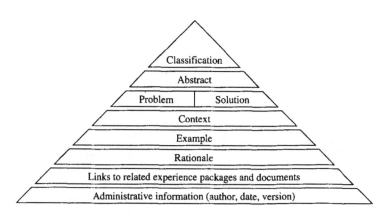

Fig. 4. Structure of a Quality Pattern.

According to the evolutionary model mentioned above (Section 3.1), there are three subtypes of this generic quality pattern structure, called observation pattern, practice pattern, and theory pattern. They differ somehow in the various sections of a quality pattern. For instance, the section 'solution' in an observation pattern can be refined to 'observation' (what did really happen) and 'hypothesis' (what may be the reasons for it).

Figure 5 and 6 provide examples of a practice and an observation pattern, respectively. The next step using these pattern could be the creation of a new practice pattern describing the process of Figure 5 augmented with the strong recommendation to distribute the artifact under inspection via paper in the kick-off meeting. The new practice pattern will have at least two links to other experience packages: one to the old practice pattern (to show the evolution of experience) and one to the observation pattern (to give a justification for the refined solution).

4 Experience Acquisition

We used experience packages according to the evolutionary quality patterns within various application projects (see also Section 6). Here, we made several observations:

- People like experience documented in quality patterns. Typically, these experience packages are quite short but very concrete. They provide immediately applicable solutions.
- The incorporation of new experience, which leads to maintenance activities in the 'experience base', is well manageable due to the evolutionary model.
- It is hard to write good quality patterns. Writing a quality pattern is time consuming due to the preparation of information towards the quality pattern structure. Writing the redundant parts (e.g., the abstract) is boring, too.
- Quality patterns cannot be written spontaneously. Instead, a writer has to think about the particular needs a future reader may have.

Classification	Experience package type: Practice pack.
	Provided experience: Process
	Object: Reviews and inspections
	Problem: Kick-off meeting
	User: Inspections manager
Abstract	An inspection kick-off meeting consists of three steps: (1) distribution of review material, (2) explanation of inspection process, and (3) introduction of review material.
Problem	How do I perform an inspections kick-off meeting?
Solution	There are three steps in a kick-off meeting, with the third step being optional.
	(1) The moderator distributes the review material, i.e., the artifact under inspection (AUI), reference documents, checklists, and forms for defect detection.
	(2) The moderator explains the goals of the inspection process.
	(3) (Optional) The AUI author explains his product and technical details.
Context	Environment XYZ
Example	Here is an agenda of an inspection kick-off:
	5 min, welcome
	5 min, distribution of documents
	10 min, explanation of goals and process
	10 min, presentation of the AUI
	10 min, discussion
Rationale	Mainly IEEE 1028; step (2) is non-optional, because inspections are performed rarely in this environment so there is the need to recapitulate the inspection process each time.
Links	Exp. Package: inspections form
Admin. info.	Author: W.C. Linton, December 18th, 1998

Fig. 5. Practice pattern example.

Despite — or especially because of — the advantages of quality patterns in reading, the inhibition threshold to write a quality pattern is high. To lower both the writing efforts and the inhibition threshold, we defined an 'experience acquisition form', implemented both on paper and using web technology [15]. The main idea of this form is that it can be used spontaneously. The sequence in which information is gathered differs from the sequence information is provided in a quality pattern. In these forms, the writer is asked for information she is able to provide quite easily, like a concrete observation or the description of her particular context. Redundant information (like the abstract) is not covered at all.

The experience acquisition form is used by project members. Every time they observe something remarkable, they can fill out such a form. In a later step, the information gathered is reprocessed by experts towards quality patterns as described above. By this, a kind of quality assurance process for quality patterns is established, as several people are concerned with writing quality patterns and reviewing other people's work.

Experience acquisition forms are mainly used for capturing observations. Capturing practice packages in this way is not very useful, since practice packages are seldom built by one person, but rather by groups of several people (like software engineering process groups, SEPGs, or quality circles).

Classification	Experience package type: Observation pack. Provided experience: Process Object: Reviews and inspections Problem: Kick-off meeting User: Inspections manager
Abstract	Consistent printouts of the artifacts under inspection (AUI) are an essential criteria for successful inspection meetings.
Problem	How do I perform an inspections kick-off meeting, even with time-pressure?
Observation	Event: Inspection meeting Dec. 20th, 1998 Due to a rapidly performed kick-off meeting, the AUI (C-Code) was distributed after the kick-off meeting electronically. Later, in the inspection meeting, every inspector had a different listing (due to different line counting in the various mail systems and different printers). This caused a lot of confusion, because the different line numbers the inspectors reported had to be reassigned.
Hypothesis	- Time pressure - Inexperienced moderator and inspectors - Heterogenious platforms
Context	Environment XYZ
Links	Exp. Package: kick-off process (Fig. 5)
Admin. info.	Author: W.C. Linton, December, 21st 1998

Fig. 6. Observation pattern example.

Figure 7 presents an experience acquisition form. The sans-serif-typed text and the marked boxes show how this form can be filled in. The example text was used to build the observation pattern is shown in Figure 6.

In the context of the transferred technology used (i.e., software inspections), we applied paper-based experience acquisition forms. Overall 24 observations within sev-

Observation on ☒ process, ☐ product, ☐ data
Date: August, 20th, 1998 Observer: Calvin Klein
Project: XYZ   Role of Observer: Inspection moderator
Particularity in the environment: Inspections have been introduced right before
Observation: The artifact under inspection (AUI) was distributed electronically. Every inspector was asked to print it out by himself. In the inspection meeting there was a lot of confusion, because the line numbering in the various printouts differed
Hypothesises (assigned with the observation)   ☒ Cause: High time preasure (no time for previous printout)   ☒ Consequence/solution: Distribution of printed material is mandatory for every kick-off meeting
Task (in which somebody may be interested in this experience):   Planning and performing an inspection kick-off meeting

Fig. 7. Experience acquisition form.

eral weeks only were collected. The amount of time to fill in one form was only a few minutes.

It is important to see, that experience acquisition forms do not replace experience documentation using quality patterns, but help to build quality patterns. They help to lower the threshold for building observations patterns. In the later step 'experience reuse', quality patterns are most preferable (see also discussion at the beginning of this section).

5 Reuse of Experience and Tool Support

The main goal of the experience transfer process is, of course, the reuse of previously captured and packaged experiences. Users of experience (and experience packages) are, in general, people requiring advice. This may be

- a project manager looking for experience on how to estimate a new project,
- a test responsible looking for information on using a particular test strategy,
- a developer who has to select a case tool for her new project and is looking for experience upon their utility in former projects, or
- a quality manager looking for quality assurance plans.

Benefits of (re-)using (documented) experience are quite obvious. To reuse experience, it has to be delivered to the potential users. In our approach, this is done in two way. First, experience packages can be provided 'as is' by, e.g., electronic channels, like web or mail. This kind of experience transfer is mainly suitable for quite general information, like benefits of inspections in this company.

Second, experience packages can be provided in junction with human experts. In this case the expert brings the experience packages with him. They are present during the whole time the expert is working together with the project people. The expert himself uses them to do his job. Also, packages are improved or created during the interaction of experts and project people. This kind of interaction is preferable for more sophisticated material, like introduction of inspection processes. The main benefit of using experience packages during the interaction of experts and project people is, that after the departure of the expert the experience persists. And, it is not new to the project people (as e.g. a experts final report). Project people have seen how to use the information packages in the experience packages.

In addition, for electronic distribution we developed several prototypes [2]. They are all web-based in order to support different platforms in several sites. Figure 8 shows a screenshot of one prototype. It contains a search-mask for quality patterns. Attributes, which are left blank, are don't care attribute. If this form is submitted, beyond others, the pattern depicted in Figure 5 is received.

6 Application of the SoftQuali Experience Transfer Approach

In this section, two applications of experience transfer are presented. The first one is about transferring experience between several companies, the second one is about improving a technology by explicit documentation of experience.

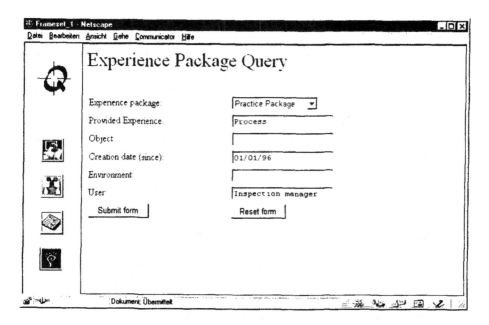

Fig. 8. Screenshot of experience base prototype.

6.1 Transferred Technology: Software Inspections

Both examples deal with inspections as transferred technology. Inspections have shown to be a very effective way of detecting defects early on in the development process. Thus, substantial effort can be saved, since defects detected later are known to be significantly more expensive.

However, there is not only one inspection technique, but several modifications of the idea of assessing a product by static examination. The implementations may differ, e.g., in the processes used, the roles involved, the artefacts inspected, and the reading technique used. In both examples the IEEE1028 definition of inspection is used, with one difference. In the first example, perspective-based reading (PBR), a new reading technique [16], based on the idea of TQM (Total Quality Management) [17] that each product has its own customers and that each customer views a product from his own point of view, was applied in the individual preparation phase and in the second example, some kind of checklist-based reading was used.

6.2 Experience Transfer between Fraunhofer IESE and Allianz

Situation. Development of high quality software satisfying cost, schedule, and resource requirements is an essential prerequisite for improved competitiveness of life assurance companies. Allianz Life, the market leader of life assurance companies in Germany, is part of the Allianz Group — one of the largest insurance groups with subsidiaries all over the world. The IT department of Allianz Life has more than 500 employees, with 350 of them being application developers. The Fraunhofer Institute for Experimental Software Engineering (FhG IESE) is acting as coach providing most up-to-date knowledge and experience on innovative reading techniques as the essential background technology.

Recent measurement programs have shown that currently quality assurance is focused on testing. At Allianz Life, about 30about 50There, a technique is sought which improves productivity by finding defects when they are cheaper to correct, reduces the number of defects which originate in phases prior to the ones they are detected in, and reduces both test and overall project effort.

Use of documented experience. FhG IESE supported the introduction of PBR as a scenario-based reading technique at Allianz Life based on its wide range of experience in the field of software inspections. This step was accompanied by goal-oriented measurement to quantitatively demonstrate the proper usage of PBR as well as its cost/benefits ratio [18]. Additionally, experiences and measurement results are reused in the follow-up projects.

A post-mortem analysis of using PBR as defect detection technique at Allianz Life showed that not only the technique involved, or the organizational context, are the main driving factors for successfully introducing state-of-the-art technology. Another important factor were the experiences with that specific technique in different contexts. On the one side, this experience influenced the introduction process (what, when, and how to do) and gave confidence in the results to expect. On the other side, these experiences allowed inspectors to learn from others and use that newly gathered knowledge to improve their personal performance.

In order to support the introduction of PBR systematically, it is not sufficient to use that kind of experience described above on an ad-hoc basis, meaning the IESE-PBR expert reuses the knowledge stored in his memory. Instead, experience packages documenting different types of experiences, at different levels of abstractions, were used for planning and communication. Both observations packages and practice packages were created using the quality pattern structure. Consequently, each experience package contains a detailed description of the influencing factors which lead to that experience. A typical example for knowledge stored in an experience package is that 'PBR-Scenarios for a specific organisation can only be defined with the knowledge of a domain expert from that organisation'.

Experiences on experience transfer. At Allianz Life, the use of documented experience[4] was found to be beneficial for technology transfer in general and for the introduction of software inspections in particular. This was mainly due to the fact that typical problems could be avoided (e.g., involving too many people in an inspection meeting) or solved in advance (e.g., scenarios, the driving factor of PBR, were developed at the Allianz Life site). Furthermore, in comparison to technology transfer at other organisations without the help of experience packages, the effort was reduced significantly. This is also reflected by the experiences made in the HYPER project [18]. In Figure 9,

---

[4] Documented experience may be of different forms. At the Allianz site, the knowledge of domain experts, described in the form of scenarios, was used to guide defect detection. In addition FhG IESE used experience made with transferring inspection technology, documented with quality patterns, to guide the implementation of software inspections at Allianz Life.

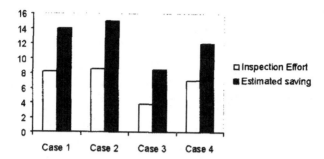

Fig. 9. Primary inspection benefits.

for each inspection the total inspection effort is compared with effort savings in terms of 'person hours'. It can be observed that for each inspection run the savings in effort are larger than the invested effort. We, FhG IESE and Allianz, believe that the reuse of documented, inspection experience is one (other possible influences are discussed in [18]) reason for the positive influence on this cost/benefit ratio.

6.3 Improvement of Inspections at DaimlerChrysler

Situation. Building mission-critical software at high quality within a tight schedule is increasingly becoming a core competency at Daimler-Chrysler. There are several divisions within Daimler-Chrysler (e.g., trucks or airplanes). And each division has its own software development unit, according to their particular needs. These units range from several dozens to several hundreds of software developers.

To improve the quality of their software development processes, the company's research division, introduced software inspections at several places. Unlike the Allianz-IESE approach, this happened mainly in the traditional way by providing teaching classes and coaching the inspection processes. This happened in several units quite simultaneously, with several researchers involved as coaches.

Use of documented experience. To improve both the introduction and the inspection process, and to avoid multiple pitfalls, experience documentation was incorporated in activities, starting in very early phases.

During their work in the application projects, the coaches documented their observations regarding inspections and the inspection introduction process. For this, they used experience acquisition forms as illustrated above. At regular meetings, the coaches discussed their observations and used them to build more mature practice packages which in turn they used in their daily work (see Figure 10). In the following the content of these practice packages is illustrated through some examples:

– Inspection process: In one unit, it is now mandatory to inform the inspectors about the goals of an inspection in each kick-off meeting, because there are quite long delays between single inspections)
– Forms: Inspections are now supplemented by role-specific inspections folders containing all material the various roles need (e.g., inspector: AUI, preparation form, inspection guidelines, checklist, experience acquisition form)

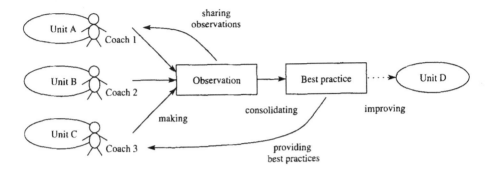

Fig. 10. Using observations and experience to improve software inspections at several sites.

– Entry criteria: It is now mandatory in one unit to distribute the AUI on paper in the kick-off meeting (see also Figure 6 and 7).

Experiences on experience transfer. The usage of observations packages (build by using experience acquisition forms) was found to be very useful. Without them, a lot of those typically small, but valuable insights in the inspection process would have been lost. This is especially important for mistakes everyone makes in the beginning when using inspections. If they would not have been packaged, some pitfalls could have not been avoided.

Another benefit is aggregating observations to practice packages. They provide not only applicable solutions but also rationales (in Section 'explanation' of the quality pattern structure). For smaller process changes, especially, the risk of reinventing the wheel twice (i.e., a change A, introduced first, is skied after a while by change B, which is replaced by change A, and so forth) was observed several times.

As in every technology transfer activity, inspection know-how is handed over gradually to the involved units. There, we see a benefit of the experience packages, too. Experiences described in such packages is:

– *very concrete.* The content of the experience packages is tailored to the specific needs and restrictions of one domain.
– *built on experience in the user's environment.* By this, the practitioners in the units are willing to accept them more than external knowledge, as they were involved in building the experience packages.
– *quite short.* Due to high time-pressure no one is willing/able to read huge textbooks or conference proceedings.
– *maintainable.* Each unit can improve their processes using the experience evolution process described above (Section 3.1).
– *transferable.* They can both be used to make new employees familiar with the established processes and to exchange experience with other units in order to improve their overall understanding.

The coaches will use the documented experiences both to train new researchers and to establish inspections in new units (as depicted by unit D in Figure 10). Starting on a more mature foundation of knowledge and experience, many troubles and pitfalls can hopefully be avoided.

7 Summary and Future Work

With the rapid rate of innovation in and around software technology, one might have expected to have seen significant improvements in the area of organizational learning and reuse of experiences. In practice, however, this has only started to begin due to the problems in capturing and reusing knowledge. The recent advent of experience factory technology [4] and its accompanying technology seems to be a promising approach to overcome those problems. In this paper, we have presented the experiences made with that technology in the SoftQuali project.

We described the basic technology of experience documentation and evolution. We introduced a crisp classification of experiences in three different types, providing a generic pattern (i.e., Quality Pattern) to document such types of experiences, and presented a practical approach for acquiring experiences. Finally, we presented the results of using this technology in two real-world examples, both related to introducing inspection technology. In general, the reuse of documented knowledge/experience to plan and control the software technology transfer process was found to be useful in both projects.

Our next activities cover several directions. First, we see the need for gaining more practical experience in using our approach in several domains. Then, we plan to build more sophisticated tools to support humans in their experience maintaining activities. Last, but not least, we need to evaluate the quality pattern structure more thoroughly. Especially our assumption that quality patterns are more comprehensible and written towards a readers needs, has to be validated empirically. As a first step here, we are performing a long-term study in a laboratory environment at the University of Ulm. There, we have asked students to write both quality patterns and reports on particular topics (namely inspections and modeling reactive systems). At a later point in time, we will give these documents to other students, asking them to perform these particular tasks and observe the time and depth of understanding. Subsequently, we plan to use these findings to start such an investigation in an industrial setting.

Another interesting question concerns the reinfusion of documented experience in development processes. Section 5 covered some technical aspects of this activity. However, there are also social aspects to cope with. Literature on reuse initiatives (e.g. [19]) often mention the problem, that people are not willing to externalize their knowledge as they fear to get unimportant. In this case, often incentives are proposed as a solution. In our environments, we observed another interesting phenomenon: people are willing to share their experience, but they are less willing to accept advice by others. As a long term goal, we are interested to investigate this contradiction to see, whether there are (social) patterns explaining this fact.

Acknowledgements

The authors would like to acknowledge the contributions of all SoftQuali partners. Thanks are also extended to Sonnhild Namingha for her efforts in editing this paper.

This work was founded by the German Federal Ministry of Education, Science, Research, and Technology under contract number 01 IS 518. It does not necessarily reflect the position or the policy of the government and no official endorsement should be inferred. The responsibility for the content of this paper remains with the authors.

References

1. Lexikon-Institut Bertelsmann, Dictionary, Bertelsmann, Gütersloh, 1979 (in German).
2. F. Houdek and H. Kempter. Quality Pattern — An approach to packaging software engineering experience. In M. Harandi (ed.): Proceedings of the 1997 Symposium on Software Reusability (SSR'97), Software Engineering Notes, ACM, Mai 1997, pp. 81-88.
3. M.Y. Jona and J.L. Kolodner. Case-based reasoning. In S.C. Shapiro (ed.): Encyclopedia of Artificial Intelligence. John Wiley & Sons, 1987, pp. 1265-1279.
4. V.R. Basili, G. Caldiera, and H.D. Rombach. Experience Factory. In J.J. Marciniak (ed.): Encyclopedia of Software Engineering. John Wiley & Sons, New York, 1994, pp. 469-476.
5. The PEF model. A booklet from the PERFECT EPSRIT project 9090, 1996.
6. The SoftQuali Consortium. SoftQuali Project Documentation. 1999. Online available at http://www.iese.fhg.de/SOFTQUALI/.
7. H. Kempter and F. Leippert. Systematic Software Quality Improvement by Goal-Oriented Measurement and Explicit Reuse of Experience knowledge. BMBF-Statusseminar 1996, pp. 281-297, DLR (German Center for Aerospace, in German).
8. H.D. Rombach, V.R. Basili, and R.W. Selby. Experimental Software Engineering Issues: critical assessment and future directions. Lecture Notes in Computer Science 706, Springer, Berlin, 1993.
9. V.R. Basili, G. Caldiera, and H.D. Rombach. Goal question metric paradigm. In J.J. Marciniak (ed.): Encyclopedia of Software Engineering. John Wiley & Sons, New York, 1994, pp. 528-532.
10. T. DeMarco and T. Lister. Peopleware. Prentice Hall, 1995.
11. D. Harel. Statecharts: A visual formalism for complex systems. Journal of Science of Computer Programming, vol. 8, 1987, pp. 231-274.
12. D. Landes, K. Schneider, and F. Houdek. Organizational learning and experience documentation in industrial software projects. In Proceedings of the 1st Interdisciplinary Workshop on Building, Maintaining, and Using Organizational Memories (OM-98), Brighton, UK, August 1998, pp. 47-63.
13. C. Alexander. The Timeless Way of Building. Oxford University Press, Oxford, 1979.
14. B. Minto. The Pyramid Principle — Logic in Writing and Thinking. Minto International, London, 3rd edition, 1987.
15. W. Bierer. A Process for Building Quality Patterns. Masters thesis, University of Stuttgart, May, 1997 (in German).
16. V.R. Basili, S. Green, O. Laitenberger, F. Lanubile, F. Shull, S. Sorumgard and M.V. Zelkowitz. The Empirical Investigation of Perspective-Based Reading. Journal of Empirical Software Engineering, 1997.
17. R.E. Zultner. TQM for Technical Teams. Communications of the ACM, 36(10), October 1993, pp79-91.
18. L. Briand, B. Freimut, O. Laitenberger, G. Ruhe, and B. Klein. Quality Assurance Technologies for the EURO Conversion — Industrial Experience at Allianz Life Assurance. Proceedings of the Software Quality Week Europe, Brussels, 1998.
19. C. McClure. Extending the software process to include reuse. Tutorial given at the Symposium on Software Reusability, May, 1997, Boston, MA.

Lecture Notes in Computer Science

For information about Vols. 1–1892
please contact your bookseller or Springer-Verlag